Praise for

Powerful Professionals

*"**Powerful Professionals** has equipped many of the innovators at 3M Company to optimize the results of the businesses they support. Our R&D, manufacturing and engineering professionals have learned value-adding influence skills. The notion of relationship building as equally important to one's subject-matter expertise was particularly enlightening. Even when an organization reengineers itself, and staff functions may be decimated, the departments and the individuals who have delighted their internal clients are the ones who thrive in the refocused enterprise. Later, when workloads increase to the breaking point, the prioritization/selection tools in Chapter 13 have prevented many a serious burn out."*
Frank Berdan, P.E.
3M Company
Manufacturing Strategy Manager

"Guaranteed to help you think about your work differently. A rich resource. Years of experience and work went into this book and you are the beneficiary."
Geoff Bellman
Consultant, and author of *The Consultant's Calling* and *Getting Things Done When You Are Not In Charge.*

*"My workteam has utilized the tools and insights offered in **Powerful Professionals** for the last several years. (We took Murray Hiebert's consulting skills course.) I have no doubt that these practical skills have helped us improve our quality, customer understanding of what we do, and increased requests for further services. I recommend this book to any group looking to improve customer satisfaction as well as differentiate their services from external consulting organizations."*
Duane Kortsha
Amoco
Environmental, Health & Safety

"This is a book for ALL professionals who want to become more influential."
Bob Ratay
Avery Dennison
Director, Logistics Consulting

"Dog-eared, coffee-stained and much-loaned. What a high commendation for any book like this. Nothing short of the best reference manual for professionals applying consulting skills inside their own organizations or any other. Guaranteed to be a timeless resource on your bookshelf."
Brenda Spilker
Suncor Energy Inc.
Human Resources

"No consultant should go on any assignment without this book by Murray Hiebert. It may save your life and that of your client."
AC Ho
Consultant

Singapore

"We have successfully trained over 600 people in our organization using the skills outlined in Murray Hiebert's Consulting Skills Program. Our Education Solutions department has received overwhelming positive feedback and support for this consulting approach from our consultants as well as Senior Management. This consulting model provides a simple, yet profound approach to the customer/consultant relationship. Initially, we customized this program to the consultants that worked with our external healthcare customers, yet due to it's word-of-mouth success, we receive numerous requests from our internal departments as well. The consulting model, tools/techniques and processes are an excellent addition to anyone that provides consulting services."
Sheila Diggs
SMS (Shared Medical Systems)
Education Solutions

"Murray Hiebert has taught me more about consulting and managing professionals than anyone else. Read this book."
Norman Smallwood
Co-founder, Novations Group Inc
Co-author of *Real-Time Strategy* and *Results Based Leadership*

*"For me, this is the most valuable and personally useful single source on how to take those extra steps from expertise and knowledge to deploying them within your organization. What makes **Powerful Professionals** stand out from the many other books dealing with these issues, is that Hiebert takes the extra step from the 'what to do' to 'how to do' and backs this up with an enormous amount of supporting information. Of course, there are similarities between internal consultancy and consultancy from outside an organization, and **Powerful Professionals** will be of value to you in either role."*
Graeme Dick
Environmental Science & Research Ltd, New Zealand
Project Manager

"An important primer for those of us who feel we have valuable knowledge, skills and experience to pass on to our internal clients, but who are unaccustomed to marketing ourselves."
Ross McNaughton
Government of Canada
Learning Advisor

*"**Powerful Professionals** is very practical and thought provoking, an excellent resource to help me leverage my expertise in my organization. It's like having a powerful coach by my side at all times! I've enjoyed reading it from cover-to-cover and it will be valuable as a reference tool as I need it."*
Robin Sober
The Mutual Group
IS Training

"This book will help you succeed. It has great wisdom. The author spent years working with technical and administrative professionals in every industry imaginable. He has continuously perfected the ideals and models in this book. Now they're all yours, in one package! Page after page, this book is loaded with practical, well-tested guidance for making things happen inside organizations."
Bruce Klatt
Co-author of *Accountability: Getting a Grip on Results* and author of *The Ultimate Training Handbook*

"This is a 'must read' for all professionals—full of powerful ideas, pertinent and practical examples, and excellent tools for dealing with a world of rapid and challenging change."
Paul Thompson

Powerful Professionals

Getting Your Expertise Used
Inside Your Organization

2ND EDITION

©2001

Murray Hiebert
Eilis Hiebert, editor

DISCLAIMER

Visit the Web Site for the latest information:
http://www.consultskills.com

National Library of Canada Cataloguing in Publication Data

```
Hiebert, Murray, 1943-
  Powerful professional


    Previous ed. has title: Powerful professionals.
    Includes bibliographical references and index.
    ISBN 1-55212-880-6


    1. In-house services (Business)  2. Knowledge workers.  3.
Professional employees.  4. Customer service.  I. Hiebert, Eilis.
II. Title.
HD8038.A1H52 2001         650.1'3         C2001-911209-2
```

COPYRIGHT AND TRADEMARK ACKNOWLEDGMENTS

TRAFFORD

This book was published *on-demand* in cooperation with Trafford Publishing.
On-demand publishing is a unique process and service of making a book available for retail sale to the public taking advantage of on-demand manufacturing and Internet marketing.
On-demand publishing includes promotions, retail sales, manufacturing, order fulfilment, accounting and collecting royalties on behalf of the author.

Suite 6E, 2333 Government St., Victoria, B.C. V8T 4P4, CANADA

Phone	250-383-6864	Toll-free	1-888-232-4444 (Canada & US)
Fax	250-383-6804	E-mail	sales@trafford.com
Web site	www.trafford.com	TRAFFORD PUBLISHING IS A DIVISION OF TRAFFORD HOLDINGS LTD.	
Trafford Catalogue #01-0282		www.trafford.com/robots/01-0282.html	

10   9   8   7   6   5   4   3

QUICK LAUNCH

Is This Book For You?

If you are a professional, or if you manage professionals, this book is for you!

Professionals and their managers using the ideas in this book to ensure their expertise was valued and used in their organizations include:

- Engineers of all types
- Systems Analysts, Systems Engineers
- Public Affairs/Communications Professionals
- Scientists of all types
- Training & Development Advisors
- Record Management Professionals, Librarians
- Lawyers, Legal Professionals
- Psychologists & Counselors
- Economists
- Planners and Social Scientists
- Quality/Process Advisors
- Internal Consultants

- Technologists of all types
- Human Resource Professionals
- Finance Professionals, Auditors
- Geologists/Geophysicists
- Safety Advisors
- Forestry and Environmental Advisors
- Nurses, Medical Professionals
- Industrial Relations Advisors
- Marketing Advisors
- Research & Development
- Organizational Effectiveness Advisors
- Contractors/Insourced Professionals

- Anyone with an expertise!

What Can You Expect to Get Out of This Book?

✔ This is a 'how-to' book, meant to assist professionals with practical models, dozens of checklists, worksheets, assessments, flowcharts, insights, examples, dos and don'ts …

✔ This book is written to support the modern role of a professional working inside an organization.

✔ This book provides field-tested advice for the most common challenges faced by professionals.

How to Use This Book:

➲ Read the rest of this Quick Launch. On Page vi is located a 'finder' list of typical professional concerns and specifically where you can find assistance to deal with them in this book.

➲ Do read the first two brief chapters, which create a context for the whole book. After that, each subsequent chapter stands alone, although sequentially the chapters build a coherent strategy for becoming a *Powerful Professional*.

➲ Our ideal would be that you read the whole book, then leave it on your desk to use as a real-time hand book.

➲ For a more traditional start, Page vii lists a *Table of Contents*.

➲ At the end of this book are useful appendices, an *Index* and a *Competency/Skills Matrix*.

Have fun while learning! We have included many humorous quotes and cartoons for an occasional chuckle!

FINDING WHAT YOU NEED

If your need is:	Look for assistance:
✓ meeting a new client	⇒ Chapter 3, page 24
✓ asking great first questions	⇒ Chapter 3, page 34
✓ selling a recommendation to managers	⇒ Chapter 6, page 82
✓ 101 ways to market your expertise	⇒ Chapter 14, page 253
✓ preparing a professional strategy	⇒ Chapter 13, page 216
✓ leading change	⇒ Chapter 9, page 144
✓ reducing the stress of change	⇒ Chapter 9, pages 152
✓ dealing with resistance	⇒ Chapter 6, page 93
✓ establishing credibility	⇒ Chapter 1, page 11
✓ saying "no"	⇒ Chapter 13, page 234
✓ clarifying expectations	⇒ Chapter 4, page 48
✓ clarifying roles	⇒ Chapter 12, page 200
✓ sorting out complex situations	⇒ Chapter 5, page 66
✓ establishing rapport	⇒ Chapter 3, page 39
✓ changing to a consulting role	⇒ Chapter 1, page 6
✓ improving your listening skills	⇒ Chapter 11, page 178
✓ knowing where to put your time and effort	⇒ Chapter 13, page 218
✓ dealing with multiple stakeholders	⇒ Chapter 8, page 123
✓ getting at the underlying concerns	⇒ Chapter 3, page 30
✓ enhancing your career as a professional	⇒ Chapter 12, page 205
✓ establishing an influential role	⇒ Chapter 12, page 209
✓ coaching professional performance	⇒ Appendix 1, page 279

TABLE OF CONTENTS

Dedicated to
Paul & Quinn

Acknowledgments

No worthy book can be the result of the thinking and work of a few people. Much of the usefulness of this book is attributable to its many contributors. Here we name some of these people—at the risk of omitting someone!

- The more than 9,500 participants in over 700 workshops and presentations who taught us so much about 'real-life' professional issues. The practical value of this book is attributable to you, our end users.
- Our client organizations, particularly the early ones, who had faith in us. Among the earliest are: the City of Calgary, Amoco, Imperial Oil, Champion, Husky, and Pacific Gas and Electric. We deeply appreciate our clients and would have liked to list all of you—not to mention your financial support!
- Our associate-instructors who gave great improvement feedback and supported us over the years. Among these, alphabetically, are: Doug Boyle, Nigel Bristow, John Davis, Mike DeGiorgi, Vern Della-Piana, Sheila Diggs, Tom Doris, Michel d'Orsonnens, Sarah Hawkes, Ivan Holland, Kelly Howser, Lyle Lachmuth, Sheldon Loar, Terrie Lupberger, Val MacLeod, Janet Mairs, Drina Nixon, Urs Nussbaumer, Erwin Peters, Sarah Sandburg, Bill Sefcik, Robin Sober, David Utts, and Ursula Wohlfarth.
- Bernie Novokowsky, David Irvine, Bruce Klatt, George Campbell, Don & Dolores Ebert, George Melnyk, Clem Blakeslee, Andy Marshall, Shaun Murphy and the Milis family—Hans, Therese, Fiona & Lisa—for their support and feedback.
- People who took time from their hectic schedules to read drafts of the book and provide improvement feedback are Geoff Bellman, Mel Blitzer, George Campbell, Lou Charlebois, Wilf Hiebert, David Irvine, Peter Justo, Bruce Klatt, Bernice Mattinson, Bernie Novokowsky, Bob Ratay, Bill Sefcik, Robin Sober, Brenda Spilker, and Ursula Wohlfarth.
- Dianne Fortier, Peter Justo, Syd Waring, Quinn Hiebert, and Sharan Sutherland, who provided timely and accurate administrative support.
- Caroline Brown, who provided line-editing and proofing skills.
- NOVATIONS Group Inc., for their support, particularly Norm Smallwood for his infectious, enthusiastic encouragement. Joe Hanson, Paul Thompson, and the late Gene Dalton lent us much-needed support. NOVATIONS also inspired the 4 Stages Model™, the Strategic Resourcing Model and the *Consulting Skills Profile* from which our database is drawn.
- The 'gurus' of the internal consulting field, particularly Geoff Bellman and Peter Block.
- AC Ho of Singapore, for his inspiration of a 'learning system' approach.
- Lastly, and most importantly, our sons Paul and Quinn, who put up with endless out-of-town days and computer hours, and dealt with the thousands of frustrations typical of an undertaking of this magnitude.

Thank you
Murray & Eilis Hiebert

1

"My life so far has been a long series of things I wasn't ready for."
© *Ashleigh Brilliant*

CHAPTER 1

HIGH PERFORMING PROFESSIONALS

Quick Snapshot

Did You Know?
- most, but not all, professionals 'peak out' mid career?
- what is driving change in the professional role?
- professionals are being asked to change, yet most don't know how?
- what specific skills professionals need to deliver their expertise?

How-to:
- create an influential professional role and position your role strategically.
- use 'power' as a professional.
- establish a client-credible role in your organization.
- deliver your expertise.

The Bottom Line:
- You will have more influence as a professional, making effective use of the models, checklists, principles and skills of this chapter.

Being a Professional 'Ain't What it Used to Be'...

" 'Yikes! The nerds have won'; 'All value comes from the professional services'; 'We are all in the professional service business,' " trumpets management guru Tom Peters, while headlines in business publications herald 'The New Worker Elite,' and tell us 'Knowledge Workers Are THE Asset of the New Century.'

"It ain't like that around here," is what ordinary professionals inside organizations are saying. Down-to-earth, real-world engineers, scientists, systems analysts, financial and human resource professionals—professionals of all stripes—are feeling the other side of the coin:

"I don't understand what my organization expects of me anymore."

"Isn't good professional work valued around here anymore?"

"By the time I do all this nontechnical work I don't have time to do my real job."

This book is all about the skills you need to deliver your expertise inside your organization.

The truth is that the role of professionals working inside organizations has changed dramatically over the last few years. Professionals, like managers, are being coaxed, cajoled, pushed and pulled to adapt to the world of competitive advantage:

- internal & external customer service
- shortened cycle times
- teamwork
- shared services
- real time systems
- outsourcing
- continuous innovation
- cost cutting
- re-engineering

Whether or not you believe these trends will endure, changes are being made in organizations which will fundamentally change the role of professionals. For years, professionals have yearned for more influential roles. Ironically, offered these roles, many are getting cold feet! In the face of this, one engineer in a Fortune 500 Company remarked ruefully "We didn't learn any of *this* in college."

Reacting to an in-depth study of the changing role of information technology (IT) professionals in Singapore, one authority stated "If you are an applications programmer, you only need to manage your computer ... When you become a systems analyst, you no longer face a computer, but hostile clients and demanding superiors. The IT profession is no longer a technical profession, it is a helping profession."

This book addresses the dramatic shift in the role of professionals working inside organizations. We present a modern model to revolutionize professionals' view of themselves and their way of working. To get into a more powerful frame of mind, we encourage professionals and professional groups to think of themselves as an internal consulting business, offering skills and services inside their organization. This entails re-evaluating themselves—thinking of themselves as internal consultants delivering their expertise to internal customers or clients. Used effectively, the skills and models of this book will ensure professionals get their expertise used and valued within their organizations.

We know of what we speak. We have experience working with over 6,500 white collar professionals in hundreds of organizations worldwide. We have amassed the largest survey database of its kind in the world on what internal customers view as high performance from such professionals as engineers, scientists, systems analysts, finance and human resource professionals—to name but a few.

What Ever Happened to The Good Old Days?

Spurring change in the work of millions of professional experts working inside organizations are drives to:

- **Be innovative.** Innovation as a modern basis for competitive advantage begins with knowledge workers.

- **Total quality solutions.** Every facet of a modern organization has to be centered on flawlessly delivering its fundamentals. Professional work is no exception.

- **Customer service.** Organizations worldwide are becoming more focused on external customers. What of internal customers? To stay employed, professionals must deliver internal customer service equivalent to, or superior to, services offered externally.

- **Stay competitive.** The design cycle for new cars is but one example. Until recently, a typical auto maker needed five years to design a new model. Now less than half that time can be spared for design. The changing role of the design professional is core to this kind of productivity increase.

- **Business solutions, not technological solutions.** Professional experts, because of their allegiance to a profession, have typically offered 'techie' solutions to organizational problems. Productivity gains, however, require professional solutions connected to the strategic direction of the organization.

- **Work in teams.** The explosion of knowledge is forcing work to be done in groups. For a project of any significance, no single person is likely to have all the needed knowledge. The Lone Ranger, working late hours in an office, is a rapidly shrinking professional archetype.

- **Commitment—of all.** In the past, if senior management approved, the project went through. To secure commitment to change, a wide range of stakeholders is now demanding involvement.

- **Managers' changing roles.** Flattening of organizations has eliminated many managerial roles, changing the roles of those remaining. Many of the functions previously performed by layers of managers in organizations are now expected to be done by professionals themselves.

In this chapter ...

- *Changing role of the professional*
- *Thinking 'You, Inc.'*
- *Asking strategic questions*
- *Professional delivery model*
- *Professional careers*
- *A change in perspective*
- *Author's credibility*
- *How clients see professionals*

THOSE WERE THE DAYS, MY FRIEND

"It seems to me that in the past, the professional's role started with someone else framing the problem and assigning the technical problem to be solved. The professional picked up gift wrapped problems. The professional's job ended with the presentation of the recommendations. It was up to the line manager whether the recommendation was accepted and change took place. NO MORE! What organizations need now are 'full cycle' consultants, professionals who can take responsibility for the full consulting cycle, from clearly establishing the business issue, through selling the recommendations, to sustaining the change as the result of the recommendations."

– From a workshop client

Enter the Powerful Professional!

This book is designed to help all internal professionals develop powerful professional roles—to become more effective deliverers of expertise to their internal clients and external customers. Professional experts are well trained in their technological fields, but generally woefully untrained and unskilled in delivery of that expertise to their organization. This book does not teach technical skills, rather it presents the skills that transcend any brand of expertise—processes for successful delivery of professional expertise. Organizations need these skills to succeed. Professionals need these skills to enhance their own work satisfaction.

'You, Inc.'

A helpful analogy is that of a small professional services firm, thinking of itself as a professional practice delivering a service to customers e.g. a lawyer or a dentist. Although internal professionals in organizations have not traditionally seen themselves thus, these features place them firmly in the category of professional practice:

✓ They have a product or service—their expertise;

✓ They have customers or clients—some direct, many indirect;

✓ They need customer feedback—they need to know how their work is valued by their clients;

✓ They have delivery systems—they need to deliver their expertise to their market. Some need to market themselves. Others need to say "no" to low value work.

Professionals need to offer the most effective and competitive service in their internal market, delivering it in a way that will ensure they will always be the 'professionals of choice' to their clients. They *should* be valued more than external professionals—after all they have insider information!

Professionals are increasingly expected to get strategic results without exercising direct control. To do this, they need:
- clear models for these new roles
- consulting skills
- persuasion skills
- 'people' & relationship skills
- supportive organizational systems.
- to understand their client's business.

If professionals are to produce much-needed, positive impact on their organization, they need to understand:
1. how to position their roles strategically inside their organization and how to manage an internal consulting practice.
2. how to deliver their expertise.
3. how to remain a valued (and satisfied) contributor over a career.

1

Ready to Begin?
Ask—and Answer—Strategic Questions

Powerful professionals need to begin by stepping back and looking at their roles strategically. They need to ask—and answer—lots of searching questions about themselves:

- "What are the external pressures on, and strategic direction of, our organization?"
- "What can we offer that is more strategic to the organization?"
- "Where do we currently spend our time? With which internal clients? External customers?"
- "How do we help our clients with strategic changes in our domain of expertise?"
- "Who *are* our major clients? Who *should be* our clients? What services do we offer them?"
- "How do we market value-added services inside our organization to our clients?"
- "To which requests should we say "no," because they are low value; which do we outsource?"

Note that all of the above questions are asked in the plural. Although we challenge individual professionals to think through their individual strategies, it is much more powerful for an entire professional group, rather than just its individuals, to clarify these strategic issues. The benefits of a clear professional group strategy are immense. We hear professionals complain about inadequacies of their clients and of their organization. They often don't realize they have not looked at themselves with the same critical eye. Assistance with professional strategies and internal marketing are covered in Chapters 13 & 14.

Modern organizations are expected to be strategic and respond to a rapidly changing environment. We would hazard a guess that most readers of this book have, on occasion, criticized senior management for the direction of their organizations; yet we will bet that many readers have not thought through their own personal strategies. This book will help those readers to do just that.

Learn How to Deliver Expertise

After clarifying a business strategy for their specialty, professionals need a *professional services delivery model.* Our general purpose model proposes five stages for a typical professional project:

1. **Exploring the Need**
   – getting clear on underlying needs before proceeding.

2. **Clarifying Commitments**
   – making sure all parties are clear on results and processes before action is launched.

3. **Gathering Information**
   – gathering further information on the defined problem.

4. **Recommending Change**
   – recommending what and how clients change.

5. **Taking Stock or Closing**
   – effectively wrapping up the project and/or planning improvements.

We will examine this model in the next chapter. Subsequently, each stage of this model is assigned a chapter in this book.

This Expertise Delivery model is on the Web Site: www.consultskills.com

We will look at professional careers, roles and role transitions in more detail in Chapter 12, Enhancing Your Role and Career.

You're Not Getting Older, You're Getting Better

Most professionals peak in productivity around age 35 according to Gene Dalton and Paul Thompson, in their landmark book, *Novations: Strategies for Career Management.* Note the word 'most,' not 'all.' Some keep their high level of productivity over their whole career. What is their secret? The research is clear. As their experience increases, those professionals who continue to be productive *change the way they look at their role*. Professionals need a way of understanding how their new professional roles are supported by an overall career strategy.

Highly productive (and personally satisfied) professionals progress through four discrete levels. Each level is like a quantum leap, requiring a new outlook and different skill sets. Specifically, high performing professionals must widen the perspective of their role, from that of specialists whose success is personal success, to a role where their success becomes the success of others.

A Powerful Way of Looking at Power

'Power' is a strange word, open to many interpretations. In this book power *does not* mean 'power over' or 'control.' Power *does* mean 'power with'—with clients, stakeholders, the organization. Shared power and commitment can work wonders. We want professionals to be influential and powerful in their organizations, without personally having to exercise direct control. Yet we have interacted with thousands of internal professionals who feel that they have little power. We assume professionals want influence. We assume professionals want to be helpful to their organizations. We assume professionals have good ideas—good for their organizations, good for their clients and good for the professionals themselves.

In this book, we will continually emphasize that the most powerful professionals see themselves in a 50-50 partnership role with their clients. One end of this partnership, where a professional assumes the client 'knows best,' usually leads to an ineffectual, one-down, 'pair of hands' professional role. The other end, the assumption that 'the professional knows best' usually leads to a frustrating, ineffectual, 'expert' professional role with low client commitment. Professional power and influence reside in the skill of professional and client *jointly* helping the organization to be more successful. This book will help you do just that. Throughout the book, we will introduce models and skills for building a powerful, 50-50 partnership with your clients.

66 Quotable Quotes **99**

"Power to move things and to get things done is diminished by the concern of power over others."
– George Campbell

"The role you perform is a function of both the power that comes with your position and the power that comes with the way you choose to perform within your position."
– Geoff Bellman
Getting Things Done When You Are Not in Charge

THE POWER & INFLUENCE SPECTRUM

The Pair of Hands	The Partner	The Expert
One-down	50/50	One-up
Client knows best	We are better together	Professional knows best

1

Internal Consulting

Thinking of yourself as an 'internal consultant' instead of a 'content expert' can help make the transition to a new role easier for yourself. Internal consultant is a powerful way to understand or frame the new professional role.

- Consultants see themselves as having customers or clients.
- Consultants see themselves managing their own professional practices.
- Consultants have influence.
- Consulting encapsulates the concept of a partnership.

Consulting is more than the sum of its parts: more than logical, rational, systematic methods; more than personal relationships. Effective consulting is an integration of head skills and heart skills, of logical skills and interpersonal skills.

Unfortunately, the word 'consultant' also has negative baggage. Many managers and professionals have had negative experiences with external consultants. We are not hung up on the word 'consultant.' As a matter of fact, most of the thousands of professionals we have worked with do not have the word 'consultant' in their title, nor is the word 'consulting' in this book title. Whatever your professional title, this book is about increasing your effectiveness.

The Brave New Professional World

The most important, over-arching skill of this book is the need to bridge the gap from professional expertise to organizational, client and business results. From working with thousands of internal professionals, we realize how unclear and distant the change in perspective can seem from professional specialist to internal consultant. By education, most professionals have been immersed in the specialist model, where problems and solutions are seen from the perspective of their expertise. Although a prerequisite of internal consulting, this perspective can also get professionals into trouble. New to a job and yearning to establish a professional reputation, the professional ironically often ends up being entrapped by that same yearning.

Some examples:

- An economist working in a large organization is becoming frustrated. Two years into his role, he is becoming a worldwide expert in his area of specialty. He receives calls every day asking him for information. He is perceived as the expert—the specialist. Yet he doesn't want to be pigeonholed. Satisfying as it is to be seen as an expert, it would limit the mobility and variety he wants. What is he to do?

  This book can help him become a powerful professional.

- Many say the role of the Human Resource professional must change dramatically if it is to survive. Professionals and management alike are questioning the changing role. One of many external forces, on-line systems for individual employees to access benefits plans and other information are developing rapidly. On-line systems for managers to access compensation, promotion and other information are decreasing the need for 'transactional' human resource activities. Yet there will always be a need for human resource professionals.

  This book can help them develop into powerful professionals.

Every profession has similar role issues. The table on the next page describes some of the major transitions to being a powerful professional. Which apply to you?

Clients or Customers?
In this book, we will refer to people to whom you deliver your expertise as:
- *internal = clients*
- *external = customers*

MOVING FROM PROFESSIONAL SPECIALIST
TO INTERNAL CONSULTANT

Specialist Perspective	Resulting Difficulties in Modern Organizations	Consulting Perspective
• Thinks mainly in terms of professional expertise.	• Overwhelmed, avoids or simplifies too quickly; keeps role narrow, frustrates clients who want a broader perspective.	• Thinks in terms of professional, organizational and business needs.
• Recommends technical solutions.	• Recommendations not accepted or acted upon; does not see the broader implications of change; finds marketing, selling and commitment-building difficult.	• Recommends business change. Sells and leads organizational change.
• Feels job is done when recommendations are presented.	• Recommendations not accepted or acted upon; change is 'the client's problem'; the problem reappears.	• Takes shared and appropriate responsibility for change.
• Likes structured work, quickly simplifies ambiguity, is detail oriented.	• Tries to make problem fit expertise; wants client to ensure problem and project are structured; suggests solutions too early; avoids problems or causes outside expertise; pair of hands role.	• Works well in unstructured situations, works with ambiguity, is strategically oriented.
• Work is planned in advance.	• Wants to know too much detail in advance, clarifies too much or too little.	• Work is adaptive and strategic.
• Rewards analytical problem solving skills.	• Frustrated, expects to be recognized for professional prowess rather than results; sees 'politics' as a huge barrier.	• Rewarded by value-added results.
• Builds on individual skills.	• Thinks mainly of own professional skills, rather than the skills of others.	• Builds on business and system skills; gets results by involving others.
• Focuses on personal success.	• Thinks mainly in terms of own professional success rather than seeing the success of others as personal success; blames others; talks in terms of 'they'; threatened by others' expertise.	• Focuses on success of others and business successes.
• In control or wants control.	• Fights for control, intentionally or unintentionally; raises resistance.	• Works by influence, in control at process level.
• One-at-a-time change, project orientation.	• Misses big picture; does not see the impact of professional change on the system; changes fail or have little impact.	• Systemic and larger scale change.
• Pushes too much or too little.	• Takes on too much ownership, or not enough; advocates or withdraws; doesn't know how to 'live at the edge.'	• Pushes enough (and at proper times) but not too much.
• Wants others to define needs and market skills.	• Blames others, is not strategic, perceived as a 'techie.'	• Takes responsibility for own career and strategy.

What's happening to REAL Professionals Working in Modern Organizations?

From our work with thousands of professionals over 20 years, what follows is one actual and typical list of challenges elicited from a group of professionals working in a modern organization. This book will deal with most of these challenges.

Area of Challenge	Specific problems within area of challenge
Building Credibility:	• Creating influence so internal customers will call upon internal professionals • Establishing credibility as internal professionals • Having expertise to communicate knowledgeably.

Professional Strategy/ Services/Priorities:	• Prioritizing, given the overload of information
	• Creating opportunities—how to do this when:
	    – clients are so busy
	    – directions are changing
	    – so many extra time pressures
	• Measuring value-added when considering projects
	• Dealing with short time frames
	• Identifying the demand for services
	• Delivering services, given increased demand
	• Having clear expectations:
	    – within the professional group
	    – with clients
	• Defining organizational needs versus client needs; then integrating both of these
	• Establishing long term internal clients.

Influence/Persuasion:	• Being able to sell professional ideas
	• Judging what is appropriate amount of:
	    – persuasion/influence
	    – finesse
	• Learning how to empower others with ideas
	• Recognizing when to push and when to hold off
	• Being able to create acceptance of ideas.

Resistance:	• Encouraging resistant and uninterested clients to listen • Providing compelling advice, yet meeting resistance.
Professional Growth:	• Dealing with the reality of opportunity for professional career growth stunted by limited resources • Filling the gaps in professional skills repertoire.

Remember clients need professional expertise because they have problems.

Internal or External, Is There a Difference?

In this book, we emphasize those aspects of consulting appropriate to working *inside* an organization. In modern organizations, whether you are on the permanent payroll, a contractor, or an external consultant, the skills and perspectives are similar. The core skills of internal consulting described in this book are applicable to contractors and external consultants as well. If we were writing a puErely external consulting book, we would include such additional topics as writing proposals and determining fees.

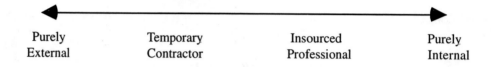

| Purely External | Temporary Contractor | Insourced Professional | Purely Internal |

We assume you are skilled professionally. This book will help you deliver that expertise.

How Do We Know What We're Talking About?

How do we know the skills of this book are valuable to professionals working in organizations?

✓ **With our associates, we have presented over 700 workshops to almost 10,000 professionals** in English, German, French and Spanish over a span of 20 years, worldwide. We have upgraded the workshop over six versions. We have worked with almost any profession you can think of within an organization. In every workshop, we glean from participants specific challenges they face when delivering their expertise within their organization. In this book we deal with most of these actual challenges.

✓ **We have amassed the world's largest database of its kind** on how professionals are seen by their internal clients, managers, peers and others. At the time of writing, our database consists of responses from statistically reliable surveys of over 7,500 professionals rated by over 50,000 clients, peers and managers. The database is growing rapidly. Our statistical analysis of this database led us to design a *Credibility Sequence for Professionals,* presented over the next two pages.

✓ **We have consulted to many professional groups and talked to hundreds of their internal clients.** Dozens of their anecdotes and actual examples are included in this book. We have consulted with clients from the Arctic Circle to below the Tropic of Capricorn and around the world. We have clients ranging from Fortune 500 corporations through government organizations to small entrepreneurial professional consulting firms.

✓ **We have researched extensively the area of professional expertise.** We have included quotes from many references. You will find our *Selected Further Reading* section at the end of this book.

✓ **We have been visited at our web site by thousands of professionals who have found the tools presented in this book to be helpful.** Throughout this book, you will be directed to this web site http://www.consultskills.com.

What our Consulting Database Tells About What Clients Value

From analysis of our large database, from our research and from talking with thousands of professionals and their clients, here is how we see professionals rated by clients for effectiveness. Following this outline and down-to-earth summary, the next page presents supporting detail.

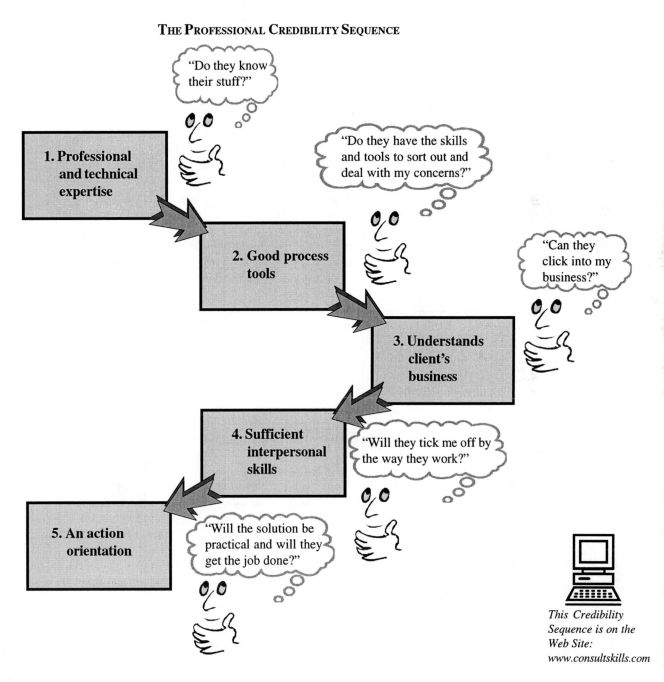

THE PROFESSIONAL CREDIBILITY SEQUENCE

"Do they know their stuff?"

1. Professional and technical expertise

"Do they have the skills and tools to sort out and deal with my concerns?"

2. Good process tools

"Can they click into my business?"

3. Understands client's business

4. Sufficient interpersonal skills

"Will they tick me off by the way they work?"

5. An action orientation

"Will the solution be practical and will they get the job done?"

This Credibility Sequence is on the Web Site: www.consultskills.com

THE PROFESSIONAL CREDIBILITY SEQUENCE:
DETAIL VERSION

What Clients Look for in Professionals:	What Our Database Tells Us	Our Database Evidence (Italics = actual survey items)	Related High Rated Competencies
1. Professional and technical expertise	First of all, clients look for strong professional and technical expertise, asking: "Is this person technically competent?"	From the database, three of the top four most discriminating items are professional/technical skills: • *Is considered an expert* • *Demonstrates good knowledge of the job* • *Is up-to-date in his/her field*	• Professional knowledge and skills • Technical excellence • Industry knowledge
2. Good process tools	Second, they ask: "Can this person understand and process my problem?" or "They have the expertise, but can they use it to solve my problem?"	From the database, the next four most discriminating items are process skills: • *Has the ability to lead groups* • *Is able to quickly analyze complex situations* • *Exercises a high level of professional judgment in applying methods, theories & tools to novel problems* • *Comes up with creative, resourceful solutions to problems within his/her area of expertise*	• Group leadership • Analytical skills (but not too much) • Complexity handling skills • Coaching skills • Creativity skills • Strategic thinking • Group problem-solving skills • Critical thinking
3. Understanding of client's business	Third, "Can this person understand my 'real world' with its constraints and provide a business solution, not a 'techie' solution?"	Clients give professionals a very low rating on this item: • *Has a wider perspective than his/her professional expertise* Professionals who relate their skills to their client's business stand out.	• Understanding the organization • Client focus • Marketing skills • Business literacy • Strategic alignment
4. A sufficient amount of inter-personal skills	Fourth, clients ask: "Can they understand my personal situation?" and "Can they get people to buy in?"	From the database, two of the top eight most discriminating items include interpersonal competencies: • *Many people seek his/her opinion* • *Is able to persuade others*	• Influence skills • Openness • Commitment skills • Dealing with resistance and conflict • Rapport building
5. An action orientation	Lastly, "Will this professional follow-through, produce the optimal solution and set up the change?"	Clients and staff groups are increasingly talking about: • 'full cycle' consulting • consultants leading the change resulting from their recommendations.	• Change leadership • Innovation skills

1

Clarifying Expectations for this Book

We feel this book presents a unique view of the modern professional role, touching upon related topics which are dealt with in depth in other literature. At the end of this book, the *Selected Further Reading* list gives you places to go for detailed discussions of topics in the right hand column.

This symbol will direct you to further information.

THIS BOOK PRESENTS UNIQUE INSIGHTS ABOUT:	THESE INSIGHTS OVERLAP WITH:
✓ Delivering your expertise inside your organization	• Project management
✓ Selling your ideas in your organization	• Presentation skills; Sales
✓ Dealing with resistance	• Dealing with conflict; Risk management
✓ Leadership as a professional	• Group leadership; Teamwork
✓ Managing a meeting with clients	• Meeting management
✓ Internal consulting	• External consulting
✓ Managing your career as a professional	• Career management; Career choices
✓ Being strategic in your role	• Time management; Strategy formulation
✓ Clarifying commitments with your clients	• Negotiation skills
✓ Establishing rapport, listening to clients	• Interpersonal skills; Communication skills
✓ Establishing a 50-50 partnership with your clients	• Assertion skills
✓ Helping coach others in these skills	• Coaching skills
✓ Marketing your professional skills	• Marketing
✓ A logical, how-to approach to consulting	• Consulting as a personal avocation
✓ Dealing with different kinds of clients	• Dealing with difficult people
✓ Gathering information by asking good questions	• Interviewing skills
✓ Sustaining change as a professional role	• Change management

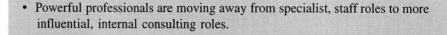

WHAT YOU HAVE LEARNED SO FAR...

- Powerful professionals are moving away from specialist, staff roles to more influential, internal consulting roles.

- There is a definable process and there are specific skills for delivering professional expertise.
    1. *Exploring the Need*
    2. *Clarifying Commitments*
    3. *Gathering Information*
    4. *Recommending Change*
    5. *Taking Stock or Closing*

- Being a powerful professional requires a unique understanding of your organization's strategy and definition of your own professional strategy to support it.

- The consulting database shows clients evaluate professionals on their effectiveness in five areas:
    1. Professional and technical expertise
    2. Good process tools
    3. Understanding the clients' business
    4. Sufficient interpersonal skills
    5. An action orientation

- Many staff groups are redesigning themselves as internal consulting groups. They are defining new professional strategy based on a more powerful role—as world-class internal consulting groups.

"There is nothing so practical as a good theory."
– Kurt Lewin

2

CHAPTER 2

EXPERTISE DELIVERY MODEL

Quick Snapshot

Did You Know?
- the more you know and love what you do, the more difficulty you may have getting your recommendations accepted?
- clarifying commitments means never having to say you're sorry?
- most professionals don't know how to manage the delivery of their expertise?

How-to:
- use the crucial first few minutes of a client conversation effectively.
- ask the right questions to establish a powerful role.
- sell your ideas.
- use a model to structure delivery of your expertise.

The Bottom Line:
- You will work more effectively and more confidently with your clients, using the models and skills of this chapter.

Don't Just 'Wing It' ...

To be influential and powerful, a powerful professional needs to possess more than expertise. A professional also needs to deliver that expertise. Delivering expertise inside an organization doesn't just 'happen.' It requires professionals to have a deliberate, distinct procedure or framework to follow. We call this a 'model.' This model is like a road map, a mental roadmap you would follow as you consult with your clients. Although rarely followed scrupulously, a mental model provides professionals with rationale for what they are doing and why they are doing it. When needed, they can confidently explain their consulting processes to clients.

A mental model is like a road map.

Without a well thought-out mental model or 'road map,' the tendency is for professionals:
- to 'wing it'
- to expect their clients to take the lead in structuring the consultation
- to have no clear process in place at all.

Model It!

We have developed a field-tested, effective, five-stage model, designed to deliver professional expertise inside an organization. Thousands of professionals presently use, adapt, customize, internalize and make this model their own, confident that their consultations are following a process that leads to success.

What follows is a thumbnail sketch of each stage of the model. Each stage has a chapter of this book devoted to in-depth understanding, including how-tos, examples, checklists to keep the process on track, roadblocks and how to deal with them, practice sessions and ways to adapt each stage to your unique situation.

When you see this symbol, you will find information on the Web Site: www.consultskills.com

THE EXPERTISE DELIVERY MODEL

The Consulting Stage	Key Logical Issue	Key Relationship Issue
Exploring the Need	Framing the problem	Establishing rapport
Clarifying Commitments	Negotiating outcomes & processes	Clarifying relationships
Gathering Information	Data gathering & diagnosis	Building ownership
Recommending Change	Selling your recommended change	Dealing with reservations
Taking Stock or Closing	Wrapping up a project or re-clarifying roles	Transferring ownership & personal improvement

Stage 1: Exploring the Need

➡ *Getting to the underlying business and organizational needs before proceeding with the consultation.*

In the Beginning ...

The initial few minutes of contact over a new project have a truly disproportionate impact on the success of that project. Most consulting problems can be traced back to these first few minutes. The first sentences set the tone for the whole consultation. Keeping all this in mind, it is crucial to immediately begin establishing a working partnership with internal clients, so that together you can thoroughly explore the underlying need.

Road Blocks

Time pressures and the clients' fears of not getting what they feel they need—these are the two main impediments to accomplishing this stage, *Exploring the Need*. Factors like these drive clients to present problem symptoms, or to come up with a hurried problem solution, rather than taking the time and care to surface underlying problems and business need. Another impeding factor is that professionals and clients both enter into a consultation with trepidation, professionals often concerned that clients have hidden agendas, clients concerned that professionals need to have problems 'put in neat boxes,' or that they will not understand 'real world' client constraints. This first stage of the model, *Exploring the Need*, helps clients open up to describe underlying causes, problems, needs and concerns. A result of thus opening up, however, is increased complexity. For this stage, professionals need skills and tools to deal with this complexity.

What You Hear First

Clients will often make a request like this one. "Please load a spreadsheet on my computer." An IT professional can do just that. It's simple, it's easy—but it may not be the best solution for the client's problem. With a few thoughtful, probing questions, the IT professional may find that the client's need would be better served by a database application.

Or a client may call the organization's Public Relations professional, exclaiming "We need a brochure just like this one I picked up at a conference." It's easy to produce a brochure, but the real need may be design of an overall marketing strategy.

Enter Your Role!

Constrained problem definitions such as those just cited lead to constrained roles. Without skills to surface underlying issues and establish a 'line of sight' to organizational strategy, professionals are in danger of relegating themselves to a narrow, pair of hands role. Since clients typically find it difficult to express their underlying needs, professionals need the skill of establishing sufficient rapport, so they can surface and deal with delicate matters of trust, openness, fears, hidden agendas, confidentiality and conflict.

This first stage, *Exploring the Need*, is crucial to the success of 'business partner' professionals. Besides finding the right problem to solve, they work on establishing a productive role and relationship with their clients.

2

The first few minutes of a consultation are crucial.

In this chapter ...

- *Why do you need a model?*
- *Exploring the Need*
- *Clarifying Commitments*
- *Gathering Information*
- *Recommending Change*
- *Closing/Taking Stock*

ASSUME makes an
ASS of U and ME

Don't just think it. Ink it!
– Bob Pike

18

Stage 2: Clarifying Commitments

➠ *Making sure all parties are clear on results and roles before action is launched.*

Clarifying—'Soft'; Commitments—'Firm.'

The softer part, Clarifying, ensures both internal consultant and client understand what they will get from the consultation and how they will work together. The firmer word, Commitments, is used to emphasize the importance of asking for, and offering, specific commitments to action.

This *Clarifying Commitments* stage of the model saves a consultation from two demons:
  • the disastrous effects of unclear or assumed expectations
  • professionals complaining bitterly about clients' lack of commitment to change.

Having Clarity Means Never Having to Say You're Sorry …

Many professionals confess that they clarify poorly. We will challenge you to *always* clarify, consciously and explicitly. Clarification can be as simple as a verbal restatement "So what I'm going to do is … and what you're going to do is …" We strongly suggest professionals end every client meeting, telephone call or conversation with this verbal statement of mutual expectations. Getting into the habit of exercising this skill alone can save days of misdirected work, not to mention frustration of clients and professionals when unwanted work is done. Verbal contracts are typically appropriate for consultations spanning a few minutes to one day's work.

The Pen is Mightier than the Word

Longer than this time span, professionals need to prepare short, easy-to-read confirming documents. The point of these is not protection; it's clarity. This way, professionals don't do unwanted or misdirected work. This straightforward, written, confirming document consists of one page or one e-mail screen (people don't read more than this!)—a point-form description of the need and a listing of the key activities to fulfill the need. We find that most clients are relieved and grateful to receive a brief, non-punishing document confirming commitments.

Stage 3: Gathering Information

➠ *Gathering information on the defined problem while building commitment.*

If it Weren't for the People …

Gathering information sounds simple, doesn't it? It is—until we examine non-rational aspects of doing it. The rational side of gathering information is that without good data, it's impossible to make a good analysis and to substantiate recommendations. The non-rational side of gathering information is that data-gathering is a thoroughly human issue, a great rapport-builder and a key part of the critical commitment-building process. Many professionals tend to have more difficulty with the 'people' aspects of gathering information. Powerful professionals possess excellent data-gathering techniques which also build commitment.

That's a Good Question!

Asking good questions to gather data is more than a rational request for data. In many organizations, even to *admit* having a problem is threatening. Asking questions with an air of superiority will lead to negative consequences. We have heard stories of blue collar workers dealing with condescending 'ivory tower' professionals by conveniently 'forgetting' some critical information. An internal consultant needs to understand the art of asking good questions in a nonthreatening way.

Fuzzy Logic?

Another complication is the difficulty that is encountered when professional specialists have to gather information under ambiguous, fuzzy, uncertain conditions. When the problem is clear, the information gathering and diagnostic processes are usually clear. But problems are not always so clear-cut. As professionals grow in their careers, they deal with increasingly complex problems, ambiguous situations, and unclear processes. Our database shows clients placing high value on the skill of effectively assessing a complex situation and coming up with clear priorities and actions. It is incumbent upon professionals to learn to clarify these complexities before proceeding to commitments.

In Chapter 5, *Gathering Information*, we will present models and skills for dealing with these important issues.

Stage 4: Recommending Change

➡ *Recommending what and how clients need to change*

Recommending = Selling Change

Realistic professionals admit they need to learn to *sell* their recommendations for change. Nothing happens in an organization unless someone sells others on change. Professional education has led specialists to believe 'if it is logical it will sell itself.' This would be nice and easy, but it's rarely true.

We have been involved with training professionals as internal consultants for over 20 years. In the first decade, we rarely heard requests for persuasion or selling skills. We now hear it consistently. As a Systems Analyst in one large petroleum company put it "It's becoming increasingly common to hear 'If you think it is important, sell me on it!'" In our data, surveying 35,000 internal clients, persuasion skills distinguish top performing professionals. Yet, while persuasion skills are very highly valued, our surveys show them being poorly done! There's a big gap here.

Much has been written on selling, almost exclusively from the perspective of an external salesperson—and the stereotypes of salespersons we hear are very negative! When asked what comes to mind when the words 'selling' and 'salesperson' are mentioned, professionals derisively mention, among other things, 'sleazy,' 'plaid sports jackets,' and 'pushy.' This book will present a thoroughly professional selling model for internal professionals.

It's Benefits That Sell, Not Features!

A *feature* is an intrinsic aspect of something, e.g. computer memory size, the RAM. A *benefit* is how that feature is of benefit to the person buying something, e.g. how the user can make excellent use of increased RAM. You don't have to list benefits to computer enthusiasts for the feature of increased RAM, but you do have to stress benefits to someone who does not understand the mechanics of computers.

This may not be the exact Expertise Delivery Model for your professional services. We encourage you to adapt the model to your specific needs.

❝ **Quotable Quotes** ❞

"Put yourself in the client's shoes and ask yourself 'What's in it for me?' " (WIIFM)
– Robin Sober

Professionals need to distinguish features (technical characteristics of the recommendation) from benefits (how a feature fulfills the client's business needs).

Professional experts, by definition, have bought into the *benefits* of their own area of expertise. They believe passionately in what they do and are excited to share with, or show others, all the features—the 'bells and whistles'—of an idea or recommendation. For this reason, it is difficult to separate features from benefits, because they appear one and the same to the expert. Furthermore, it may appear unnatural, political, condescending or manipulative to the professional to state clearly the benefits their recommendations will have for clients. ("It's so clear to me and my colleagues," thinks the professional. "Why wouldn't it be natural and clear to the client?") It is even more challenging to be able to state the specific benefits for varied stakeholder groups.

"It's so clear to ME; how come you can't see it?"
To clarify, here is a story told by a Senior Ph.D. Chemist for a multinational company. "For the last three years, I've been trying to get this organization to increase the purity of a chemical from approximately 99.70% to 99.85%. Now I realize why I couldn't get my recommendation approved. I talk only to other chemists who are as excited as I am about the chemical elegance of the 0.15%. Now I understand the need to describe the specific benefits that resonate with *non-chemist* managers!"

"Yeah, But ..."
As soon as professionals list the benefits of their recommendations, it is normal for clients to think of the downsides. Professionals then have to deal with client reservations; with risks and resistance.

It is often tricky to identify resistance, since it first manifests itself as more of an intangible 'climate,' making it hard to pin down and to actually deal with it. That is because resistance is first felt on an emotional level by both client and consultant, before they can logically understand or articulate it.

Nothing is as frustrating for a professional as having recommendations sitting on some shelf gathering dust— recommendations that are good for the client, good for the organization and good for the professional.

If professional recommendations involve significant change, reservations and resistance are natural. In fact, if professionals do not get resistance, they may have a problem! If clients do not offer any resistance, perhaps they do not understand the changes the consultant is recommending; or they are stonewalling and are planning not to do anything with the recommendations!

Resist Resisting Resistance!
'For every action, there is an equal and opposite reaction' is one of Newton's Laws. If professionals feel resistance from clients, they tend to push back harder. As they push harder, their clients push back even harder. A good principle of consulting is 'you won't win pushing matches with your clients,' so the skill is *not* to push back. Instead, as in martial arts, make the resistance work for you.

In Chapter 6, *Recommending Change*, we will emphasize selling your ideas and dealing with direct resistance. Additional chapters, *Sustaining Change* and *Dealing with Resistance,* will also delve more deeply into the challenging skills of this stage.

Stage 5. Closing or Taking Stock
➠ *Effectively wrapping up the project*

Professionals describe consulting projects ending by not really ending. They just 'fizzle out' or are 'beaten to death.' In most cases where a professional is delivering expertise within the organization, many concurrent projects are part of an ongoing client-consultant relationship. In this kind of relationship, we use the term 'Taking Stock' to describe the periodic checkups required. These taking stock sessions ensure recognition, role improvement and job satisfaction. Professionals need to judge when and how to ask the client for a taking stock meeting at the optimum time—when things are going well. The worst possible time to take stock is when something has gone wrong—yet that's when taking stock usually occurs. Crisis and problem solving sessions are the worst time to review progress toward mutual goals, to renegotiate outcomes, to ask for feedback, or to renegotiate roles. We use the term 'Closing' to refer to a project where the professional and client actually wrap up a discrete consulting project.

Models: Living with them, living without them!

'Internal consulting' is the term we will use to describe the process of delivering expertise inside an organization. Internal consultants require a model to provide framework and direction. They need to develop a range of consulting skills in order to implement the stages of that model.

Rarely do projects sequentially follow the five-stage model just outlined. When it comes to dealing with human beings and complex organizations, it's unlikely that any model works in every case. Yet a professional does need a model as a touchstone. This five-stage model, like any model, needs adaptation to the circumstance. Here are two examples:

1. If the problem is complex or large, you may need to cycle through the first three stages a few times. For example, when presented with a complex problem, you and your client may agree on a starting hypothesis, then you go out and gather data as to whether the hypothesis is correct. When you have gathered and analyzed the data, you will go back to your client and explore how to proceed on the problem using the additional data.
2. Another common consulting job often handed to professionals is selling an improved system. For Human Resource professionals, it may be selling an improved compensation system; for Systems professionals, it may be selling an upgraded spreadsheet. Placing these requests in the context of the model, the professional is actually starting at the *Recommending Change* stage.

Throughout this book we will encourage you to design your own personal model, one that works for you in your personal situation. We hope it includes elements of our model, but we would be delighted if you design your own, based on the principles, ideas, checklists and skills in this book.

In the chapters devoted to each stage of the Expertise Delivery Process, we will assume only one consultant and one client. Although not a good assumption for a modern organization, we are consciously simplifying in order to focus on the stages of the five-stage model. However, we do deal extensively with multiple client or complex stakeholder systems in *Mapping Client Systems,* a chapter dedicated to this issue.

2

Some authors use the words 'change agent' instead of consultant to accentuate the bottom line of successful professionals, that is, clients making effective and lasting changes as a result of professional recommendations.

If the Shoe Fits ... A person with large feet understands that one model of socks or panty hose does not fit all—even if it is advertised as such. We encourage you to adapt our Expertise Delivery Model to your needs ... and to buy hosiery that fits!

WHAT YOU HAVE LEARNED SO FAR ...

- You need a model to effectively deliver your professional services.

- Our recommended model has five stages:
  1. *Exploring the Need*
     – getting to the underlying business need before proceeding.
  2. *Clarifying Commitments*
     – making sure all parties are clear before action is launched.
  3. *Gathering Information*
     – gathering further information on the defined problem.
  4. *Recommending Change*
     – recommending what and how clients need to change.
  5. *Closing or Taking Stock*
     – improving your role or wrapping up the project.

- We encourage you to adapt the model to your specific situation.

THE EXPERTISE DELIVERY MODEL

*"You never have a second chance
to make a first impression."*
– TV Ad

CHAPTER 3

STAGE 1:
EXPLORING THE NEED

3

Quick Snapshot

Did You Know?
- most consulting problems can be traced back to the first meeting?
- many clients present solutions rather than problems?
- one little word 'why?' can scuttle your project?
- client and consultant fears result in strange behaviors from both?

How-to:
- get at underlying issues and causes.
- establish rapport; work with client fears.
- set up an influential role.
- ask opening questions that not only keep you out of trouble but establish your credibility.

The Bottom Line:
- You will set your projects up for success by using the models, checklists, assessments and skills in this chapter.

Why this First Stage is so Crucial

Exploring the Need, the first stage of the Expertise Delivery Model, sets the stage for the whole project. We compare it to a hologram. Like multiple facets of a hologram, all the issues of consulting are present in every sentence that you and your client speak.

Exploring the Need begins the first time a potential project is raised and ends when you start making commitments, or alternatively when you say "no," rejecting the project. Pressured by time and driven to 'get down to work,' professionals and clients often gloss over this first stage. Yet many consulting problems can be traced right back to the first discussion. "If only I had handled that differently at the very beginning!" is a commonly heard remark among professionals.

During the first few minutes of client contact, you have the most leverage you will ever have: leverage over the problem scope, how the problem will be worked, even over your impending role. Mistakes made here will haunt you for the whole project. From the onset, you will need every skill of internal consulting to get your project off on the right foot. Ultimately, this is your big opportunity. Use it or lose it!

In this Chapter ...

Because every facet of the Expertise Delivery Model is present in this first stage, *Exploring the Need,* we cover a disproportionate amount of material in this chapter. For ease of use, we have divided the chapter into a number of sections. Depending on your needs and expertise, you may wish to focus on one or more topics.

These chapter sections will raise many of the issues faced by a professional at this first stage. We will present models, skills, hints, checklists and other tools for understanding and dealing with the dynamics of *Exploring the Need*. We will tell you where you can find more detailed information for all these topics within this book.

66 Quotable Quotes 99

"When consultants talk about disasters, their conclusion is usually that the project was faulty in the initial ... stage."
– Peter Block
Flawless Consulting

When you see this symbol, you will find information on the Web Site: www.consultskills.com

Getting Into Consulting Mode

The first stage can be initiated in a number of ways. Exploratory conversations with potential clients—where you hear about a new project for the first time—can take place in such varied locations as the hallway, a client's office, during a meeting, over the phone, or by e-mail. The first stage may also vary a lot in length. By telephone, *Exploring the Need* may only take a few minutes. If, however, a proposed project is expected to last for a long time, the first stage may span a number of meetings and a number of weeks.

A Jumble of Questions

Whatever the nature or length of the exploratory meeting, while answers are needed to a million questions, it's possible to ask only a few! Below are questions which will probably occur to most professionals and clients:

About the Concern:
- Is the problem correctly defined?
- Is the client presenting a solution rather than a problem?
- Is the client presenting the underlying problem, or just a problem symptom?
- If I think it is just a symptom, how can I get at the underlying issues and causes?

About the Client:
- Do I really understand what the client needs?
- Is this client committed to this or trying to 'get rid of a monkey off someone's back'?
- Are there hidden agendas here? Is the client presenting the full story?
- What doesn't feel right here?
- I'd really like to do this, but in different way. Will the client look at other options?
- Are there sufficient client resources and talent in the client organization?

About the Work:
- Does the proposed work fit with my professional group's strategy?
- Should I ask questions which will enlarge, or narrow, the problem scope?
- How much time will it take to do this well? Do I have the time?
- Should I say "yes" or "no" to the proposed project?

About Myself:
- Am I the right person for this project?
- Is the implied role the best role for me?
- Does this client trust me? Do I trust this client?
- Do I like this person? Does this person like me?
- Am I looking dumb or smart by asking these questions?

3

In this chapter ...

- *First stage, Exploring the Need and why it is important*
- *Typical fears and their implications*
- *A typical first meeting*
- *Reframing the presenting problem*
- *Establishing rapport*
- *A 'try-on' example*
- *Self assessment skills checklist*

The 'Classic Consulting' Mode

In 'classic consulting' mode, your client presents the problem and you, the professional, respond by listening, negotiating the problem and establishing how you and the client will work together—illustrated in the flowchart on the next page. In early parts of this book, for simplicity, we will assume this 'classic consulting' mode.

Some characteristics of this typical consultation are:

- It starts with rapport building. Powerful consultations have powerful human as well as technical elements.
- The presented problem is paraphrased or summarized to show your client you have understood.
- Exploration is clearly separated from commitments. Once you start making commitments, you are in the next stage, *Clarifying Commitments.*
- If a project is to be turned down, the earlier the better.

If you feel you cannot say "no," or you don't know how to say "no," see Chapter 13, Your Strategy: Saying Yes or No.

Before making a decision to accept or reject a project, three areas need examining:

1. *Explore the underlying need.* What is the best way of understanding and stating the need? There is usually tremendous pressure for the professional and the client to jump to solutions before thoroughly clarifying the underlying needs and causes.

2. *Explore the best processes and relationships for solving the need.* What are various approaches to solving the problem ? What roles are best for you and for your client?

3. *Clarify whether the work will add value to you and your organization.* To work effectively as a professional, you must be clear on your own personal consulting strategy, that of your professional group and that of your organization. If uncertain about this, see Chapter 13, *Your Strategy: Saying Yes or No.*

Keep in mind ...

- Many assumptions must be made at the beginning of a consultation. While it's impossible to clarify every assumption, be aware of their presence.
- The underlying business issues must be identified. There is nothing as frustrating as working on a symptom of the 'real' problem—dealing in Band-Aid™ solutions.
- The scope of the problem can be broadened or narrowed at this stage. Changing the problem scope becomes much more difficult later.
- You can establish a powerful role. Just like problem scope, scope of roles is established early—often by implication—and is difficult to change later.
- Your goal is 50-50 responsibility for the success of this consultation. The ideal 50-50 commitment to the success of this project starts right from the beginning.
- The interpersonal basis for the consultation is established early. No matter what your professional expertise, a personal relationship is crucial.

Effective consulting means you are neither 'one-up' nor 'one-down.' The best consultations are 50/50 partnerships.

FLOWCHART OF A TYPICAL FIRST EXPLORATORY CONVERSATION

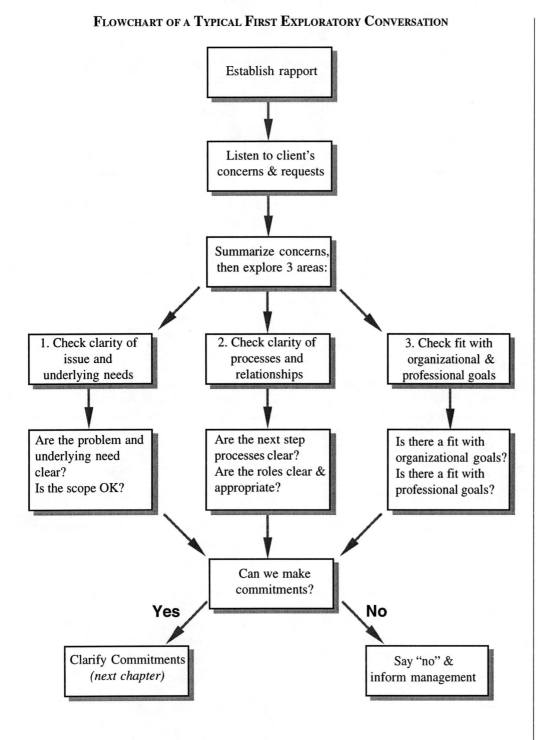

Establish rapport

Listen to client's concerns & requests

Summarize concerns, then explore 3 areas:

1. Check clarity of issue and underlying needs

2. Check clarity of processes and relationships

3. Check fit with organizational & professional goals

Are the problem and underlying need clear?
Is the scope OK?

Are the next step processes clear?
Are the roles clear & appropriate?

Is there a fit with organizational goals?
Is there a fit with professional goals?

Can we make commitments?

Yes

No

Clarify Commitments
(next chapter)

Say "no" &
inform management

This flowchart assumes a lone client presenting the concern. Other consulting variations are dealt with later; some are summarized on the next page.

When and how to say "no" are dealt with in chapter 13.

27

Alternative Formats to 'Classic Consulting'

In this chapter we are dealing mainly with a 'classic consulting' mode—one client and one professional. Here are thumbnail sketches of some other formats:

Alternative Formats

1. Classic:

One client/one consultant
Client presents concern

2. Persuasion:

One client/one consultant
Consultant 'sells' solution

3. Groups:

Group & one consultant
Group owns concern
OR
Group & consulting team
Both own concern

4. And Other Formats.

- **Professionals persuading clients.** Examples of this might include:
  - human resource professionals selling an improved compensation or career development program to managers and employees.
  - engineers selling a new preventative maintenance program to field locations.
  - accounting professionals selling a new financial program to district accounting professionals.

  Many professionals find selling new or changed programs more difficult than responding to a client's need—more about this in Chapter 6, *Recommending Change*.

- **Consultations involving a group of clients** faced with a challenge; for example, dealing with a management team consisting of multiple clients rather than with a single client. Examples might include:
  - a purchasing professional investigating an inventory problem common to a number of field locations.
  - a pulp and paper chemist consulting to a number of divisions, all with interests in a waste water reduction process.

- **Consulting teams or project teams working with many stakeholder groups.** More and more consulting is carried out this way. A team-based consultation may have a project leader, team members from two or three technical specialties, two or three user representatives—in addition to representatives of staff groups like Safety and Human Resources. Group consultations are more challenging—more about this in Chapter 8, *Mapping Client Systems.*

- **The immediate contact client is a third party.** This is where you, the professional, work through a *contact* person, who represents the *final* clients. Often, head office professionals have a contact person in field locations. In these cases, it's imperative to keep in mind who the *final* clients are: the people being represented by the contact. To clarify your client complex systems, read Chapter 8, *Mapping Client Systems.*

- **Manager or group leader has contracted** services on behalf of the professional—another consulting variation. A professional's ability to influence a better statement of the problem or a more powerful role will be more difficult in this situation. The consultant's hands are tied. If this is happening to you, we recommend that after reading this book, you negotiate a more powerful role with your manager. As you will see, powerful professionals need room to reframe issues and roles.

How does this First Stage Fit into the Expertise Delivery Model?

A powerful professional clearly separates the exploration of a concern from commitment to action. One hallmark of an inexperienced consultant is a 'jump to action.' Here's how the first stage fits into the Expertise Delivery Model and how it differs from the next stage, *Clarifying Commitments*.

Consulting Stage	Typical Activities for the Stage
Stage 1: *Exploring the Need*	• Establishing rapport, credibility and trust. • Listening to understand client's presentation of the problem. • Exploring with your client the underlying needs and issues. • Reframing the problem, if necessary. • Establishing a 50-50 partnership for the project. • Discussing alternative ways to process the problem. • Saying "no," if necessary.
Stage 2: *Clarifying Commitments*	• Negotiating the outcomes for the project. • Clarifying constraints for the project. • Negotiating the project plan. • Negotiating roles. • Making commitments. • Saying "no," if necessary (your last graceful opportunity). • Documenting agreements.
Remaining Stages of the Consulting Model	

When you start making commitments, you are in Stage 2. When you start recommending change, you are in Stage 4.

Separation of exploration from commitment is a powerful consulting tool. Often this separation is not conscious for either consultant or client.

Giant steps for professionals and clients rarely come from jumping to causes and solutions.

Fears and Their Impact

Fears Can Cause Roadblocks

Believe it or not, examining the consultant and client fears can give valuable insight into the dynamics of *Exploring the Need*. Below is an abbreviated checklist of possible fears you and your clients may feel as you discuss a new project.

- Check off those that usually apply.
- Identify those missing from the list.
- Anticipate how these fears could affect your projects.

This symbol will remind you of our numerous, practical, adaptable checklists.

Most checklists are on the Web Site: www.consultskills.com

TYPICAL CLIENT FEARS	TYPICAL PROFESSIONAL FEARS
❏ Loss of control to the professional	❏ Client looking for a scapegoat
❏ Risk of failure	❏ Client has hidden agenda
❏ Not getting what I want	❏ Client will not negotiate
❏ Professional doesn't understand my business	❏ Scope creep
❏ Professional will recommend more expensive solutions than the problem requires	❏ Client has one-track mind around a certain solution
	❏ Client doesn't know what is needed
❏ Professional does not understand my constraints, e.g. budget	❏ Client's behavior is part of the problem
❏ Professional will mess up	❏ Client won't give enough time to problem
❏ Solution will cost too much	
❏ Consultant does not have professional expertise	❏ Client wants an easy solution to symptoms rather than dealing with the cause
❏ Professional will get transferred before the end of the project	❏ Client has reputation of being hard to work with
❏ Professional will not deliver on time	❏ Unrealistic deadlines—"Have it done yesterday."
❏ Professional will discuss our private problems with others	❏ Client wants something outside my professional group's priorities
❏ Project will go over budget	❏ Organizational politics
❏ Project will be late	❏ Lots of 'people problems'
❏ It's not OK to ask for help	❏ Problems will come up outside my area of expertise
❏ Lack of confidence in staff departments	
❏ Embarrassment or loss of self-esteem	❏ Embarrassment or loss of self-esteem
❏ Don't like the professional	❏ Client not committed
❏ I'll look stupid/incompetent	❏ I can't say "no" to a poor project
	❏ I'll look stupid/incompetent

Fears Influence Behavior

Misunderstood fears can place significant roadblocks in the path of an effective consultation. Let's look further at client fears and their impact on how a client might present a problem.

Even one fear on the preceding page will compel a client to present the problem in a narrow way. Here are just a few examples:

IMPLICATIONS OF CLIENT FEARS

SOLUTION PRESENTED INSTEAD OF THE PROBLEM	WHAT THE CLIENT WOULD REALLY LIKE TO SAY
• "Phone the vendor about their leaking seals."	• "We've had a rash of worrying maintenance problems recently. We're trying to track down the causes. I suspect the new seals are causing some of these problems. Could you investigate?"
• "Install Excel on my computer."	• "We've been running into lost inventory on the construction project and probably need to keep better track of inventory. Could you help me set up a simple, effective inventory tracking process? We don't want to spend a lot of time on this because we are very busy." (At this point, the client might not be ready to mention suspicions of employee theft.)
• "We never get those month-end reports from Accounting on time. Could you 'get after' Accounting?"	• "Recently our Accounting reports seem to be later and contain more errors. I have tried to talk to people in Accounting but they keep saying they are short-staffed. Can you quickly get to the bottom of this and report back with your recommendations?"
• "Can you put on a communications workshop next month for my team?"	• "We've been having a lot of conflict on my team recently and people say I don't listen to them. What could you do to help me?"

It is helpful to distinguish what clients want from what they need.

Clients may not even recognize they have fears, much less their implications.

Client Fears Can Hinder *Exploring the Need ...*

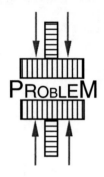

Client 'helpfulness'—telling you what to do, can often translate into professional 'helplessness'—feeling you are locked into ineffective action.

Besides being an expert par excellence in your field, to be a more powerful professional, you need to *understand and manage your consulting processes to better deliver your expertise.* Since clients are not usually aware of how to make the best use of professionals, it's up to you, the professional, to effectively and appropriately deliver your expertise in consulting situations. Keeping this in mind, your challenge, however you receive the initial problem information, is to help clients surface the underlying business and relationship issues. Often clients are actually trying to *help* you, the professional, by keeping the presenting problem simple. The unintended consequence of this 'helpfulness' is that the problem is often framed in an *unhelpful* way!

The way a client presents a problem to you can be connected to almost every client fear on the Fears Checklist on page 30. Often acting out of a human need to keep control, clients may not even be aware they have fears at all. A problem may be presented as hopelessly narrow, jumping to a quick-fix solution, instead of presenting the real problem. If a client fears loss of control, presenting a narrow problem is the best way to take care of that fear.

An example of jumping to the solution being presented, instead of exploring the underlying problem, might be a statement such as "We need a faster computer network." In this case, the professional needs to ask probing questions to find out how the client reached this solution. Sample questions to help you and the client look at the underlying needs are on page 34. Other reasons for jumping to a solution might include:
- allaying other fears, e.g. fear of going over budget,
- genuinely thinking they already know the answer,
- not thoroughly analyzing the problem and alternative solutions.

The flip side of narrow presenting problems is that fearful clients sometimes state problems in a broad, ill-defined manner. For example, a client may present a very general statement of the issue, hoping there is a generalized, less painful solution that doesn't involve surfacing the underlying communication issues in the team. Another example would be "Do something about accounting; we never get reports on time." In this case, you need to help your clients get more specific. You can do this by asking for examples and specific issues, prioritizing, then planning action. We will go into more detail on 'fuzzy,' broad problems in Chapter 5, *Gathering Information.*

JUMPING TO SOLUTIONS

"Many professionals are rewarded for and/or respected for their problem-solving ability with respect to their area of expertise, so it's easy to jump to solutions to describe the problem."

– *Robin Sober*
The Mutual Group

DON'T PUSH THE PANIC BUTTON!

"Consultants need to remember that by the time managers call for consulting help, they may be frustrated and irritated. Their comments may reflect these feelings. No matter how dramatically and impatiently managers declaim their wishes, however, consultants should not be panicked into taking self-defeating action."

– *Robert Schaffer*
High Impact Consulting

One consequence of professionals' frustrations and fears is that they may blame their clients for things that they, not their clients, should change.

HOW FEARS CAN AFFECT A FIRST MEETING

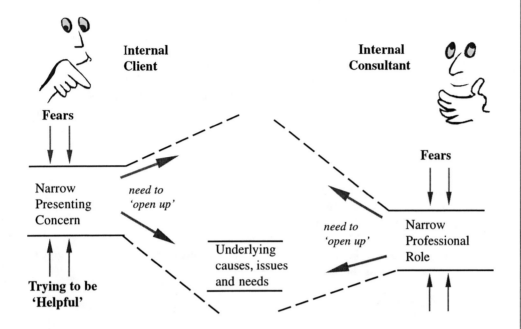

Professional Fears Can Seriously Narrow Your Professional Role

So far, we have left out a very important person who also has fears—the professional. Similar to clients, consultants' favorite method of keeping fears under control is often to define a narrow professional role. Ironically, consultants often blame their clients for narrow roles, yet these are often the by-product of the professional's own fears. It takes caution not to unintentionally collude with clients to keep the problem narrowly defined, based upon fears, acknowledged or unacknowledged. We delve deeper into consultant fears in Chapter 10, *Dealing With Resistance*.

Both professional and client need to 'open up' and explore:
* the underlying issues and causes,
* how to 'scope' the working problem,
* a range of options for solving the problem.

To get clients and professionals out of narrow definitions and roles, we now suggest:
1. asking effective opening questions,
2. redefining the presenting problem,
3. establishing rapport.

"Internal professionals often get a narrow concern presented in the form of a solution. This is usually due to client fears. The professional, eager to please, implements the solution without checking the frame. This leads to a downward spiral of the professional being seen as a pair of hands; this perception then becomes an expectation in the next project, with the professional complaining about the client perception and so on and so on and so on. To halt this spiral, check the frame!"

– Bill Sefcik, CPA

A DO-NOT ...

Don't ask 'Why?' too early. It puts your clients on the defensive. To avoid looking bad, your client has to:
1. *disown the initial problem definition*
2. *create justifications as to why they have the problem in the first place!*

Don't dig yourself into a hole by inadvertently setting your clients up to look bad.

Characteristics of Powerful Opening Questions ...

- *They do not put clients on the defensive.*
- *They help uncover underlying issues and causes and help express difficult issues.*
- *They help you look beyond your own specialty and role*

66 Quotable Quotes 99

A novel opening question:
"What is the itch you want to scratch?"
  – Teresa Wilcox

This Checklist is on the Web Site: www.consultskills.com You may wish to produce an edited version of this Checklist for your specific use.

Questioning to Redefine/Reframe a Presenting Problem

POWERFUL OPENING QUESTIONS

First questions are crucial to your success as a professional. They get at underlying needs, open up options and set up a powerful professional role for you. For these reasons, you cannot afford to 'wing it.' You need to plan the typical questions you use in your area of expertise and in your organization. Below is a suggested list of questions. Some questions may resonate with you more than others. Some questions will work better with some clients than with others. Modify this list to suit your needs or add your own specific questions.

One of the best applications for this checklist involved a Training Advisor in a large organization who received most training requests over the telephone. She would often hang up the telephone and then think of better questions she should have asked. She composed an edited subset of the questions below, taping it to the wall above the telephone. Now as she talks to her clients, she scans the list and asks much better questions to get at the underlying need and appropriate solutions.

After establishing rapport, you might ask:
- ❏ "What led you to this solution?"
- ❏ "What got you interested in this approach?"
- ❏ "You seem enthusiastic about _____. How do you see it helping you solve your concerns?"
- ❏ "Which concerns do you see being solved by this approach?"
- ❏ "Give me some examples of your concern."
- ❏ "Can you give me some examples of how this would help you with your concerns?"
- ❏ "Please give me some (more) background."
- ❏ "I would like to be sure I understand the underlying issues here. Can we talk about the need for this approach?"
- ❏ "Let's step back, examine the big picture and look at other approaches to this problem."
- ❏ "Can we explore some other means of dealing with your concerns?"
- ❏ "Can you foresee any concerns this approach might not deal with?"
- ❏ "What benefits do you see for solving this problem?"
- ❏ "What would you like to see in place when your concern is solved?"
- ❏ "What do you like and dislike about the ways things are handled now?"
- ❏ "What is it about this approach that makes it useful to you?"
- ❏ "Is there another perspective that someone else might have?" or "How would others look at this?"
- ❏ "What is working now?"
- ❏ Your specific questions for your role:

Framing and Reframing

Framing a problem involves clarifying an often vaguely defined set of assumptions, which determine the scope of the problem. Drawing a frame renders complex information into a manageable problem statement.

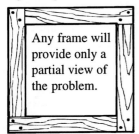

Any frame will provide only a partial view of the problem.

Once a problem frame is accepted, it is very difficult to change.

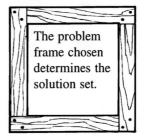

The problem frame chosen determines the solution set.

3

This said, fortunately it is possible to change the problem frame. It is easiest to do it early in the process by *reframing* the problem—consciously changing that original set of assumptions. Reframing is a powerful tool in your consulting tool kit. By reframing a problem with your client, you are actually reframing your own professional role, as illustrated in the figure below.

TYPICAL EVERYDAY LIFE EXAMPLE	A NARROWER FRAME (AND ROLE)	A WIDER FRAME (AND ROLE)
"Let's get a different car."	"Let's buy a new, red sports car."	"Let's consider our transportation needs for the next two to three years."
"We need a spreadsheet for our computer."	"Let's ask Systems to load Excel™ on the workstation."	"We need to look at our financial forecasting and reporting process."
"We need our engineers to be more customer-focused."	"Let's buy all our engineers the *Powerful Professionals* book."	"How do we help our engineers connect their skills more tightly to their customers' needs?"

BENEFITS OF REFRAMING

• Reframing can increase the range of solutions when problems are presented too narrowly, often leading to much more effective action.

• Reframing can focus your attention, as well as that of your client, when problems are presented too broadly.

• Defining the best problem frame is critical for getting a consultation started on the right foot.

• As you reframe the problem, you are also reframing your role. Narrow problems set up narrow roles. Unclear problems set up unclear roles.

• The most powerful consultations usually occur where neither you nor your client could have produced as powerful a problem frame without the input of the other.

• Highly valued by clients are professionals who come up with creative, resourceful solutions to problems within their area of expertise. Reframing is key to reaching this kind of solution.

66 Quotable Quotes 99

"Feeling 'one-down,' internal consultants often don't challenge the client's frame of the problem. If we don't check the frame, however, we allow the client to control both the process and the content, thereby being forced into a pair of hands role and losing our leverage."
– Bill Sefcik, CPA

Problem frames are generally not well thought-out by clients. Clients are usually delighted with professional help to enlarge, narrow or change the problem scope to a more effective one.

Defining the Business Need: Reframing the Problem

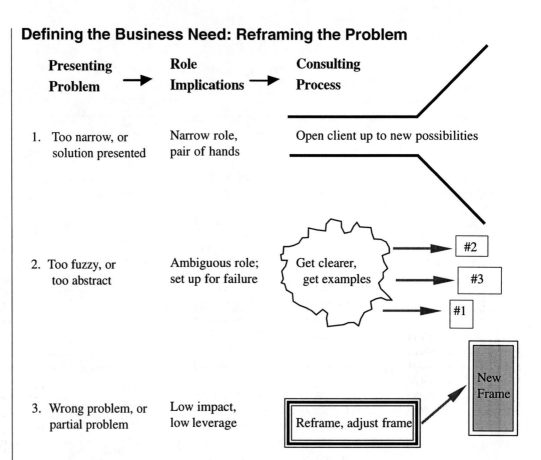

Presenting Problem	→	Role Implications	→	Consulting Process
1. Too narrow, or solution presented		Narrow role, pair of hands		Open client up to new possibilities
2. Too fuzzy, or too abstract		Ambiguous role; set up for failure		Get clearer, get examples → #2, #3, #1
3. Wrong problem, or partial problem		Low impact, low leverage		Reframe, adjust frame → New Frame

In Chapter 5, Gathering Information, is a method for sorting out fuzzy and complex situations.

Reframing Techniques

Here are some practical skills and principles for increasing your reframing skills:

✓ First, separate understanding from agreement. Listen to your clients by summarizing their statements without committing yourself to a course of action.

✓ Remember, for any number of reasons, most clients are presenting the problem as they truly see it. These reasons can range from the pressures of time—"We need it fixed now," to truly trying to be helpful—"I didn't want to burden you with that."

✓ If your client has presented you with a solution, start the reframe with the solution— "You seem enthusiastic about the ABC computer. What are some ways you would use a system like this?"

✓ Don't ask the habitual, interrogation question, "Why do you want that?" putting your clients on the defensive. You do, however, need to determine causes. Use less threatening questions like "What led you to that?" It leads clients to tell you non-threatening stories which will probably include causes.

✓ Keep in mind that your client's frame may ultimately be the best one. Checking for the best frame may mean you may come back to the original problem statement as the best statement.

Often clients are unsure what problem they are trying to solve. Strangely, this can actually be a benefit. When clients are unsure of the problem, they are more open to reframing it!

CHECKLIST OF TECHNIQUES FOR
REFRAMING CLIENT NEEDS

❏ Resist the temptation to go with the first definition of the problem. Experience shows that a better definition of the underlying need and the potential solution will nearly always emerge after you invest time to redefine the issue.

❏ Problem too narrow? Ask your client some of the 'opening up' questions found on the Checklist, page 34.

❏ "Why?" questions ask for justification, putting the client on the spot, possibly causing loss of face. Instead, ask "What led you to …?" This allows a simple explanation, leading easily to a reframe.

❏ Problem too broad?

  1. Ask the client for examples of the broad concern. Brainstorm specific issues that make up the broad concern until all the issues are out on the table. If possible, make this list visible.

  2. Summarize the specific issues and set priorities on the top few.

  3. Plan action on these.

  We will deal with this topic in more depth in Chapter 5, *Gathering Information*.

❏ Listen for, and be aware of, both the content of the situation—the technical and business issues, and the process of the situation—how you and your client are dealing with the content.

❏ Use open-ended questions. Allow your client to talk about the issues surrounding the presenting issue. Be patient! Rarely do potentially more threatening, underlying issues get out on the table during the first pass, or even the second.

❏ Know your own tolerance for ambiguity. Low tolerance for ambiguity—fear and ambiguity of not knowing the right answer for a while—will often cause a consultant to collude with the client to keep the problem narrowly defined. Powerful professionals have learned to work with unstructured and ambiguous problems.

❏ Model the behavior you expect from your client. If you want your client to be open to new ideas and approaches, you need to show you are open to new ideas and approaches.

Low tolerance for ambiguity— consultant's and client's—often severely limits the search for underlying issues and the range of options considered. This usually comes from fear of not immediately knowing the 'right' answer.

PROBLEM & ROLE ICEBERG

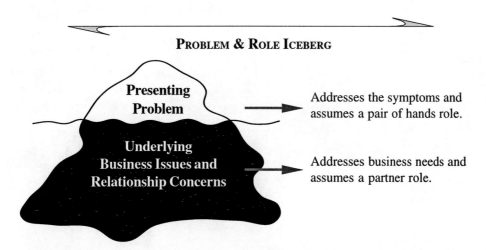

Like an iceberg, often only the tip of the problem can be seen. You need to get below the surface to find the real needs and set up powerful roles—not to mention avoiding Titanic failures!

One of the first challenges for a professional is to test whether the presenting problem is too narrow or too large.

❝ Quotable Quotes ❞

Actual positive feedback to a professional from a client: "Looks at alternatives and uses judgment to determine best course of action. Doesn't jump to conclusions but considers a range of possibilities."

DEFINING THE PROBLEM SCOPE

Clients can present a wide range of problem definitions or frames. No matter how the problem is presented, the end results you want are the same—a problem definition which:

- meets the underlying needs
- is logically defensible
- has mutual commitment
- is strategic
- enhances your role as a powerful professional.

Very Narrow ←——————————————————→ **Very Broad**

Characteristics:

• a solution is offered	• very complex, fuzzy or messy
• a symptom is described	• multiple causes
• client assumes cause is known	• no one action will solve the issue

▼ ▼

Examples:

Systems:	*Engineering:*
• "Please load Excel™ on the workstation."	• "We have a maintenance problem."
Human Resources:	*Training:*
• "How can we fire Mr. Doe?"	• "Do you have a communications workshop?"
Public Affairs:	*Financial:*
• "Can you design a brochure for us?"	• "Accounts Receivable are in bad shape again."

▼ ▼

Professional Role Impact:

• Pair of hands role	• Potential for broad roles
• Solution may fail	• Need to handle ambiguity
• Short term, non-strategy reputation	• Without further clarity, recommendations may fail

▼ ▼

Consulting Strategies:

• Ask questions which open up options.	• You may wish to deal with emergencies first—but be careful.
• Avoid asking "why?" type questions, thereby putting the client on the defensive.	• Ask for examples of the concern to make the concern more concrete.
	• Manage the ambiguity by summarizing often.

Establishing Rapport

No matter what your professional expertise, consulting is a personal service business. Establishing rapport is crucial to the success of this service. There is direct correlation between establishing rapport and effective uncovering of difficult, threatening issues. Whatever the nature of your client, time and effort spent in rapport building is time well spent.

We are not denying the existence of the ogre client, overly aggressive, who would probably perceive establishing rapport as 'touchy-feely stuff.' The majority of your clients, however, are decent human beings. Like you, they are trying their best to be effective.

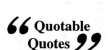

As much effort should be put into 'rapport' talk as 'report' talk.

WHY ESTABLISHING RAPPORT IS SO IMPORTANT

- Clients, like professionals, have basic human needs—the need to be respected, the need to be treated as an individual, the need to belong and the need for self esteem. Building personal rapport is crucial to fulfilling these needs.
- If you want your clients to 'open up' and express potentially threatening issues, you need to establish trusting relationships.
- If you want your clients to face difficult realities, you must first create supportive and personal relationships.
- Establishing and building trust is crucial to healthy business relationships. It starts at first contact.
- Establishing rapport at the first and every meeting is crucial to establishing a 50-50 consulting relationship.

❝ Quotable Quotes ❞

Rapport Not Needed? One professional told us of a sign above a client's desk reading: "Spit it out and get out."

"*As internal professionals, we have the false sense that we do not need to spend much time building rapport for two reasons:*
    a. Clients seem very busy and don't have time.
    b. Clients will use us anyway, because we are internal and they have to use us.
We have to keep in mind that as rapport increases, so does the opportunity to become business partners to our clients.

External consultants spend a lot of time building rapport as a matter of survival with clients. Internal consultants should not spend less effort in the area of rapport."
                           – *Bill Sefcik, CPA*
            Consulting Skills for Professionals workshop instructor

*Be recursive!
'Recursiveness,' a
mathematical term,
would translate into
'non-math' as
'model the behavior
you wish to elicit.'*

*A wider list of
effective consulting
principles are
presented in the last
chapter.*

*Use face-to-face
communication as
much as possible,
especially at the
early stages of a
consultation. It is
much more difficult
to build relationships
using telephones and
e-mail.*

Principles for Establishing Rapport

Techniques are hollow without the foundation of principles. Just think of how most of us recoil from phony smiles sometimes practised by insincere salespeople. Here are some principles for establishing rapport:

- *Treat your clients the way you would like to be treated.* Remember that clients are human, with fears, control needs and acceptance needs.
- *Remember, there is always a reason why people act the way they do.* What appears to be bizarre client behavior is usually rational behavior in the client's mind.
- *Model the behavior you expect in your clients.* For example, be open if you want your clients to be open. Explain your agendas if you want your clients to be clear on their agendas.
- *Communicate about communication difficulties.* That is, talk about the communication difficulty objectively, one level above where you are communicating. For example, "I think we are locking horns here; could we step back for a moment and talk about the impasse?"
- *Separate people from the problem.* Don't personalize the problem for either you or your client. Be tough on problems but supportive of clients. Focus on the problem, not the person.
- *Remember that commitment building starts at first contact with your client,* is built by establishing rapport, reinforced at every client contact and does not end until the project is wrapped up.

Telephone & E-Mail Rapport

Because communication is mainly nonverbal, written or telephone communications are more challenging from a personal perspective. Additional items specifically related to telephone and e-mail rapport are:

- ❏ *Smile.* Even over the telephone and in an e-mail message, people can almost 'hear' or 'read' a smile and sincerity.
- ❏ *Tone of your voice or your writing is more important* because people do not have the usual 'body language' cues. Research confirms that much of communication is nonverbal.
- ❏ *Change your telephone message daily, if possible.* When you record your message, remember first impressions are lasting.
- ❏ *You can often verbalize carelessly without undue repercussions.* Saying something and writing it are two different things. People generally accept some verbal ambiguity. The written word, however, carries more impact, is more direct, and does not have the forgiving modification of tone or humor, so watch what you write!
- ❏ *Always reread your e-mail before your send it.* Although many people like the brevity and informality of e-mail, think of the human side of your message as thoroughly as the head side. As one professional said, "We can peeve one person by what we say; we can peeve many more with one e-mail message."

CHECKLIST FOR ESTABLISHING RAPPORT

To many professionals, the person-to-person contact required to establish an effective consulting relationship does not come easily. Here is a 'coaching' list for establishing personal rapport:

3

Before Meeting Your Client:
- ❑ Ask around to find out something about your client—a hobby or something that interests both you and your client.
- ❑ Know and use your client's name. People appreciate the effort of remembering names. Be sure your client's name is spelled properly in any documents.
- ❑ Know and use the basic etiquette of your organization in speech and dress. Even if you have a tendency to push back against some organizational norms in speech and dress, first contact is probably a poor occasion to do so.
- ❑ Avoid meeting new clients at times when you are not in top form, for example at the beginning or end of a stressful day.

Remember, all these techniques must be built on good principles and values. A phony smile won't 'cut it.' But don't forget to smile if you mean to be friendly. Rapport is established heart-to-heart, not head-to-head.

Strategies for Rapport Building:
- ❑ Take time to talk about something other than the business at hand. Put as much effort into rapport talk as report talk.
- ❑ For the first few minutes, use open-ended questions to get the client talking. See Chapter 15 for listening skills.
- ❑ Use active listening: paraphrase and summarize often.
- ❑ Know that different people have quite different styles. What works well with one client may bomb with another. Be alert, flexible and open.
- ❑ Use personal communication as much as possible. It is more difficult to build relationships using memos and e-mail.

Techniques for Building Rapport:
- ❑ Make and maintain eye contact.
- ❑ Smile. Clients respond to consultants who respond to clients.
- ❑ Shake hands.
- ❑ Use humor.
- ❑ Find some nonbusiness topic you both like to discuss, or comment on some timely topic.
- ❑ Chat about someone you both admire.
- ❑ Tell your client something personal about yourself. Speak sincerely.
- ❑ Listen—hear clients out—before jumping into critique or solutions.

This Checklist is on the Web Site: www.consultskills.com You may wish to produce an edited version of this Checklist for your specific use.

If Your Client is Emotional or in a Bind:
- ❑ Remember, you can't fix feelings. You can only help your clients express their feelings.
- ❑ Support your client. Recognize efforts the client has already made to resolve the problem.
- ❑ Support the client if it is difficult for the client to admit a problem.
- ❑ Support clients if they feel trapped. Look for the positives they may not see.
- ❑ Do not have people lose face. Clients will defend their self esteem beyond all else.

If Your Client is Upset or Defensive:
- ❑ Don't take it personally. Don't get defensive in return.
- ❑ Take the time to let clients express their feelings. Allow them to let off steam.
- ❑ Work hard to get at the issues and needs *underneath* the feelings.
- ❑ Work hard to find objective criteria for solving the problem.
- ❑ Stand your ground while negotiating a 50-50 role.

Trying It on for Size: A Typical First Contact Example

What follows is a simulated first 'meeting' with a client. Assume this exploration conversation takes place over a telephone. The client is the Technical Training & Safety Manager—tough and aggressive, but not unreasonable—of a medium-sized organization. The consultant is a Computing Support Desk Analyst. Purchase Orders for computing equipment or software must be initialled by the analyst.

As you 'listen in' on this first conversation, keep in mind these four questions:

1. What is the analyst doing successfully? What would you do differently?

2. What choices does the analyst have and where would those choices lead the consultation?

3. How successful is the analyst in surfacing the underlying needs?

4. How successful is the analyst in establishing a 50-50 relationship, neither one-up nor one-down?

EXAMPLE OF A BRIEF BUT TYPICAL FIRST CONTACT

Dialogue	Comments
The telephone rings in the analyst's office. *Analyst:* Good morning. This is Del Wong at the Computing Support Desk. How can I help?	• The best way to have enthusiastic clients is to show enthusiasm. What do you say when you answer the telephone?
Client: Good morning. I'm Chris Sharma, Manager of Technical Training and Safety. Your boss told me you would be able to take care of my request. I'm sending down a Purchase Order for a new Strato Cirrus 5000 computer. Your boss said you need to initial it so we can get the computer delivered tomorrow.	• Note the client may be name dropping. Did your boss say you *would* or *could* initial the PO? Often the first person you need to clarify your consulting role with is your supervisor. • The client has jumped to a solution and acted on it—a particular kind of computer. The client wants you to rubber stamp the solution and has already arranged for vendor and delivery.
Analyst: Hi Chris. I believe we have met before—on the Corporate Information Project. You gave a presentation on the need for tracking safety statistics.	• The consultant is trying to establish rapport by finding some topic in common. Establishing rapport can be particularly difficult over the phone. • The corporate policy is to severely discourage equipment like the Strato Cirrus 5000 which does not network well with the rest of the computing system. The Systems Department does not support its hardware or software. The analyst is not raising that issue yet but will need to do so soon.
Client: I'm in a big hurry. Can I send down the Purchase Order?	• The client is in no mood for rapport building—drop the attempt for now.

Analyst: I'll try to be brief. As you know, our organization doesn't support the Strato Cirrus. But if it is the best machine for your needs, we can prepare a business case. But let's leave that aside for now. I'm curious what features of this specific system excited you?

- Note the consultant is putting on the yellow light—not a red light saying "no," nor a green light saying it is OK. You don't want to be a road block nor do you want to be walked over. You want to maintain a 50-50 stance.
- One way of gathering information in a nonthreatening way is to co-opt the client by having the client describe the features which led to the solution.

Client: I was at a Safety & Training Conference last week and the Strato Cirrus people showed me how this machine can produce great graphics for the training materials we produce. I've got to go. I'll get our assistant to bring down the PO.

- The analyst has ferreted out one need so far, graphics for training materials, hardly sufficient reason for an unusual, unsupported machine.
- The client is putting the analyst under great pressure. You must be able to hold your ground to get at the underlying issues.

Analyst: I understand you are in a hurry. But I would like to understand all your needs. You mentioned graphics for training manuals. I'm sure you'll want to make wider use of this machine, for example, safety record keeping and statistics?

- The temptation will be great to quote corporate policy at this point. But the analyst chooses to try again to 'ferret out' the underlying needs.
- Note the analyst's use of active listening techniques—recognizing the client's time pressure and summarizing the one need mentioned so far by the client. People are much more likely to listen to someone who listens. Model the behavior you expect in your client.

Client: Look, I've talked to my Vice President and got the budget approved. And your boss said you'd take care of this for me.

- More pressure and more name dropping. Note the client does not say your boss said you would sign.
- What are the analyst's choices here?

  1. Sign off the Purchase Order

  2. Get off the phone and ask for a face-to-face meeting

  3. Try again for more data about the underlying needs

  4. Explain the policy about non-compatible equipment

  5. Communicate about the impasse

     And more options you may think of.

Analyst: Look Chris, I'm concerned that we are going in different directions here. The reason for signing off on computing equipment Purchase Orders is we want to be able to support the Strato Cirrus 5000 and its software. Unfortunately, we don't support this particular system. In order for me to sign off, I would need to work with you to justify this non-compatible equipment. If the Strato Cirrus 5000 is the best machine for your needs, I will sign off, but I need some of your time to gather information. Could we get together this afternoon?

- The analyst began with a communication about the developing impasse. This will give the client an opening to discuss how the consultation is going so far.
- The analyst tried to explain the corporate policy in logical and nonthreatening terms. Was it a good attempt?
- Notice again, how the analyst tries to offer a 50-50 relationship. I'll do some work if you will work with me. How successful is the Analyst?
- Many participants in our workshops suggest that face-to-face meetings are needed in situations like this. Asking for the meeting also allows you to prepare, to talk to your boss and to be able to find out about the

43

Client: (Silence for a few seconds) You people in Systems always seem to slow down things around here. But if that's what we need to do to get the Strato Cirrus 5000, I have got a few minutes this afternoon at three o'clock.

Analyst: Three is fine with me. I'd like to bring with me a portable computer that we do support to give you a demo of the graphics capabilities and our network. Could we also discuss the proposed uses of the machine?

Client: I can't spend much time. I'll have the Purchase Order ready.

Analyst: See you soon. Bye.

- Silence is very difficult for most people to handle. Note the slur on Systems. Keep the problem separated from the person. Note the first concession by the client but with a string attached—"If that's what we need to do to get ..."

- Be careful to hold your 50-50 ground here, neither being too soft nor too hard.

So, how did you do in considering the four questions set out at the beginning of this example? We will give you an opportunity to rate yourself on the next page.

BIRD'S EYE OF THE FIRST STAGE—EXPLORING THE NEED.

While still in this first stage, it's a good idea to step back and get a bird's eye view of the situation. You can be most helpful as a professional when you come up with aspects that your clients, immersed in the situation, may not have considered.

Framing the Concern:
❑ Can we clearly state the business need?
❑ Is the issue framed too broadly, leading to fuzzy solutions?
❑ Is the issue framed too narrowly, leading to a partial solution?
❑ Are we sure the problem frame will deal with the underlying causes so the problem does not recur?
❑ Are we sure that we understand and agree to the cause(s) of the concern?

Recommending Change:
❑ Will people see the need to deal with this issue?
❑ Will other people see the benefits of solving the concern?
❑ Is solving this problem worth the change effort?
❑ Where can we expect barriers, reservations and resistance?

Commitment:
❑ Who else has information related to this concern?
❑ Who else has a stake in this problem and/or its solution?
❑ Whose support is needed now or in the future?
❑ Who might be threatened or hurt if this concern is dealt with?
❑ Who else needs to be involved with this issue?
❑ Is the situation complex enough for us to diagram the multiple stakeholder system?

The System:
❑ If this concern is dealt with, what other interacting systems may aid or inhibit the change?

Potential Problems:
❑ How will we back out or change direction if further information leads to a different problem definition?

LOOKING IN THE MIRROR:
A SELF ASSESSMENT OF EXPLORING THE NEED SKILLS

Rate your *Exploring the Need* skills.

1 = *Needs much improvement* to 5 = *Very skilled.*

Highlight your development needs. If you are serious about your development, seek feedback from your professional peers, your clients and your supervisor.

3

General Skills:
1 2 3 4 5   I understand and can work with both the rational and personal dynamics of Exploring the Need.

1 2 3 4 5   With my clients, I can quickly establish a 50-50 partnership, neither one-up nor one-down.

1 2 3 4 5   I understand the importance of the first few minutes of client contact.

1 2 3 4 5   I know how to ask powerful questions to get at underlying problems.

1 2 3 4 5   I know that commitment building is something that starts in the first few seconds of Exploring the Need and doesn't stop until the project is closed.

Rational Skills:
1 2 3 4 5   I can demonstrate to my clients that I thoroughly heard the presenting problem.

1 2 3 4 5   I always summarize or paraphrase before responding to what my clients say.

1 2 3 4 5   I know what questions to ask to get at the underlying issues in a nonthreatening way.

1 2 3 4 5   I know when and how to reframe client problem statements.

1 2 3 4 5   I can 'hear' both content and process when my clients are speaking.

Interpersonal Skills:
1 2 3 4 5   I can easily establish rapport.

1 2 3 4 5   I understand my own tolerance for ambiguity. I don't rush to action due to fear of ambiguity.

1 2 3 4 5   I understand and can work with my own fears and client fears at first contact.

1 2 3 4 5   I understand and can deal with the common need for control, both in myself and in my clients.

1 2 3 4 5   I understand the dynamics of client resistance and can make resistance work for me.

1 2 3 4 5   I can deal with difficult clients.

Strategic Skills:
1 2 3 4 5   I know what I need clarified before making a commitment.

1 2 3 4 5   I know how to say "no," with options, to clients when the work is not strategic.

1 2 3 4 5   I know when to say "yes" to a project because it is value-added work for my organization.

1 2 3 4 5   I thoroughly understand the strategy of my organization and my professional group so I know when to say "yes," when to say "no," with options, and what to market.

If Your Client Initiates the Consultation:
1 2 3 4 5   I do not say "yes" without understanding the underlying business issue to be solved.

1 2 3 4 5   I understand the dynamics of a first client meeting which often results in my client presenting a narrow view of the problem (often a solution rather than a problem).

1 2 3 4 5   I know when and how to help my clients narrow or broaden the problem frame.

1 2 3 4 5   I balance what I should 'own' with what my clients should 'own.'

1 2 3 4 5   I know how to clarify the process by which the problem will be solved.

If You Selling a Proposal to Your Client:
1 2 3 4 5   I know how to prepare and present a persuasive proposal.

1 2 3 4 5   I know how to present both features and benefits of a proposal.

1 2 3 4 5   I know how to surface and deal with client reservations and concerns.

1 2 3 4 5   I know how to help my clients deal with resistance and change.

1 2 3 4 5   I can ask for a decision.

This Assessment is on the Web Site: www.consultskills.com.

WHAT YOU'VE LEARNED SO FAR ...

in**BRIEF** →

- You have the most leverage you'll ever have at the very beginning of a consultation. Use it or lose it!
- Both clients and consultants have fears. These fears can cause dysfunctional behavior in both clients and consultants.
- It is natural and OK for clients to present a too-narrow or too-broad view of a problem. Often a problem solution is presented instead of the problem.
- By asking appropriate questions you can broaden or narrow the scope of a consultation, and consequently, your role.
- You, as a consultant, have considerable control over the questions you ask, thus over the direction of the consultation.
- Avoid asking "Why?" questions too early and risk putting your clients on the defensive.
- Establishing rapport is very important to building the trust you need to get at the underlying issues.

THE EXPERTISE DELIVERY MODEL

Taking Stock or Closing

EXPLORING THE NEED

Recommending Change

Client Commitment

Clarifying Commitments

Gathering Information

"Clarifying commitments means never having to say you're sorry."

STAGE 2: CLARIFYING COMMITMENTS

4

Quick Snapshot

Did You Know?

- your last opportunity for high leverage is at the Clarifying Commitments stage?
- the most common reason for low client commitment is that clients were never asked?
- misunderstandings are costly and can undermine your career?
- clarifying expectations is a powerful conflict reduction tool?

How-to:

- determine the appropriate amount of clarification.
- manage the ambiguity of agreements.
- set up an influential role.
- clarify verbally and in writing.

The Bottom Line:

- You will be more effective by clarifying commitments with your clients using the models, checklists, assessments and skills of this chapter.

Second Stage: Clarifying Commitments

Having explored the problem and processes with your client in *Exploring the Need*, you will now want to move to making commitments. In this chapter, the most important word is 'clarifying.' Clarifying means never having to say you're sorry. Clarifying Commitments signifies moving into the action phase *with enough clarity to proceed*—clarity on expectations, outcomes, processes and roles.

In most consulting books, the term 'contracting' is used to describe this second stage in the Expertise Delivery process. We do not recommend the use of legal contracts internally, yet the legal concept of contracting can be a powerful touchstone for the clear commitments needed to function effectively as a professional. A contract:

- spells out clearly what each party will get from the agreement,
- commits the parties to action,
- requires 'consideration'; benefits both parties,
- cannot be signed under duress.

A client always has the last word, a powerful professional ensures it is the right word.

The word 'contract,' however, can be intimidating to internal clients. Some of these words are 'softer' and may be more appropriate to use in your organization:

- agreement
- understanding
- terms of reference
- confirmation.
- mutual agreement
- project scope
- expectations clarification

The concepts and principles of clarification are paramount to effective consultation; the words are of less consequence.

The goal for this second stage is to establish a 50-50 partnership, professional and client sharing equal commitment to the project. In this vein, clarification by and from both sides ensures highly valued work. This requires an explicit agreement between consultant and client, preferably written, outlining:

- overall results expected
- what you expect from each other
- how you will work together.

Why Bother Clarifying?

"I thought you wanted ..." "If only I had cleared that up right away ..." These statements occur like echoes throughout many consultant stories, echoes of unclear expectations at the root of numerous consulting problems and conflicts. One mark of high-performing professionals is taking responsibility for clarifying commitments. This is not the case with the following two sad stories!

"That'll be $40,000 please!"

A Project Engineer in a large utility company telephoned an in-house Systems Analyst to ask how much a feasibility study for an engineering project would cost. The Systems Analyst understood the engineer *to ask for* the *actual feasibility study to be carried out* and asked "When do you want it?" The engineer, expecting *just a cost estimate figure* to carry out the feasibility study, said "Next Friday will be fine." Neither side clarified any further.

To meet the Friday deadline, the Systems Department hired external help. The feasibility study arrived on the project engineer's desk on time, with a $40,000 internal bill! The Design Engineering group found out the cost of the study, but certainly not in the way they had expected!

Repercussions of not clarifying expectations were horrendous. The Systems group started to insist on formal documentation with numerous sign-offs. The Engineering group was furious. Besides blaming the Systems group for this incident, they dredged up many other long-standing complaints. Long after the managers of the Systems and Engineering groups were replaced, the feud went on.

"My only CEO Communication was about a screw-up!"

An Audio Visual (AV) Professional in a large organization often received requests for presentation slides from the CEO's Administrative Assistant. The usual slides were 35 mm. One day a request for "presentation slides" was made by telephone. The AV Professional, as usual, prepared 35 mm slides and sent them to the CEO's office. Later that day the CEO himself phoned the AV Professional directly, saying "There's a problem with the slides you sent me. They're 35 mm, I need overhead slides." With bruised professional pride, the AV Professional remarked ruefully "I had never communicated directly with the CEO before, and perhaps never will again. My only conversation was about a screw-up!"

Most organizations have equivalent stories. Clarifying Commitments is a crucial skill for a professional. Misunderstandings are costly to your organization and your career.

Not only does clarifying commitments reduce problems, it also produces immense benefits.

4

"A minute of clarification can save hours of work later."
– *Robin Sober*

In this chapter …

- *Clarifying Commitments pays off!*
- *Levels and guidelines for how much and what to clarify.*
- *Clarification checklists.*
- *Ambiguity!*
- *Confirming (one page!) usable sample documents*
- *Asking for what you want*
- *Consulting roles*

Clarifying Commitments Pays Off!

For a small investment of time, the benefits of clarification are great:

- **You have most leverage early.** Up-front is the best time to ask for and clarify what you want and need for a successful 50-50 project; also to influence the direction of the project.

- **You have most influence early.** Professionals yearn for influence, inherently believing that the *technical* wizardry of their profession will suffice—*performance* wizardry is what is actually valued.

- **Roles are established early for the life of the whole project.** Internal consultants often complain about the inadequacy of their roles. The best time to negotiate and establish roles is early in the consulting process.

- **You and your clients will have many assumptions and expectations.** You need to be sure the critical items are clarified and agreed-to.

- **If you or your clients have any of the fears** discussed in Stage 1, *Exploring the Need,* you can partly alleviate them by clarifying commitments.

- **Most clients appreciate clarity.** Clients will often express appreciation when clarification is done well.

- **Clarity sets up the later stages** of the Expertise Delivery Model, especially *Recommending Change* and *Closing.* Ironically, the best time to negotiate Closing—the last stage— is at this early *Clarifying Commitments* stage.

- **Clarification enhances client commitment.** One consulting peeve we often hear is lack of client commitment to projects. Some reasons might be that clients weren't asked, weren't clear, or didn't know what was expected of them. Commitment and ownership are built early and reinforced often.

- **Clarification reduces conflict.** One organization we work with has a saying '80% of conflict arises from unclear expectations.' Clarification is a simple and effective conflict prevention tool.

Next, we will distinguish two kinds of clarification:
1. Roles and services clarification—the long term concern
2. Project clarification—a short term concern.

This chapter is concerned with shorter term project clarification. In Chapter 13, *Your Strategy: Saying Yes or No*, we will deal with the longer term issue of roles and services agreements.

❝ Quotable Quotes ❞

"One of the greatest sources of problems between consultants and customers is the lack of mutual understanding about what was to be done ... As I try to keep everything conversational and informal, I overlook the key agreements that are needed. Clear contracting mitigates many potential problems down the line."

– Geoff Bellman Getting Things Done When You Are Not In Charge.

TWO LEVELS OF CLARITY

In modern organizations, at least two kinds of clarity are needed to be successful:

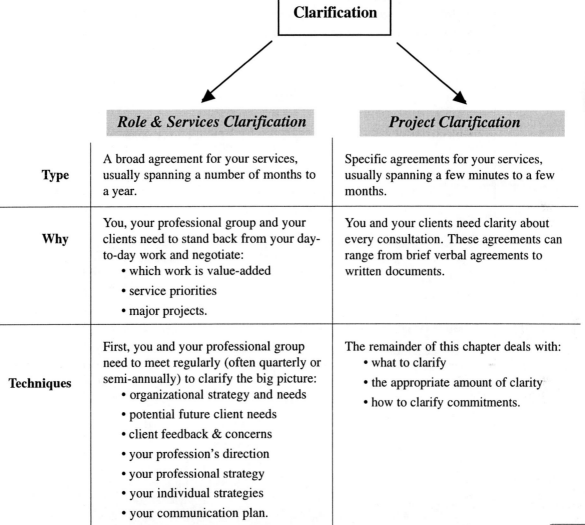

	Role & Services Clarification	**Project Clarification**
Type	A broad agreement for your services, usually spanning a number of months to a year.	Specific agreements for your services, usually spanning a few minutes to a few months.
Why	You, your professional group and your clients need to stand back from your day-to-day work and negotiate: • which work is value-added • service priorities • major projects.	You and your clients need clarity about every consultation. These agreements can range from brief verbal agreements to written documents.
Techniques	First, you and your professional group need to meet regularly (often quarterly or semi-annually) to clarify the big picture: • organizational strategy and needs • potential future client needs • client feedback & concerns • your profession's direction • your professional strategy • your individual strategies • your communication plan. Second, on a semi-annual or annual basis you meet with your key clients to discuss and negotiate: • their needs and expectations • your professional strategy and offers • your service priorities & projects • your communication plan.	The remainder of this chapter deals with: • what to clarify • the appropriate amount of clarity • how to clarify commitments.

4

We will be dealing in more detail with role and services agreements in the Chapter 13, Your Strategy: Saying Yes or No.

CLARIFYING COMMITMENTS CHECKLIST

The following checklist is much too long except for very large projects. The checklist is in two parts. The first is problem-related, the second, relationship and commitment-related. You may find it useful to:
- ✔ Check the items which typically create misunderstandings.
- ✔ Check items you feel are critical to a successful project in your area of expertise.
- ✔ Amend or add items specific to your situation.

PART 1: NEGOTIATING THE PROBLEM SIDE

Can you identify which items sometimes fall between the cracks, resulting in misunderstanding?

Consultants & clients can get into trouble by ignoring these items.

This Checklist is on the Web Site: www.consultskills.com.

Objectives:
- ❑ business problem to be solved
- ❑ business/technical objectives—musts/wants
- ❑ organizational objectives related to the project
- ❑ client's objectives —musts/wants, short/long term
- ❑ consultant's objectives—musts/wants

Results expected from the project:
- ❑ definition of success
- ❑ specific product or service to be delivered
- ❑ scope of project
- ❑ measures of success
- ❑ risk/benefit

Quality level:
- ❑ quality level expectations
- ❑ quality measures
- ❑ service/support expectations

Resources:
- ❑ information sources
- ❑ research available or needed
- ❑ technical data source
- ❑ outside help

Values:
- ❑ fit with organizational values

Costs and economics:
- ❑ budgeting and approvals
- ❑ who is funding this?
- ❑ budgets and charge codes
- ❑ support services: e.g., clerical, technical—who provides, whose budget?
- ❑ economic benefits and payback
- ❑ economic requirements

Data collection:
- ❑ acceptable/non-acceptable methods
- ❑ technical information sources
- ❑ feedback of data to sources—who, when, how much, what format?
- ❑ confidentiality

Schedule/project plan:
- ❑ timelines
- ❑ completion/turnover date
- ❑ number of days estimated
- ❑ critical path
- ❑ major decision points about continuing the project
- ❑ absolute deadlines
- ❑ review/reporting target dates

Underlying issues:
- ❑ wider implications of this project
- ❑ organizational politics related to the project
- ❑ sensitivities

Constraints/restrictions:

- ❏ financial
- ❏ people resources
- ❏ other resources
- ❏ labor contracts
- ❏ legal and government requirements
- ❏ what to avoid

Potential problems:

- ❏ what could go wrong?
- ❏ back out clause
- ❏ preventive actions
- ❏ contingency plan

PART 2: CLARIFYING RELATIONSHIPS AND PERSONAL COMMITMENTS

Key stakeholders and clients:

- ❏ sponsor or funding client(s)
- ❏ working client(s)
- ❏ end user client(s)
- ❏ indirect clients (e.g., Purchasing, Human Resources, etc.)
- ❏ other stakeholders
- ❏ vendors and suppliers
- ❏ contractors

Dealing with problems:

- ❏ how will problems be identified and handled?
- ❏ process to resolve conflicts

Ensuring acceptance and commitment:

- ❏ who will be impacted by this project now or in the future?
- ❏ who needs to be involved?
- ❏ level of involvement
- ❏ whose acceptance and commitment is critical?

Feedback from clients and customers:

- ❏ by whom?
- ❏ when?

Roles and responsibilities:

- ❏ consultant
- ❏ project team
- ❏ working client
- ❏ others (e.g. clerical, research, data sources, etc.)

Decision making:

- ❏ how decisions will be made
- ❏ who will be involved in key decisions?
- ❏ level of decision making authority
- ❏ who has final approval?

Change management:

- ❏ how will changes be made?
- ❏ how do we get out of this (gracefully) if project becomes unfeasible or collapses?

Communication:

- ❏ who needs to be informed for commitment?
- ❏ how will they be informed?
- ❏ how often will they be informed?
- ❏ status reports

4

❝ Quotable Quotes ❞

"We are usually much better at dividing up work than drawing people together under a common banner."
– Geoff Bellman
Getting Things Done When You are Not in Charge.

"I have often noticed that a personalized clarification checklist list is very important. Most successful consultants often have two lists: a detailed list for larger projects and an abbreviated list for small projects."
– Bill Sefcik CPA

On-Job Application

One very successful professional consulting organization uses this checklist to assess where misunderstandings typically occur, then emphasizes the need for increased clarity in these areas. Many professionals have edited this checklist to produce a personal version and inserted it into their notebook to make sure they have clarified all crucial items with their clients.

How Much to Clarify

Having just covered a long, long list, *now* we tell you that brevity is the soul of a good agreement! Given that:

– each project and client is unique, requiring different levels of clarification;

– you and your clients are under time pressure;

– you don't want to make the clarification process cumbersome and bureaucratic;

you still want to be sure you have clarified the critical items.

❝ Quotable Quotes ❞

"The 80/20 rule applies to clarification. Find the 20% to clarify that has the 80% impact."
– Bob Ratay
Avery-Dennison

One way to address this question is the idea of 'minimum critical specifications.' A term used in engineering or scientific work, it means *defining the minimum number of critical pieces of information required to specify a problem or a whole system.* The analogous question for the consulting process is "What minimum items do I need to clarify in order to ensure a successful project under these circumstances?"

Below are some variables and approaches to consider. The more rational and business-related issues are relatively easy to define. The amount of clarification needed will increase as these variables increase:

- The size of the project
- The length of time from project inception to completion
- The visibility of the project
- The number of people involved
- The impact of the project.
- The amount of people's time in the project
- The risk of the project

Increase the amount of clarification

Insight from a workshop participant:
"I've identified some 'red flag' areas where I tend not to clarify as much as I should:
- *I like the work,*
- *the client likes me doing it, and*
- *it's easy."*

Most professionals are skilled at these more quantifiable variables. Those below, involving emotions and personal relationships, are usually more challenging.

- Trust
- Tolerance for ambiguity:
  - your client's tolerance
  - your own tolerance
- Perception of relative power
- Past experiences with client:
  - your own
  - reputation with others

Assess the impact on the amount of clarification

The connection is usually clear for the first set of rational variables; for example, the bigger the project, the more clarification needed. For relationship and emotional issues the connection is less clear. For example, if the trust level is low, an intuitive reaction is to try to clarify further. Asking a wary client to clarify further may make the client's trust spiral even lower.

Here is a case in consulting where commonsense and intuition can get you into trouble. It's good to be aware that some critical pieces of consulting are not intuitive. In fact, intuitive behavior can be dysfunctional and become the cause of difficulties!

A general principle to remember is that 'more of the same' is rarely as effective as a different strategy.

4

The Leaning Tower of Pisa & Commonsense Consulting

Some of the greatest advances in science and mathematics have gone against what was accepted commonsense. Take the story of Galileo. From time immemorial, it was accepted wisdom that a denser object falls at a faster rate than a less dense object. Galileo, we are told, dropped objects off the Leaning Tower of Pisa to show that small, less dense objects fall at the same rate as large, denser objects. He suffered considerable insult and injury from the authorities who defended the accepted wisdom. Even today, if you asked a random group of people whether a larger, denser ball falls more rapidly than a smaller, less dense ball, most people would say the larger ball falls more rapidly. Normally this assumption won't get people into much trouble. Unless, that is, they are designing a bungee jump!

For other intuitive and 'commonsense' behaviors that get professionals in trouble, see pages 33, 75 and 264.

In this book we will point out numerous situations where commonsense, intuitive behavior can get you into trouble.

We now move on to another personal variable, Tolerance for Ambiguity.

We will specifically explore the issues with complex or multiple clients in the Chapter 8, Mapping Client Systems.

The Challenges of Clarifying

Low tolerance for ambiguity means being unable to proceed without 'definiteness.' The more effort to establish the future in a definite way, the more likely the unexpected will arise. The unexpected tends to play havoc with 'definiteness.' The tendency is then for the consultant to push the client further to clarify with more detail—or alternately, to give up on clarification altogether because 'It doesn't work.' To further complicate the situation, the client's tolerance for ambiguity often differs from the consultant's. In these situations, a consultant's natural tendency is to blame 'dumb' clients. Beware of that!

What for one client may be too much clarity, for another may be too little.

- **Fit the amount of clarification to the situation and the client.** Either too little and too much clarification is dysfunctional. Too little risks misunderstanding; too much risks alienating clients by creating the perception of mistrust. Detailed clarification is often interpreted as a consultant's unnecessary need for control.

- **Document the minimal critical 'specs.'** *Always* document the few critical items that need clarification to ensure project success, but use only the minimum amount of clarification to get the job done. If at all possible, keep a written agreement to one page of paper or one e-mail screen.

- **The greater the number of clients, the greater the divergence of individual clarification needs.** For multiple client situations, finding the optimal level of clarification is even more challenging. One method is to openly explain the reasons for the amount of clarification needed. Most people will go along with you if you can tell them why.

CLARIFYING COMMITMENTS:
AMBIGUITY AND RISK GUIDELINES

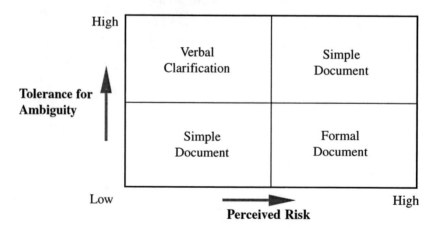

56

Confirming Commitments

Having considered the variables on the amount of clarification needed, the understanding then needs to be confirmed with your clients. *This stage is extremely important.* Some simple-to-complex guidelines for confirming commitments are:

- **No agreement at all is always a no-no.** Unless you love danger and living at the edge, *always confirm your understandings*. A minimal agreement is better than none!

- **The minimum verbal agreement is a restatement of what you understand to be the key expectations.** At the end of the telephone conversation or meeting, "So what I understand is that I'll do X and Y, while you'll do A and B. Is that how you see it?" This statement should be nonthreatening and clear, promoting a 50-50 partnership.

- **The minimum written documentation is a one-page memo or one e-mail screen** for one day to a few weeks work. The next section deals with construction of this kind of document, used in most internal consultations.

- **A formal project mandate.** If your project is very complex, high profile, risky or involves a lot of people, you would need to produce a formal project mandate. Project Management books deal with this situation in more detail.

- **A legal document.** We rarely hear of legal documents being used inside organizations. In such cases, professional legal advice would be used.

> 66 **Quotable Quotes** 99
>
> *"Powerful profession-als always confirm understandings and agreements before proceeding."*
> *– George Campbell*

4

We guarantee you will save hours of work and frustration with the use of this simple tool—explicitly clarifying expectations.

HOW MUCH CLARITY? SOME GUIDELINES

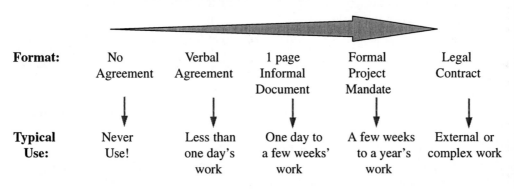

Format:	No Agreement	Verbal Agreement	1 page Informal Document	Formal Project Mandate	Legal Contract
	↓	↓	↓	↓	↓
Typical Use:	Never Use!	Less than one day's work	One day to a few weeks' work	A few weeks to a year's work	External or complex work

The Pen is Mightier than the Word

Your power and role as a consultant can be enhanced by making it *your* responsibility for actually writing the agreement. Benefits to you include:

- constructing it to reflect the 50-50 partnership you want, while including the key items you want and need included.

- relieving clients of a bothersome, but extremely important, activity.

- expressing the project and your own role in your terms, while providing documentation for other stakeholders to the consulting project.

- providing written documentation as protection—often helpful in the event of disputes.

Gary Karrass, in Negotiate to Close, suggests volunteering to write the agreement yourself. Besides relieving the client of that task, you can emphasize what you want, and make it specific to avoid misunderstanding later.

We are sticklers for keeping the confirming document to one page. People won't read more than that unless it is very important to them.

Just as computers use verification processes to make sure information sent to a disk or modem was actually received, so also consultants need to reflect back to their clients understandings of commitments reached.

Confirming (Brief!) Documents

One of the most frequently used methods for clarifying commitments is to write a one page document or a single screen e-mail message. For internal consulting within the time frame of a few days/weeks, the one-page document is a powerful and useful tool for effective consulting.

Features
- One page or less! Busy people, like your clients, will not read much more.
  It is very informal. Use lists and bullets. Make it easy to read!
- The consultant assumes responsibility for misunderstandings. "Just to be sure I understand the commitments we've made, here's how I see the project ..."
- It is non-punishing and doesn't sound or feel like you are trying to protect yourself.
- It has a 50-50 partnership tone. The lists of client commitments and consultant commitments should feel equal.

Benefits
- ✔ It will raise your chances of doing valued work.
- ✔ It will raise your chances of having a satisfied customer.
- ✔ You will have more influence over the scope and tone of the project and an opportunity to frame the project and your role in a powerful way.
- ✔ You will have more influence over your role, your commitments and your priorities.
- ✔ Clients will often compliment you for well written confirming documents. Most clients also like brevity and clarity.
- ✔ If disagreements do occur, you will have documentation of your good faith intentions.

Outline
1. Re-establish rapport. "Thank you for the meeting ..."
2. Remind clients of the underlying issues. "My understanding of our goal (or purpose or business need) is ..."
3. List consultant commitments. "What I have agreed to do is ..."
4. List client commitments. "What you have agreed to do is ..." (This list should be approximately the same length as the consultant's).
5. Ask for feedback. "If you have any concerns, please call ..."
6. Follow up. "I'll call or see you ..."

One department collected and now keeps a large number of these one page confirming documents on file. Professionals in the group can pick the best model for their particular project.

CONFIRMING DOCUMENT EXAMPLE 1
ONE CLIENT AND ONE CONSULTANT

To: Client
From: Professional
Re: The XYZ System Improvement Project

Thank you for this morning's meeting. Just to be sure I understand what we have agreed to do, here are the major deliverables for us to complete for Phase I.

Phase I business goal:
- To produce a feasibility study for improving XYZ System including recommendations and a cost/ benefit study.

I am responsible for:
- getting approval for this project from my manager. If there are any difficulties, I will let you know by the end of this week.
- spending about five days data gathering about the XYZ System needs, by interviewing 3 or 4 of your specialists and 3 or 4 of your users.
- analyzing the results of the survey and compiling them into a report with recommendations.
- researching what other departments like yours are doing to make the XYZ System more efficient.
- producing a cost/benefit report for my top two recommendations, by April 20.
- completing the above within 15 person-days of effort. My traveling expenses will be submitted through your department for reimbursement.

You are responsible for:
- producing the Project Initiation Report and communicating why we are initiating this project to your staff and to your manager, by April 2.
- notifying the specialists and users you want me to interview, by April 2.
- providing me with the current XYZ System documentation.
- getting approval for me to access any data within the current XYZ System, by April 5.
- being available for consultation if we run into any roadblocks we cannot now anticipate.
- starting the budgeting procedures for Phase II.

We will meet on April 23rd at 1:00 pm in your office to review the data, analysis and recommendations. We will then scope out Phase II of the project.

If I have missed any key points or if you have any concerns about the above, please call me at extension 2222.

These samples are on the Web Site: www.consultskills.com

4

In these three examples of a confirming document, you may wish to:
- *identify ideas to use in your consulting practice: which to modify to fit your typical consultations, and to fit your organizational culture*
- *check the documents for the right tone and how they fit with the criteria presented in this chapter*
- *check that they reflect the professional doing this for clarity and to raise the chances of a successful consultation*
- *check whether it feels like 'consultant protection.'*

CONFIRMING DOCUMENT EXAMPLE 2
CONSULTANT TEAM LEADER TO CLIENT SPONSOR TEAM

To: Client, Head, XYZ System Improvement Project Steering Committee (S.C.)
From: Project Leader, XYZ System Improvement Project Team (P.T.)
Re: The XYZ System Improvement Project

Thank you for this morning's meeting. Just to be sure we all understand what we have agreed to do, here are the major deliverables for us to complete for Phase I.

Phase I business goal:
   • To produce a feasibility study for improving XYZ System including recommendations and a cost benefit study.

Major Phase I milestones and responsibilities:

Action/Item	Timing	Who
Produce a Project Initiation Report and discuss it with your staff and executives.	by April 2	S.C.
Notify and inform us of the specialists and end users you want us to interview. We will select the remainder to get a good cross section of opinion.	by April 2	S.C.
Get approvals for the Project Team to access any data within the current XYZ System.	by April 5	S.C.
Spend about five days data gathering about the XYZ System needs by interviewing 10 to 12 XYZ specialists and 10 to 12 end users.	by April 12	P.T.
Provide us with the current XYZ System documentation.	by April 8	S.C.
Research what other organizations are doing to make the XYZ System more efficient.	ongoing	P.T.
Analyze the results of the research survey and compile them into a report with recommendations.	by April 20	P.T.
Produce a cost/benefit report for the top two recommendations .	by April 20	P.T.
Do the above within 25 person-days of effort. Traveling expenses will be submitted through your department for reimbursement.	ongoing	P.T.
Be available for consultation if we run into any roadblocks we cannot now anticipate.	ongoing	S.C.
Start budgeting process for Phase 2	April 20	S.C.

The Project Team will meet with you on April 23rd at 1:00 pm in your office to review the data, analysis and recommendations to complete Phase I of the Project. We expect to start Phase II shortly thereafter. If I have missed any key points or if you have any concerns about the above, please call me at extension 2222.

If you were a client, would you feel this confirmation to be:
 helpful?
 too detailed?
 clear?
 daunting?

CONFIRMING DOCUMENT EXAMPLE 3
FORM BASED —TO BE COMPLETED BY PRINTING IN SPACES PROVIDED

Project Name:	**Date:**
Project Sponsor:	
Project Leader and Team Members:	
Other Stakeholders: (customers, end users, government, etc.)	
Brief Project Description: (e.g., business need, background, benefits, etc.)	
Results Expected: (make them as specific and observable as possible)	

Resources Required:
  Budget
 	
  People Support (skills, names and time commitment)	

Project Plan—Major Steps: (include communication and commitment building)

Action	Who is Responsible	Deadline

Follow-Through: (amendments, mileposts achieved, updates, etc.)

A form like this one is used by a professional group in BTAmoco. You may wish to adapt it to your own use.

Asking For What You Want

The best way to get what you want is to ask for it! There is a balance, though: ask for too little and you won't get what you want; ask for too much and you won't get what you want. Our data from thousands of internal clients show that most professionals are too weak with their requests and consequently often feel one-down. It is difficult, however, to judge the strength of one's own requests. The illustration below may help you begin assessing. Thus, we also suggest:

1. Asking clients and others who work with you for feedback.
2. Seeking coaching from people who can observe you in action, clarifying expectations and commitments with clients.
3. Practising with coach professionals to become comfortable with the strength of your requests; also with the tone of voice accompanying the words.

ASKING FOR WHAT YOU WANT

Strength		Typical Statements
Too Wimpy		"Maybe you could see your way to ..."
		"Perhaps you could ..."
Too Weak		"We couldn't do the project without ..."
Just Right		"I need ..."
		"Project success requires ..."
Too Strong		
		"You have to ..."
Too Demanding		"Let me tell you ..."

Probability of Getting What You Want

Payoffs for asking appropriately for what you want:

✔ You will more often get what you want!

✔ You will be more satisfied as an internal consultant when you act with 50-50 power with your clients.

✔ Your clients will also be more satisfied because when you make direct requests, they will often mirror direct requests of you.

✔ You will do less unwanted or misdirected work.

✔ Ultimately, your organization is a huge winner because powerful and clear agreements are negotiated.

Influential Professional Roles

Professionals yearn for influential roles within their organizations. Often professionals feel one-down to line management and especially to senior management. Role negotiation is not necessarily an independent item, negotiated apart from *Exploring the Need* and *Clarifying Commitments*. By thinking powerfully about yourself, you establish powerful roles before you meet with your clients, and these roles are reinforced in every interaction with them. It is better to perform in the role you want, and then to formalize it, than it is to perform in less powerful ways and try to negotiate a more powerful role. It is better to act in powerful ways than to expect others to give you power. No client can give you a powerful role. Either you act in powerful ways or you don't.

Don't shoot yourself in the foot! Take this story, for example. An external consultant had worked hard to coach a relatively new internal consultant to work with a division in a large health institution. This professional had often complained "They aren't making good use of me around here." Toward the end of a meeting with a senior manager, the manager turned to the internal consultant and asked "I'd like to sit down with you and discuss some other issues that we might work on together." The consultant replied "I'm busy the rest of the week. Could you send me a list of your concerns?" Talk about shooting yourself in the foot!

If you are given the opportunity to be powerful, you must take the opportunity. This book challenges you to step out and manage your consulting practice in ways that build effective and powerful roles.

A Continuum of Roles

The range of roles you can assume as an internal consultant can range from a pair of hands role, through to a 50-50 partnership, to a professional expert. Below is a model to help better understand the range of roles on a continuum between too weak and too strong—for long term effectiveness. In the short term, any of these roles can be effective. When you are new or inexperienced, the pair of hands role is not only appropriate but helpful.

These roles are described here in a first-pass, broad brush way—more on this later. Because roles are so crucial to your consulting success, we will look at roles from many different perspectives throughout this book.

A CONTINUUM OF CONSULTING ROLES

A Pair of Hands	The Business Partner	The Expert
◄―――――――――――――――――――――――►		
Too wimpy (except for new consultants)	Assertive	Too Pushy
"Tell me …" One-down to clients	"Let's work together." Equals over project	"What you should do …" One-up to clients

WHAT YOU'VE LEARNED SO FAR ...

Chapter 3, *Exploring the Need,* established the need to spend time exploring issues and building rapport.

In this chapter, *Clarifying Commitments*, it was time to clarify before making some commitments:
- using levels, guidelines, checklists,
- dealing with ambiguity,
- using verbal confirmations,
- writing confirming memos,
- asking for what you want, and
- establishing your own consulting role.

What is needed next is to gather more information on the clarified problem before making your recommendations. The next chapter also deals with a crucial item—greatly valued by clients—which we postponed from Stage 1, *Exploring the Need*.

THE EXPERTISE DELIVERY MODEL

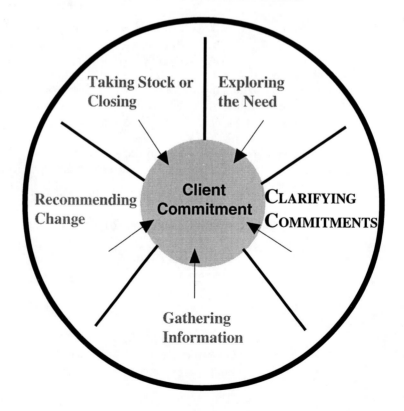

"Questions are the answer."
– Zig Ziglar

 **5**

STAGE 3: GATHERING INFORMATION (ASKING POWERFUL QUESTIONS)

5

Quick Snapshot

Did You Know?
- powerful questioning is a unique consulting skill that sets up powerful roles?
- professionals asking poor questions often blame clients for 'misleading' answers?
- clients place high value on the professional skill of sorting out complex, unclear situations?

How-to:
- ask questions which simultaneously build client commitment and build powerful consultant roles.
- use probing, face-to-face questions to sort out fuzzy, messy situations with clients.
- stay away from some 'commonsense' questions, sure to get professionals in trouble!

The Bottom Line:
- You will be able to gather information more effectively, while increasing client commitment and setting up more powerful professional roles. The models, skills and techniques of this chapter will help you do this.

Have fun with the participative learning in this chapter!

As you are customizing the Expertise Delivery Model to become your personal model—to work for you in specific situations—we use terms designed to have the model usable in your head as you work. In consulting literature, this stage has various names: Synthesizing Information, Data Collection and Diagnosis among them. We call this stage simply 'Gathering Information.' What is your description?

A good introduction to other information gathering skills is the Scholtes book listed in Appendix 1.

Carving Out a Piece of a Very Large Pie

Data gathering is an immense subject, undertaken after Exploring the Need and Clarifying Commitments. Whatever your expertise, you will have spent years learning the data gathering and diagnostic tools of your profession. Training advisors will have learned needs analysis techniques; engineers, how to gather and analyze data to solve engineering problems; auditors, how to use auditing skills to gather appropriate data; systems analysts, trained in structured systems analysis techniques. Add to this skill training in related topics like Problem Solving, Decision Making, and Project Management, and you have an impressive pool of skills. We do not intend reworking such professional models of data gathering. Most professionals feel comfortable using data gathering methods in their area of expertise.

Yet professional specialty techniques, while powerful tools, often miss two important data gathering skills, both of immense value to professionals:
  1. Asking powerful questions of clients in order to set up a powerful consulting role.
  2. Sorting out complex situations verbally with clients.

In working with clients to sort out a messy, fuzzy situation, questioning skills are critical. The most common, widely used data gathering skill is simply asking people questions. Yet verbal questioning is rarely mentioned in professional education. In this book, we made a conscious decision to address the most commonly used data gathering skill—asking real people questions, face-to-face. We made this decision with the full realization that there are many more data gathering techniques (see below), thoroughly addressed in other references.

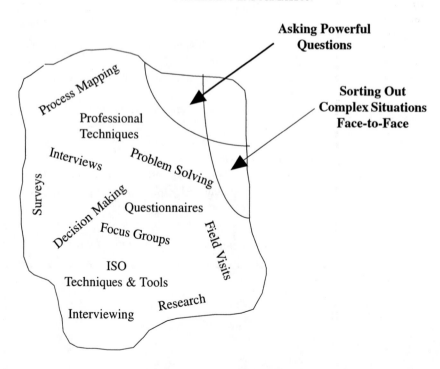

THE MOST VALUED SKILLS OF GATHERING INFORMATION

Asking Powerful Questions

Sorting Out Complex Situations Face-to-Face

Process Mapping
Professional Techniques
Interviews
Problem Solving
Surveys
Decision Making
Questionnaires
Focus Groups
Field Visits
ISO Techniques & Tools
Interviewing
Research

"My," said Alice, "you DO ask a lot of questions!"

Data gathering requires professionals to ask a lot of questions. Gerald Goodman, in his book *The Talk Book*, estimates that approximately 25% of everyday conversations is in the form of questions. In our work with professionals, workshop participants estimate that 75% to 95% of early consulting time face-to-face with clients is spent in questioning to understand their concerns and get at underlying issues. It's easy to see why high performing internal professionals need to learn effective use of questioning skills.

Asking a logical, rational question may be threatening to your clients. This may surprise you. How could a simple question be threatening to your clients? Easily!
- It's easy to make a client look dumb.
- It's easy to appear condescending.
- It's easy to raise fears of 'exposing dirty laundry.'
- It's easy to imply inadequate problem solving skills—clients thinking quietly "How come we didn't think about that ourselves?"
- It's easy to see questioning as a way of exercising power, since information is a source of power. Asking for data is asking the data supplier to share power in the form of information.

"Taking That Smart-ass College Kid Down a Peg or Two!"

In a large natural gas processing plant, remote from head office, a new electrical engineer was on his first field assignment data gathering, condescendingly asking logical engineering questions about a particular electrical problem. As part of the process, he opened an electrical panel. Being a rookie, he didn't realize that for safety reasons opening an electrical panel in a gas plant shuts down the panel completely. The panel happened to control a large gas compressor in the plant. It took about 20 minutes to get the compressor back on stream.

The plant operators, when asked later why they didn't tell the new electrical engineer this simple rule, wryly joked that it was their way of "taking that smart-ass college kid down a peg or two!" The new engineer had asked excellent, rational 'engineering questions,' unaware that the questioning technique felt demeaning to the 'hands-on' plant operators. 'People' aspects of questions are as important as logical aspects. Our goal here is to present logical models, which are also personally helpful.

In another instance, while interviewing employees for a systems project, a Systems Analyst noticed the employees were very 'antsy.' When trust built up, an employee reluctantly divulged this concern: "... the information I give you may mean automating what I do. I might lose my job!"

How To Pull a Strand Out of Spaghetti

Over 35,000 surveys in our database tell us that clients greatly value professionals' ability to sort out complex situations. In increasingly complex situations where they find themselves, clients often don't know how to express the problem, much less how to solve it. Powerful professionals need the skill of informally sitting down with a client and working through complex situations—like pulling strand after strand out of cooked spaghetti.

5

In this chapter ...

- *Why this stage is so important*
- *Why rational questions often don't yield rational answers*
- *A questioning simulation*
- *Questioning strategies*
- *A model for quickly sorting out complex situations*
- *Dos & Don'ts of questioning*

In this chapter we are dealing with just the opposite situation to Chapter 3, Exploring the Need. There the professional's role was to help a client look at a narrowly presented situation in a bigger context. In this chapter, we assume professionals are presented with a complex situation— with no easy answers. Here the professional's role is to help the client work through the complexity to effective actions.

Almost the Real Thing!

Take a few minutes to participate in the following simulation. You will benefit much more from the subsequent discussion of questioning skills if you try the exercise for yourself. The exercise simulates a typical complex consulting situation where the client, a senior manager, takes a number of minutes to present you with a complex situation. In this simulation, you work for the same organization, but you know very little about the specific situation and the client. Jot down the first two or three questions which spring to mind. Don't over analyze, or take time to mull over your first question. In a real situation, you may have difficulty letting the client finish before jumping in with a question! Do the same here.

THE INPROS SITUATION

You are a professional in your area of expertise. The Manager of Administration called your boss about a problem. Unaware of the issues, you were selected as the troubleshooter now starting your first meeting. The manager begins:

"A Project Team was set up eight months ago to coordinate the installation of an Intranet Project System [INPROS] in our organization. The successful start-up of the system is critical to the short and long-term productivity of several departments. The Accounting Division is particularly vulnerable. Within the next four weeks, they need to produce some government reports from the planned pooled reporting system.

"Today, the project is three weeks behind, with five weeks to go to the planned start-up date. Various causes have been cited: first, the length of time it took for the Project Team and Accounting to agree on standards; second, the current late delivery of software from the low bidding vendor (some people, including me, had warned against this vendor for that reason); third, the reported personality clashes on the Project Team; and finally, the recent illness of the Project Team leader, Robin Just. Perhaps the pressure of this project has been too much for Robin. Two Project Team members, Chris Rosa and Lee Wan, have been suggested as possible replacements, even at this late date.

"There is one more step on the 'critical path' of the project plan—training the users. Doubts have been cast on the ability of the training group to deliver the quantity and quality of training programs required.

"There is much concern at the highest levels of the organization. We have asked you, as an outsider, to look into the situation and give your recommendations."

What would be the first two or three questions you would ask?
1.

2.

3.

Which of these questions would be your lead question?

Twenty Questions

From working with many diverse professionals, we have chosen to print just twenty of the many actual INPROS situation questions we have heard asked over the years.

1. What do you expect of me?
2. What is the highest priority?
3. What are the most critical issues?
4. What were the original project objectives?
5. Can you tell me about the project plan?
6. How soon will Robin be back to work?
7. Can you get the accounting reports out on time this month?
8. Who else can we talk to about the project?
9. Can the start-up be delayed until we get some of these problems sorted out?
10. Can we bring in some outside trainers to take care of the training concerns?
11. Are there any other concerns that you have about the project?
12. How do you feel about the project?
13. What are some of the things that have been tried?
14. Who else is involved?
15. What are the causes for the delay?
16. Why did you choose me to work on the project?
17. What are the most immediate needs?
18. How was the vendor chosen?
19. Can I talk to the Project Team?
20. What role would you expect me to play in the project?

We can classify most of the above questions into one of five categories:

Triage or Band-Aid™ Questions	Priority Setting Questions	Big Picture Questions	Specific Issue Questions	Process Questions
	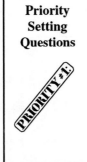			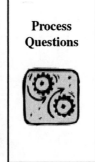

Let's look at these categories, their pros and cons, and use this information to construct a general model for effectively sorting out complex situations face-to-face with clients. To begin, can you hazard a guess as to which of the twenty INPROS questions above—and which of your own three questions—would fit in the first category, 'Triage' questions?

Quick fix actions can leave professionals in a fix.

Triage Questions

from page 69:
   # 7. Can you get the accounting reports out on time this month?
   # 9. Is there any way the start-up can be delayed until we get some
        of these problems sorted out?
   #17. What are the most immediate needs?

Triage questions do **not** fix the underlying problems. They alleviate the immediate symptoms. They are the classic 'Band-Aid™' questions. Triage is the medical term for sorting out priorities when multiple casualties come into a medical facility. Triage answers the questions: "In what order do we treat the casualties?" "Who needs attention first?" Benefits and downsides of Triage questions are summarized below.

TRIAGE QUESTIONS

Pros	Cons
• They help to get the project back on track quickly.	• They do not deal with more underlying causes of the immediate problems.
• They deal with the immediate hurts and are thus very comforting for the client.	• They can be superficial. Ferreting out the underlying causes usually results in much better solutions.
• They exemplify the benefits of a 'quick-fix.'	• They put the professional into a pair of hands, 'fire fighting' role, usually dissatisfying in the long run.
• They build credibility by being action oriented.	• The tendency is for clients, when their immediate needs are met, to say "Thanks and good-bye," leaving professionals with a very narrow role.
• Triage questions, used appropriately, in a timely fashion, can be very useful.	

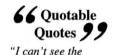
Quotable Quotes
"I can't see the forest for the trees."

"When you're up to your behind in alligators, it's hard to remember that your goal is to clear the swamp."

APPLICATION

Looking back at the questions you wrote for the INPROS situation, do any of your questions fit into this Triage Question category?

Priority Setting Questions

from page 69:

#2. What is the highest priority?

#3. What are the most critical issues?

Related to Triage questions are Priority Setting questions, which ask the *client* to establish priorities and the critical issues. Facing the complexity of a situation, wanting to quickly reduce uncomfortable ambiguity, a professional's natural tendency is to ask priority setting questions. Usually clients will be 'helpful' and tell you what they feel are the key issues. Once they have told you what you asked for, however, you may feel frustrated if *you* feel *their* stated priorities don't address 'the real issues.'

Besides, it's too early! How can you and your clients establish priorities until you have *all* the issues out on the table? We have actually heard some professionals claim that clients became angry when these kinds of questions were asked, countering with "If I knew the priorities, and what to do next, I wouldn't need your help!" Even worse, when you ask clients to state their priorities, they often tell you not priorities, but what to do! You do need to know the priorities, but later in the process, and not by asking. More later …

Client 'helpfulness' can lead to consultant helplessness.

PRIORITY SETTING QUESTIONS

Pros	Cons
• They quickly get the clients' priorities on the table.	• If the situation is complex, clients may not know what the priorities are or may have identified them poorly.
• In complex situations, priorities must be established to bring the complexity under control.	• The priorities may be on immediate needs, leaving the longer term, bigger picture priorities untouched.
• They reduce the inevitable tension of ambiguity.	• They constrain the consultant into working with the *expressed* priorities.

Both professional and client need to establish priorities to get complex situations under control. Asking them too early, however, can constrain the range of actions for dealing with the situation.

APPLICATION

Looking back at the questions you wrote for the INPROS situation, do any of your questions fit into the Priority Setting category?

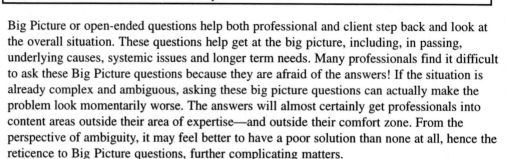

Big Picture Questions

from page 69:

\# 4. What were the original project objectives?

\# 5. Can you tell me about the project plan?

\#11. Are there any other concerns that you have about the project?

\#12. How do you feel about the project?

\#15. What are the causes for the delay?

Big Picture or open-ended questions help both professional and client step back and look at the overall situation. These questions help get at the big picture, including, in passing, underlying causes, systemic issues and longer term needs. Many professionals find it difficult to ask these Big Picture questions because they are afraid of the answers! If the situation is already complex and ambiguous, asking these big picture questions can actually make the problem look momentarily worse. The answers will almost certainly get professionals into content areas outside their area of expertise—and outside their comfort zone. From the perspective of ambiguity, it may feel better to have a poor solution than none at all, hence the reticence to Big Picture questions, further complicating matters.

Still, powerful professionals need to ask Big Picture questions.

- Big Picture questions set up 'big picture' roles. To be perceived as having a powerful and influential role, professional and client need to get the total picture of the messy situation out in the open. By contrast, close-ended questions set up close-ended roles.
- Big Picture questions, by laying the whole problem out in the open, enable you to set priorities. In order to get at effective, longer term solutions to complex situations, a professional needs to understand the problem in all its manifestations, with all its ramifications.
- As well as being good logical questions, Big Picture questions can be excellent rapport-building questions. Clients want to get messy situations 'off their chests.' Messy situations can be emotional. Clients' own mismanagement of the situation can be a sticky part of the concern they wish to express. Having a professional who can help clients talk it out can be helpful.

To capture the benefits of Big Picture questions, you must be able to manage the increased ambiguity they produce. One technique is this: on hearing the answer to a big picture question, always paraphrase or summarize what you have heard.

- It shows you are listening, able to track the complexity and handle messy situations.
- Clients can correct any misconceptions you may be receiving.
- Summarizing has the highly desirable effect of reducing ambiguity.
- Summarizing helps the client to go to the next deeper level where underlying causes and barriers are situated.

The Onion Effect

In a messy or complex situation, the first things a client usually tells a professional are the easier, less threatening aspects of the situation. It's like peeling back the first layer of an onion. In order to get to the core of the issue (and the onion), a professional needs to summarize what has been heard so far, to ensure accurate tracking of the situation, reducing ambiguity, layer by layer. The next Big Picture question will peel back the second layer. Repeat the summarizing process, then ask another Big Picture question, and repeat the process with each 'layer,' until you reach the core.

APPLICATION

Looking back at the questions you wrote for the INPROS situation, do any of your questions fit into the Big Picture category?

BIG PICTURE QUESTIONS

Pros	Cons
• Long lasting solutions are probably derived from the bigger picture. • Only with all the information out, will high priority issues be identifiable. • Big Picture questions tend to help the client express underlying—typically more difficult—information. • Big Picture questions help build a big picture role for the professional. • Big Picture questions generally help build rapport with the client.	• Asking bigger picture questions makes the consultation more complex, probably raising 'ambiguity anxiety' in most clients and in professionals. • Big Picture questions actually make the problem look worse! • Big Picture questions may result in irrelevant information—and possible biases. • Big Picture questions require both client and consultant to manage larger amounts of information.

Questioning Your Role Strategy

Questioning strategy has great impact on the type of information gathered, unexpectedly influencing the *role* a professional will play throughout the whole consulting project. Although questioning strategies and implied roles may vary by client and situation, the most effective and powerful professional role over time is that of a business partner. See Chapter 12, *Enhancing Your Role and Career,* for a more in-depth treatment of this important topic.

A RANGE OF ROLES

Pair of Hands   **Business Partner**   **Expert**

◀──▶

"Tell me what to do."   *"Let's find out together what to do."*   *"I'll tell you what to do."*

There is no point asking great questions if you don't listen well to the answers! See Chapter 11, Listening Skills for Professionals.

5

Specific Issue Questions

from page 69:

\# 6. How soon will Robin be back to work?

\#10. Can we bring in some outside trainers to take care of the training concerns?

\#18. How was the vendor chosen?

\#13. What are some of the things that have been tried?

Often related to trying to find quick fixes, specific issue questions focus attention on one aspect of the situation. They are the questions which relate to one of the specific situations expressed in the INPROS simulation.

SPECIFIC ISSUE QUESTIONS

Pros	Cons
• If you happen to hit the most critical specific issue, you will be perceived as efficient—maybe even seen as a hero.	• You *may* be dealing with a low priority issue, *without* getting all the issues out in the open.
• Specific Issue questions appeal to our professional, content-driven, expert, troubleshooting roles.	• Specific Issue questions place the professional in the expert consulting role: "Let me tell you what to do." In the long run, this is generally counter-productive for you and your clients.
• Some clients like the comfort of a professional engaging in expert consulting.	• Specific Issue questions tend to be a 'hit and miss' activity, especially early in the consultation.
• Specific Issue questions have limited value early in messy situations, but they *do* have a place.	

Troubleshooting??
Ever thought about the origin of the phrase 'troubleshooter'? We surmise it may relate to a heroic 'expert' model of consulting. Picture this: the professional comes riding into the clients' camp shooting trouble. "Ah, there's the problem. Let's shoot it! If we miss, let's find another specific issue to shoot." Of course we all know heroic gunslingers existed only on the silver screen.

APPLICATION

Looking back at the questions you wrote for the INPROS situation, do any of your questions fit into the Specific Issue category?

Process Questions

from page 69:

\# 1. What do you expect of me?

\# 8. Who else can we talk to about the project?

\#14. Who else is involved?

\#16. Why did you choose me to work on the project?

\#20. What role would you expect me to play in the project?

\#19. Can I talk to the Project Team?

We suggest that you do not ask Process Questions as your first two or three questions, and work instead to get all the issues—the content—out in the open. Process Questions relate to how the client concern will be dealt with—roles, processes and methods. We suggest you leave these questions until later in the process and ask them in more powerful ways. More later …

Not Earlier, Not Later, Not Ever!

from page 69:

\# 1. What do you expect of me?

\#20. What role would you expect me to play in the project?

\# 2. What is the highest priority?

\# 3. What are the most critical issues?

These are some questions on our typical list we suggest you do not ask—ever.

We call these "Tell me what to do, boss" questions. Unfortunately it is natural and intuitive to ask them, but what's actually happening with questions like these, is that you are asking the *client* to lower the ambiguity of the situation by telling *you* what the priorities are and telling you what your role should be. Most clients will happily tell you! Almost certainly they will assign you a narrow role and supply a solution for you to work on. In other words, *they will unilaterally determine your professional job*. When this happens, professionals often get angry at clients, claiming "My clients won't let me …"

If you want to be a powerful consultant, you must not ask simplifying questions too early. These questions can put you into a simple but ineffective role! Research shows that professionals can greatly increase their influence by handling the ambiguity of complex consulting situations.

You may be protesting at this point that a professional needs to know the priorities and needs role clarification. Yes, you do need these. But there is a more powerful way to do this. Read on…

APPLICATION

Looking back at the questions you wrote for the INPROS situation, do any of your questions fit into the Process category?

The Pot Calling the Kettle Black?

Often we hear professionals complain about clients' hidden agendas, BUT professionals can ask questions that implicitly have a hidden agenda—questions that already anticipate answers. If they get the answer they want, professionals continue that line of questioning. If they don't, they switch the line of questioning. Professionals may not even realize that they are doing this, yet it can be very frustrating to clients, who sense a 'hidden agenda,' even if the professional didn't deliberately intend one.

When asking questions in a complex situation, resist simplifying the problem too quickly.

Clarifying Ambiguity

As more surrounding information is laid out, the problem appears more complex—clients get edgy, and so do professionals. The best way to ameliorate this data anxiety is to use a listening response, a summary perhaps, before asking the next question. You can reduce ambiguity by:
- summarizing clients' data
- making notes with your clients
- making information visible on a whiteboard or flipchart.

Effective consultants have learned how to handle their own need—as well as their clients' need— to reduce ambiguity.

Sorting Out a Complex Situation: A Questioning Strategy

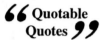

Clients and professionals will find the best answer when the best questions are asked.

We will conclude this chapter by leaving you with a how-to questioning plan or model, to apply directly to complex situations, which will undoubtedly arise in your professional practice. Professionals need a general strategy for sorting out messy situations face-to-face with clients. As always, we encourage you to adapt the model to your own needs. On the next page is our 'hourglass' model, followed by an example.

Why Triage?

You will notice the hourglass model starts, perhaps surprisingly, with Triage. Information is narrowed by asking questions about any immediate 'hurts' which need to be relieved before the consultant and client step back to the big picture. The reason for starting here is that the client may be unable to step back to the Big Picture until immediate issues are dealt with. Burning, immediate issues tend to 'take over' the client's emotions and mind, if not dealt with right away. The professional can use Triage questions to build credibility as an 'action oriented' consultant, then move out into a bigger picture setting when the waters calm.

We do not recommend Triage where you know from history or reputation that your clients will want to stop here and not go on to the Big Picture. In this case, ask Big Picture questions first—you can always revert to Triage. Usually, relieving clients of their immediate crises will help you and your client deal with Big Picture issues, which set up Big Picture roles.

DANGER!

In cases where only Triage issues—usually symptoms—are dealt with, the problem will almost certainly recur. When immediate needs are met, the temptation for many clients is to say "Thank you" and move on to other issues. If this happens, you leave yourself in a low leverage, pair of hands role. Be on your guard against this happening, particularly if you know from past history with a client that it's likely to happen. In this case, ask larger, Big Picture questions. You can always revert to Triage, if needed.

THE HOURGLASS MODEL
FOR SORTING OUT A COMPLEX SITUATION

The Mental Model	Strategy	What You Are Doing	The Impact on Your Role
	Triage	• Fixing the immediate hurts • Fire-fighting • Putting on 'Band-Aids' • Buying time • Gaining credibility and trust for your client to step back and look at the big picture.	• You are narrowing your role • You are putting yourself into a fire-fighting mode • You are creating credibility by being 'action oriented.'
	Big Picture	• Broadening the context of the problem • Getting at the context of the issue • Getting at the underlying issues.	• You are broadening your role • You are raising the level of ambiguity • You have the most power with the Big Picture.

	Critical Actions	• Narrowing the scope of the problem by jointly establishing:
		  – priorities
		  – action plans
		
		• Clarifying your agreement.
			• You are probably narrowing your role around the priorities
			
			• You are again creating credibility by being 'action oriented.'

5

The implications of this hourglass model are:
- Warning: Starting with Triage may be risky! See the 'Danger' section on the previous page.
- Every question has a role and a strategy implied in it.
- Big Picture, or open-ended questions, open the scope of the problem and expand potential roles; closed-end questions do the opposite.
- 'Tell me what to do boss' questions greatly narrow the problem and your role. It is much more powerful to propose priorities and roles at the broadest vista of the situation—the transition between Big Picture and Critical Actions.
- Recognize both client and professional tolerance for ambiguity. Don't narrow scope and role for the wrong reason—lack of tolerance for ambiguity.
- Specific questions and transitions related to the hourglass model follows in the next two pages.

This model is on the Web Site: www.consultskills.com.

If you have difficulty remembering and/or summarizing clients' spoken words, see Chapter 11, Listening Skills for Professionals, for ideas.

SORTING OUT COMPLEX SITUATIONS VERBALLY

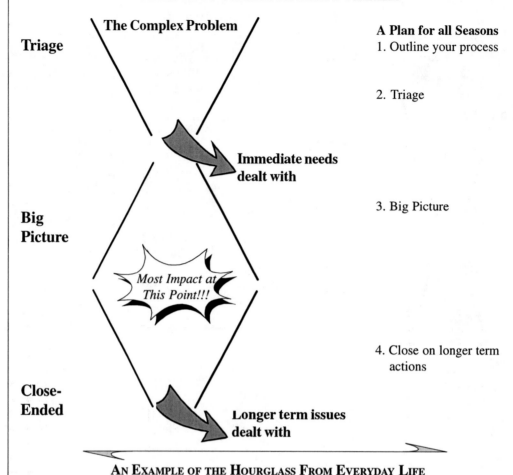

A Plan for all Seasons
1. Outline your process

2. Triage

3. Big Picture

4. Close on longer term actions

AN EXAMPLE OF THE HOURGLASS FROM EVERYDAY LIFE

Because of its universal appeal, the following example is for illustration only. *We do NOT mean to imply that 'parent-child' resembles 'professional-client'!*

Picture a five or six-year-old child playing in a playground near home. The child comes running home to the parent. The child is crying, scratched, bruised and has a minor cut. What would an effective parent do? Triage, of course. First the parent would soothe the cries, treat the cut and put bandages on the scrapes. Then send the child back? (Often children are anxious to get back.) NO! An effective parent would probably step back with the child and ask some Big Picture questions about how the situation arose and how the accident happened. After discussing how the child got hurt, an effective parent would probably finish by both parent and child agreeing to carry out some actions designed to keep the child away from further harm.

APPLICATION

Looking back at the questions you wrote for the INPROS situation, how do you feel about your questioning strategy? What would you change?

A Plan for All Seasons

To verbally clarify a complex situation presented by a client, we suggest the following hourglass questioning sequence:

Step 1: Summarize and Outline Your Process

    a. Summarize or paraphrase what you have heard so far:

      "What I understand so far is …"

    b. Outline your process:

      "In the time we have available, I suggest we first look at the most immediate concern(s), then step back and have you help me understand the big picture, and end with the best plan of action."

Step 2: Triage

    a. Transition:

      "Let's spend the next _____ minutes with the immediate needs."

    b. Typical Triage questions:

      "What is your most immediate concern?"

      "Does anything need attention right now?"

      "How much flexibility do we have with the deadline?"

      "What issues cannot wait and need to be addressed right now?"

    c. Clarify a plan for the Triage issues:

      After discussing the most immediate concern, end the discussion with "So what we will do to deal with the most immediate concern is …"

Step 3: Big Picture

    a. Transition:

      "Now that we have dealt with the most immediate need, let's step back and look at the big picture. You have mentioned these concerns so far…" (summarize the first pass concerns).

    b. Typical Big Picture questions:

      "Just so I understand the big picture, can you tell me some more about the situation?"

      "So I can understand the situation, what were the original goals for the project?"

      "How did this project get started?"

      "What end result is required?"

    c. Going deeper, if required:

      After summarizing, or better, making visible what you have heard so far, ask "Is there anything else about the situation that would help me understand it better?"

Step 4: Closing on Longer Term Actions

    a. Transition:

      (Assuming you have been asking Big Picture questions and summarizing client concerns)

    b. Typical closing questions:

      "Given the concerns we have discussed, it appears to me that your highest priority concerns are x, y and z. Is that the way you see it?"

    c. Negotiate any differences on priorities and roles.

      When you and your client agree on the priorities, propose a role or roles:

      "From these priorities, I think I could be most helpful by … Does that fit for you?"

    Note: You want to avoid both telling your client—the expert role, or asking your client—the pair of hands role.

      With our proposed questions, you are proposing priorities and roles—the business partner role.

    d. Discuss and agree to longer term actions to deal with the priority concerns.

5

WHAT YOU HAVE LEARNED SO FAR …

- Data Gathering is a huge area from which two client-valued aspects emerge:
  - asking powerful questions
  - sorting out complex situations verbally with your clients.

- A professional has almost total control over which questions to ask and when to ask them—use this opportunity wisely.

- Every question has a strategy and role implied in it.

- Many professionals inappropriately manage ambiguity by asking "Tell me what to do, boss" questions or using 'expert' roles.

- Many professionals underuse Big Picture questions, thereby losing Big Picture roles.

- The hourglass questioning strategy can assist you in sorting out complex situations.

THE EXPERTISE DELIVERY MODEL

"I desperately need some wise advice which will recommend that I do what I want to do."
© *Ashleigh Brilliant*

CHAPTER 6

STAGE 4: RECOMMENDING CHANGE

6

Quick Snapshot

Did You Know?
- being a creative professional is no longer sufficient for success: these days you must be able to persuade others to accept and implement your creative ideas?
- clients greatly value being persuaded, but professionals are lousy at persuading?
- client resistance can actually work to your advantage?

How-to:
- structure a recommendation presentation to increase client acceptance.
- present recommendations for change in a powerful way.
- change client resistance into client commitment.

The Bottom Line:
- You will greatly increase the chances of your recommendations being accepted, acted upon and adopted by using the ideas, models, checklists and worksheets of this chapter.

Start with the change in mind.

When 4 = 1
Some consulting cases actually BEGIN with the Recommending Change stage. As an internal professional, you may be required to sell change to clients who did not ask for one!
Systems professionals often need to sell changes in computer procedures to people who are quite happy with what they are used to.
Human Resource professionals can be required to sell changes in compensation or benefit plans to managers and fellow employees.
Engineers often sell process improvements to production management and employees.

Looking Over the Brink

You have had a flawless consultation to this point: a successful exploration and definition of client need, followed by clear expectations and commitments—made and carried out. You have gathered and analyzed data, and made great recommendations, which you know will benefit your client, your organization and yourself. You may now face one of the biggest disappointments a professional can face. Your recommendations don't get approved or implemented! Your hard work, summarized into a wonderful report and presentation, is sitting gathering dust on a shelf or buried in a file. (If this scenario hasn't happened to you, you just haven't been consulting long enough!)

Recommending ...

In the past, a professional's job typically entailed diagnosing predetermined problems and suggesting solutions. Whether clients adopted the solution or not was up to the clients—the professional's involvement ended with the presentation of recommendations. No more. As a consulting professional today, you are expected to sell your recommendations as well as follow through with an appropriate role in implementation.

Change ...

The second word in this stage is 'change.' Your ideas need to be implemented; that is, change needs to take place. We use the word 'change'—how recommendations will be implemented—to help professionals look beyond technically correct solutions. This is the real payoff for your work, keeping you happily employed.

One key issue for this stage is commitment—commitment to action. Unfortunately, commitment isn't something that starts at this stage. Commitment starts before *Exploring the Need*. As consultant Joe Folkman puts it, "Commitment building begins before you meet the client, at the first meeting, at every meeting, at every step and doesn't end until the project is clearly turned over to the client." If this is the first time you have thought about commitment, it may be too late.

The Grand Canyon of Professional Skills

With this step of the Expertise Delivery model, Recommending *Change, we* have the biggest performance gap for professionals. We know from our international database that clients greatly value persuasion and change leadership skills in professionals. Yet, in the same database, clients rate professionals low on these very skills! Here is room for most growth. Here is where you can stand out from your fellow professionals—*if,* besides having good ideas and recommendations, you also know how to get them approved and implemented, and how to help people with change. The first step is being able to present your recommendation persuasively.

BRIDGE THE GRAND CANYON SKILL GAP

Persuasion Greatly Valued & Persuasion Poorly Rated = Biggest Skill Gap

= Need to Improve

Selling Moves From Gaudy to Professional

The ability to sell professional recommendations has become critical to the success of professionals working inside organizations:
- As organizations become flatter and push down decision making, professionals are required to be full cycle consultants, selling proposals and taking part in the change they have recommended.
- More participative decision making means more people need to buy into a recommendation to ensure its success.
- Increasingly complex technology requires that professionals sell proposals and recommendations to clients who may not clearly understand projects from the technical perspective.
- Recommendations are increasingly tested against more stringent criteria: "Will this help our organization be more successful?" 'Nice-to-dos' just don't cut it any more.

Given the growing importance of selling recommendations, many professionals still tend to look down their noses at the skills of selling. Certainly selling has a bad name, associated with used cars, polyester and loud ties. Yet the obvious answer to the question "Does anything happen in your organization unless someone recommends and sells change?" is, of course, "No."

6

We are not talking about the seamy side of selling, but the professional side of selling: that is, meeting client needs over the long term. We are not going to discuss ways of pushing your ideas, rather we will explore ways of presenting so that your clients can see for themselves the value of your ideas. This chapter is not about pulling the wool over the eyes of unsuspecting clients, nor is it about how to package poor recommendations so they look better. It is about presenting valuable recommendations in a way that raises your chances of approval AND implementation.

The Selling Wheel—A Model for Internal Professionals

Go into the business section of any bookstore and you will find rows of books on selling, all written for the external salesperson. You will find next to nothing to assist professionals working inside organizations to sell their ideas. Our Selling Wheel addresses this void, uniquely focusing on the professional working internally. You cannot afford to 'wing' this critical step. To convincingly present and sell recommended change to your clients, you must effectively address six steps—we will call them 'spokes'—of the Selling Wheel.

Up until now in our Expertise Delivery Model, we have assumed there is only one client and one professional. Realistically, however, you need to sell recommendations to a group of clients, often at a management meeting. For the rest of this chapter we will use a management meeting scenario, although the same process is appropriate for a one-to-one situation.

In this chapter ...

- *Why this step?*
- *The Selling Wheel*
- *Powerfully presenting recommendations*
- *Dealing with resistance*
- *The Change Window*
- *A right-now example*
- *On-job application worksheets*

This stage, Recommending Change, is crucial to the success of your projects and ultimately your career success. Here's where the 'rubber hits the road.' In difficult economic times, selling skills are particularly important.

SELLING WHEEL

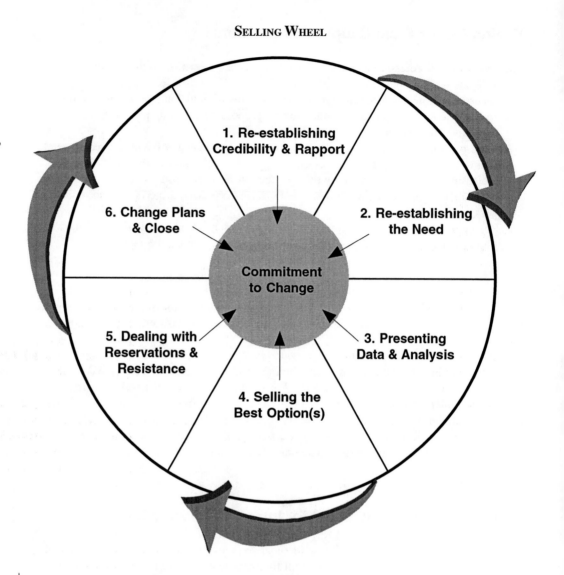

Shifting Gears on the Selling Wheel

We will now look in detail at each 'spoke' of the Selling Wheel, then follow with an example of how these spokes are used in practice, providing a worksheet you can use to plan your own presentation.

You will notice the first two steps have 'Re-' prefixes. Working internally, you almost certainly know the clients to whom you will be presenting recommendations. New clients may also be present for your presentation. 'Re-establishing' refers to familiar clients; 'establishing' to unfamiliar clients.

1. Re-establishing Credibility and Rapport

The first Selling Wheel spoke is to establish, or re-establish, rapport and credibility (previously discussed in the first stage of the Expertise Delivery model, *Exploring the Need*). In addition to rapport—human-to-human connection—consultants must also re-establish their credibility as professionals who can supply valuable recommendations.

Why bother re-establishing rapport and credibility—particularly if you know the clients?
- ✔ You want and need commitment to change. Commitment is a matter of the heart as much as the head.
- ✔ Recommending change often raises reservations and resistance in clients. Establishing human-to-human contact greatly assists with these emotional parts of change.
- ✔ In our workshops, and in many references, the phrase 'You need to sell yourself before you sell your recommendation' comes up over and over.
- ✔ Professionals often use an implicit, but entirely inappropriate principle: 'If it is logical from a professional point of view, it will sell.' Yes, logic is necessary and helpful. But it is NOT sufficient!

You can do a variety of things to establish rapport and credibility:
- ❏ Learn about your clients. Understand the key questions they are asking, their expectations, needs, preferred styles, and reservations.
- ❏ Establish and maintain appropriate eye contact. Read Chapter 11, *Listening Skills for Professionals,* for specific skills, tips and hints for this important skill.
- ❏ If you don't know some people at the meeting, introduce yourself to them. Ask them to introduce themselves.
- ❏ If appropriate, use humor or a story to put people at ease.
- ❏ Get quickly to the point. Many clients are 'action oriented.' But do take time to establish rapport and credibility.
- ❏ Give a brief overview of your presentation.
- ❏ Have a brief, point form, written summary of your presentation for clients to follow during the presentation. Note the word 'brief.' You want people to follow you, not to get caught up in reading details. If appropriate, have detailed notes available for client scrutiny following your presentation. Alert them that these notes are coming.
- ❏ Be thoroughly prepared (but not stilted).

WARNING!

In many organizations, you are required to present your final recommendation at the outset. If this is the culture of your organization, be careful. You may be setting yourself up. Since your recommendations are presented without the context and logic of how you arrived at your conclusions, clients who do not like your recommendations will move mentally—perhaps even vocally, to Spoke 5, Dealing with Reservations and Resistance—without hearing anything in between. If you must present an up-front statement of your recommendations, ask them to hear you out as to how you reached those recommendations. Remind them that you will give them ample opportunity to express their concerns.

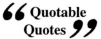

❝ Quotable Quotes ❞

"Remember the relationship side of things. You want your clients to come back."

– Robin Sober

6

Professional 'Field of Dreams' – Take 1 'If we build it logically, they will buy in.'

CAUTION

WATCH YOUR STEP

2. Re-establishing the Need

*Professional
'Field of Dreams'
– Take 2
'If we build it
professionally,
they will take care of
the business need.'*

Next, you must establish or remind your clients of the business needs driving your project and its recommendations. If these were established during the first and second steps of the Expertise Delivery Model, it may suffice to reiterate and remind clients of the needs that you have already established. Do *not* assume clients remember. Many days and hundreds of problems have intervened and competed for your clients' attention.

Why bother re-establishing needs?
- To resonate with your clients, you need to connect, or reconnect, your recommendations to the problem which gave rise to the recommendations. If clients don't know (or don't remember) the problem you are solving, they won't buy into the change.
- Staff groups have often been tagged with the epithet 'they don't understand the business.' The best way to counter this is to securely tie your recommendations to client business needs.
- In the section *'Exploring the Need,'* we cautioned against asking clients "Why?" thereby running the risk of putting clients on the defensive. Here we face the other side of the coin. If the client is to buy into your recommendations YOU must answer the question "Why?"— the first of many times and many ways in which you will have to do so.

In addition to reviewing client needs, you may find it helpful to cover some other information:
- ❑ Give a brief history of the issue, emphasizing the original business need.
- ❑ Remind your clients of the major benefits and payoffs of meeting the business need.
- ❑ Position the needs in the clients' frame of reference—why is *this* a concern for *these* clients?
- ❑ Remind clients of why the problem was framed the way it was.
- ❑ For different types of clients at the presentation, think of the needs which will resonate for each.
- ❑ Remind clients of the implications and downsides of *not* solving the problem.

*Three Wise Men?
To implement your
recommendations,
your clients need the
answer to three
questions:
1. WHAT are you
   asking us to do?
2. WHY should we do
   it?
3. HOW do we do it?
The most important
question is a "Why?"
question. Commitment
comes down to
answering Why? for
your clients. To
increase your success
rate, ensure your
presentation answers
all three questions.*

If presenting your recommendations to a diverse group, you will need to be aware that different clients may see your presentation and recommendations in very different, often contradictory, ways. See Chapter 8, *Mapping Client Systems,* for more details on analyzing and dealing with various client groups.

3. Presenting Data and Analysis

Many professionals have known the frustration of presenting proposals based on solid professional logic, only to find that their clients remain unsold and uncommitted. Professional specialists tend to focus on this analytical section, making its presentation the centerpiece of their recommendation. Important as it is, especially for analytical clients, securing client commitment involves much more than effective communication of technical analyses and recommendations. Powerful professionals keep in mind that their clients are generally far more concerned about meeting their business needs and concerns, than they are about embracing technical elegance.

The following tips can help you present technical information in a way that encourages your clients' understanding and acceptance:

❑ Present the minimum amount of data that will provide a technical basis for your recommendations. Resist the temptation to present *all* the data that you sweated over.

❑ Limit the analysis to just the amount it takes to understand where the recommendations have come from—no more.

❑ Connect your data and diagnosis directly to your clients' needs. It's the *solution* to your clients' problems which sells—not the amount of information.

❑ Take every opportunity to demonstrate your business acumen—strategic and financial—as well as your professional acumen—expertise, knowledge and skills.

❑ Use pictures and visuals wherever possible. Clients will remember about 10% of your words, but about 50% of what they see. But don't overdo visuals either—most organizations have a story of the 'techie' entering a half-hour presentation toting 50 slides.

❑ Check your presentation for technical jargon.

❑ Keep your presentation clean. If you can't visualize and keep the framework in your head, no one else will.

> Main Point #1:
>> Subpoint #1:
>> Subpoint #2:
>> Subpoint #3:
> Main Point #2:
>> Subpoint #1:
>> Subpoint #2:
> Etc.

Professional 'Field of Dreams' – Take 3 'If we present it analytically and logically, they will commit to action.

You will note that 'selling your recommendations' skills overlap with 'presentation skills.' If presentation skills are a challenge for you, find a workshop or a good coach. Most professionals require specific coaching to improve presentation skills.

6

Features are 'the bells and whistles.' Benefits are why a client needs the bells and whistles.

4. Selling the Best Option(s)

Because of its crucial importance, we will analyze and examine this selling 'spoke' in more than usual detail.

For acceptance and commitment to action, you need to answer three critical questions for your clients:
- ✓ **What?**
- ✓ **Why?**
- ✓ **How**?

Let's deal with the first two in this section of the Selling Wheel; the third later.

Features & Benefits—Vital Parts of Buying and Selling

What? = Features:
➢ Descriptors of the proposed solution to your clients' needs and problems
➢ Characteristics of the product or service recommended
➢ Typical client *feature* questions:
"What does it do?"
"Can you outline your proposed solution to me?"
"What are the main components of the recommendation?"

Why? = Benefits:
➢ Why and how your client would benefit from the feature
➢ How the feature meets an explicit business need for the specific client
➢ Typical client *benefit* questions:
"How does that help solve my problem?"
"What's in it for me?"
"How will this fulfill my needs?"
"What advantage does this feature provide for me?"
"How will this feature solve a critical need for me?"

Here's an example of how you might answer the 'What?' (features) and 'Why?' (benefits) questions when discussing a notebook computer.

RECOMMENDATION: TO BUY A NOTEBOOK COMPUTER

Features	Typical Benefits
Compact	• Can be used almost anywhere • Fits in a business case • Takes up little space • Can be used in cramped spaces, like airplanes
Lightweight	• Easy to move • Does not cause muscle strain • Easy to carry • Easy to handle

Why bother with benefits?
- Benefits (why recommendations meet your clients' needs) sell!
- All recommendations have some downsides which produce concerns. The benefits need to outweigh any inherent concerns. Your clients must see for themselves that the benefits (upsides) outweigh any concerns (downsides).
- Clear benefits help sponsors sell your recommendations to others.
- Long after the features are taken for granted, the benefits will be remembered.
- Research shows that listing too many features actually raises resistance (looks too much like a 'sales job'). If you want client commitment, more emphasis must be given to the advantages and benefits of the recommendation—from your client's point of view—than to the specific features you are proposing.

Features = Fun
Benefits = Buy.

If You Love Your Professional Area—Watch Out!

PREPOSTEROUS STATEMENT #1

"The more you know and love your area of expertise, the harder it is for you to see and express benefits from your client's point of view." Here are three corollaries:
"The more you know and love what you do:
- *#1 ... the more you love to describe detail after detail (=features) of your recommendations rather than the benefits of these features.*
- *#2 ... the more you have 'internalized' the benefits of your recommendations and assume that your clients have as well.*
- *#3 ... the more you talk with professional colleagues, the more you get into trouble when you talk with your clients. Professional talk is not client talk."*

"This system has 512 Megs of SuperRAM ..."
Most early desktop PCs were bought by 'techies'—people who understand the difference between ROM and RAM, Megs and Gigs, and a PCI or a EISA bus. To sell to a techie, a salesperson might just say "This system has 512 Megs of SuperRAM upgradeable to 2 Gigs, a SuperSCSI 120 Gig Drive ..." etc. To state the benefits of each of these features to a fellow aficionado would be condescending! To an erudite PC buyer these features are like beauty and aesthetics! Yet the current largest group of desktop PC buyers are not techies at all. They are home users. You just 'snow' home users by using these tactics. How do you explain to a home user the need for and benefits of 512 Megs of RAM? You might talk about the benefits this way:

✓ ability to run modern programs, especially games, which demand a lot of memory space

✓ plenty of room to have a number of programs running at once

✓ machine is upgradeable and will be able to expand with your needs.

These benefits may be obvious to the techie but hardly obvious to the average home user!

 Quotable Quotes
"Your job, as a professional, so to get your work implemented in a way that adds value to the organization. You must find a way to sell that fits your values and is effective."
  – George Campbell

Selling—helping others get what they need—can be fun!

You need a wide range of benefits to make sure at least one feature resonates with each client's need.

ARE YOU A PORSCHE™ SALESPERSON?

In our workshops, we simulate participants learning to be salespeople for Porsche. Guy Kawasaki, the marketing manager for Apple™ computers when the Macintosh™ was introduced, tells the Porsche™ story in his book, *Selling the Dream.* This story illustrates the difference between features and benefits. Porsche™ uses a sales training technique where the trainer places a number of little magnetic flags on the features of a Porsche™. In order for new salespeople to pass the sales training program, they must be able to relate both the particular feature and its benefits for a prospective customer. This is our simulation:

"As a salesperson, for every feature of a Porsche™ you need to be able to list at least a dozen benefits for the feature. One of the features of a Porsche™ is that it has heated external rearview mirrors. What are some benefits of heated rearview mirrors?"

The first four or five benefits come quite quickly, for example:
- safety
- doesn't fog up
- doesn't ice up
- don't have to scrape.

After the first few benefits, there is a pause. We do a time-out and ask "Why the pause? Why do we push you to a dozen?" The pause is because the first few benefits are usually those that participants themselves would see for the feature. The dozen, because effective salespersons need to push well beyond what appeals to them personally, to reach the range that would appeal to a specific customer.
"For the next group of benefits, look beyond what might appeal to you, to what might appeal to a wide range of customers."
Now the group will very quickly go to the dozen:
- don't scratch during scraping
- don't misalign during scraping
- increase resale value of car
- feel safer
- can warm up hands while fumbling for keys
- increase bragging rights with neighbors
- rewarm your breakfast bagel (appeal to customers with a sense of humor?)

"Good. You are qualified to sell Porsches!"

'Breakthrough benefits thinking' is helpful because salespeople start speculating how the feature might appeal to others. The exercise can also be a lot of fun!

What might be a benefit for one client—'bragging rights with neighbors' for example, may be a turnoff for another, so exercise care. Many professionals have remarked that this is often true in their organization. Benefits which appeal to senior management may be a turnoff for frontline workers and vice-versa.

A CHECKLIST OF TYPICAL CLIENT BENEFITS

As you use this Benefits Checklist remember the following principles:
- Powerful benefits must be benefits for the specific client; not for clients generally.
- The more specific and measurable the benefits the better.
- Ensure benefits are believable. Clients are skeptical. One unsubstantiated benefit wipes out ten substantiated ones.
- What may be a benefit for one client may be a turnoff for another.
- Like features, benefits need to be chosen and used sparingly. It only takes one benefit to sell—as long as it's the right one for that client!
- All these benefits can be short or long term.
- Don't use the list to 'psych out' your clients. The point here is not to push your client's 'hot buttons,' but to have clients give your valued recommendations the consideration they deserve!

Economic Benefits:
- ❑ Increased revenue
- ❑ Greater return on investment
- ❑ Increased cash flow
- ❑ Ease of financing
- ❑ Shorter payout time
- ❑ Higher cost/benefit ratio
- ❑ Tax advantages
- ❑ Higher efficiency
- ❑ Higher productivity of labor
- ❑ More competitive
- ❑ High growth potential

Cost Benefits:
- ❑ Minimized project costs
- ❑ Minimized design costs
- ❑ Minimized capital costs
- ❑ Minimized operating costs
- ❑ Minimized maintenance costs
- ❑ Within budget
- ❑ Reduced inventory

Resource Benefits:
- ❑ Increased productivity
- ❑ Reduced number of people needed
- ❑ Minimization of labor required
- ❑ Reduced training time
- ❑ Maximized use of in-house resources
- ❑ Fewer outside resources required

People Benefits:
- ❑ Increased commitment and ownership
- ❑ Ease of change
- ❑ Minimized change required of people
- ❑ Made jobs easier or more enjoyable
- ❑ Ease of operation
- ❑ User friendly
- ❑ Enhanced quality of worklife

Values, Principles Benefits:
- ❑ Fit within corporate values and principles
- ❑ Fit with organizational culture
- ❑ Support for organizational direction/ strategy
- ❑ Ethically/legally correct

Customer/Client Benefits:
- ❑ Increased customer service
- ❑ Increased sales/revenue
- ❑ Response to customer needs/ requests

Quality Benefits:
- ❑ Increased quality
- ❑ Fewer rejects
- ❑ System highly reliable
- ❑ Reduced losses
- ❑ Underlying causes eliminated
- ❑ Well researched

Service Benefits:
- ❑ Ease of servicing/maintaining
- ❑ Availability of after-implementation service
- ❑ Availability of trouble shooters
- ❑ Availability of replacement parts

Environmental/Safety Benefits:
- ❑ No adverse environmental impact
- ❑ Enhanced environment
- ❑ Enhanced safe operation
- ❑ Reduction of health problems
- ❑ Ergonomically correct

Timing Benefits:
- ❑ Project completed on time
- ❑ Fits well with other initiatives
- ❑ Minimized time to production
- ❑ Minimized time to market

Technical Benefits:
- ❑ Increased throughput
- ❑ Decreased downtime
- ❑ Greater reliability
- ❑ Anticipated future needs/upgradeable
- ❑ Support for future technological directions

Interfacing/Planning Benefits:
- ❑ Well planned
- ❑ Easily meshed with existing systems/ compatible
- ❑ Application in other areas
- ❑ Implementation is not disruptive of normal operations
- ❑ Risks assessed and manageable
- ❑ Contingency plans in place

Image Benefits:
- ❑ Enhanced organizational image
- ❑ Enhanced employee pride
- ❑ Enhanced employee morale
- ❑ Seen as leading edge

6

This Checklist is on the Web Site:
www.consultskills.com.

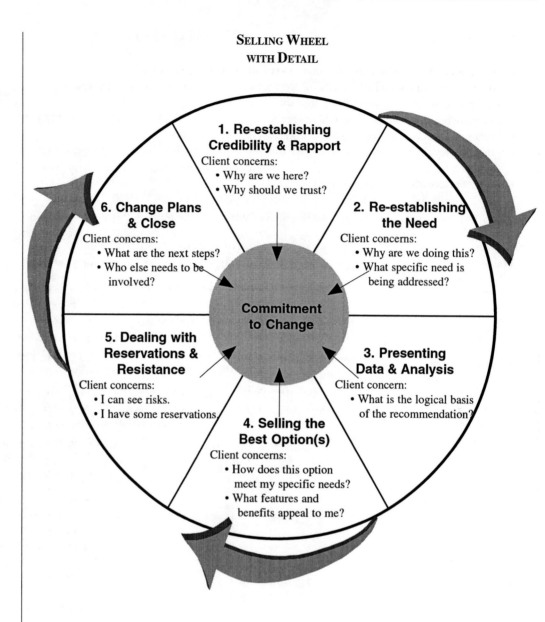

SELLING WHEEL
WITH DETAIL

**1. Re-establishing
Credibility & Rapport**
Client concerns:
• Why are we here?
• Why should we trust?

**6. Change Plans
& Close**
Client concerns:
• What are the next steps?
• Who else needs to be
  involved?

**2. Re-establishing
the Need**
Client concerns:
• Why are we doing this?
• What specific need is
  being addressed?

**Commitment
to Change**

**5. Dealing with
Reservations &
Resistance**
Client concerns:
• I can see risks.
• I have some reservations.

**3. Presenting
Data & Analysis**
Client concern:
• What is the logical basis
  of the recommendation?

**4. Selling the
Best Option(s)**
Client concerns:
• How does this option
  meet my specific needs?
• What features and
  benefits appeal to me?

*This Selling Wheel is on
the Web Site:
www.consultskills.com.*

5. Dealing With Reservations and Resistance

Now you are faced with so-called 'resistance to change.' Because it is the most widely used excuse for failure, this spoke of the Selling Wheel is the second one allotted a disproportionate amount of time.

- You've re-established rapport and credibility
- You've re-established the business need driving your recommendations
- You've presented your data and analyses
- You've presented the major features of your recommendations along with client benefits—how the recommendation will solve the client's need.

Now for resistance. 'Resistance' is a strange word, loaded with negative and emotional baggage, which can lead to negative and protective behavior. We prefer the less loaded word 'reservations.' Other words we have heard used in this context are: 'risks,' 'objections,' 'reluctance,' 'buyer remorse,' and plain old 'implementation concern.' Using a particular word may not make change any easier, but changing a label can possibly help you and your clients manage it more effectively.

Two Distinct Brands of Reservations and Resistance

Before we go any further, we need to distinguish between two kinds of resistance:

1. Direct Resistance, better called 'reservations' or 'risk management.'

   If you ask for your clients' concerns about your recommendation and they openly tell you, you are dealing with direct resistance. Although it may seem brusque at the time, this kind of direct resistance is the easier type to deal with. It is the topic of this chapter.

2. Indirect Resistance.

   If you ask for your clients' concerns and they give you a 'runaround,' 'stall,' or 'brush off,' not their real reservations, you are dealing with indirect resistance. This more challenging form of resistance is the topic of Chapter 10, *Dealing with Resistance*.

If you ask employees whether they want change in their work area or organization, they will probably rhyme off a number of suggested improvements. So what's this resistance to change anyway?

6

DIFFERENCE BETWEEN DIRECT AND INDIRECT CLIENT RESISTANCE

Direct	Indirect
•Resistance stated openly and honestly; the real concern stated.	•Resistance stated in apparently rational terms, not the real concern.
•Usually the client maintains eye contact and uses 'I' statements.	•Usually the client does not maintain eye contact and uses third party "we" or "they" statements.
•May feel hurtful at the time because it may feel blunt, but it is actually the more honest and easier to deal with.	•A put-off or runaround.
•You know exactly where you stand; the issue is clear.	•Feels out-of-focus, like foggy film. Hard to get a grip on what is happening.
▼	▼
•Leads to honest negotiation or conflict resolution.	•Leads to misdirected energy and frustration.
•You can put your energy into the real issue.	• You will be led to put energy into side issues.

Reservations will surface now, at the presentation—or later when you are absent.
It's like the saying: "You can pay me now, or you can pay me later."

We have seen commitment scuttled by professionals who were threatened by legitimate and manageable implementation concerns!

Some Principles for Dealing With Direct Resistance

- Reservations and resistance are natural and OK. If you don't surface the reservations during your recommendations presentation, they will certainly surface during implementation.
- When presented with any significant change, most people will think of reasons why the new ideas won't work. It's natural for most people to want to stay with the comfortable status quo and defend it—even when the current way of doing things is not working well. (In reading this book, you yourself may have reacted to many ideas with "This won't work for me with my clients!")
- To the degree you can, anticipate reservations that clients may have to your recommendations and plan how to deal with them. Remember, different client groups may have quite different reservations. (See Chapter 8, *Mapping Client Systems,* for more details on analyzing and dealing with diverse client groups.)
- Resistance is usually felt long before it can be articulated. Professionals often feel rising resistance of the client and either push back harder, or repress it—both dysfunctional reactions, causing the client to push harder or repress it as well. (A useful analogy is the difference between isometrics and the martial arts. With isometrics, any force is resisted with an equal and opposite reaction with little movement. In the martial arts, the principle is to make the opponent's energy work for you—in this case, you can make your clients' resistance work for you.)

Deal with Reservations!

Here are some reasons why you must surface your clients' reservations at this stage of your presentation:

- If the clients express reservations, you know that they are listening and tracking you!
- Reservations are often just concerns about how you will successfully implement your recommendations. Clients are not challenging 'What' or 'Why' but wanting to know 'How'?
- Your clients may be right! What professional can guarantee a perfect recommendation?
- You can't do anything about what you don't see or understand. You cannot deal with reservations that are not expressed.
- Even if you are unable to adequately address client reservations, addressing them shows you are interested in their 'real world' concerns.
- If you want your clients to be open to *your* concerns, you need to model openness to *their* concerns.

After discussing the need to bring resistance out in the open, a professional in a large telephone company said "We are too polite for effectiveness around here."

PREPOSTEROUS STATEMENT #2

"If you are asking your clients to change significantly and you don't meet any resistance you may have a problem!" Here's why:

- Your clients may not understand what you are asking them to do.
- If your clients don't anticipate and discuss implementation difficulties now, they will later—and perhaps blame you for selling a defective recommendation.
- Your clients may not be listening.
- Your clients may be dismissing your recommendations as 'water off my back,' with no intentions of implementing them.

Resistance is Scary!
If surfacing reservations is so beneficial, why do professionals (and clients) often have difficulty with it?

- Our database shows that professionals are woefully unskilled at dealing with conflict. (Most clients are no better at it!)

Surfacing resistance = surfacing conflict and conflict is scary!

- Surfacing reservations often results in the expression of emotions—emotions are scary!
- Surfacing reservations may result in concerns you didn't think of or you can do nothing about—being out of control is scary!
- Many professionals have not learned the models and skills we present here—these skills are *not* scary!

Tips for Surfacing Client Reservations
Clients are often willing to share their concerns about your recommendations. All you need to do is ask them. Pause frequently during discussions and presentations to ask clients to voice any concerns.

- ❏ Deal with important or easy concerns immediately. Defer the remainder, ideally by visibly recording them.
- ❏ Give many opportunities for expressing reservations throughout the presentation, rather than leaving them to the end. Summarize the reservations before moving on.
- ❏ If you are unclear about a reservation, ask for an example. Often concerns are expressed as generalizations; an example makes them concrete. To a concern of "We don't have the skills," you might ask "Can you give me an example of where they would see their skills lacking?" It's usually easier to deal with specific, concrete concerns.
- ❏ Always summarize a reservation, whether you can deal with it or not. Clients want their concerns heard. A powerful consulting skill is to make client concerns visible on a whiteboard or flipchart.
- ❏ Support your clients in clarifying confusing concerns. Often client reservations begin with a 'gut feeling' that 'something isn't right here.'
- ❏ Even though it is natural to feel defensive (after all, you've put a lot of thought and energy into your recommendations), do *not* exercise resistance in return! Keep calm. Remember that reservations are a natural reaction to recommendations for change.
- ❏ Do not punish clients for expressing their reservations, nor respond defensively to client comments. In many ways, clearly expressed client reservations are a gift, letting you know where your client stands so that you can effectively deal with any reservations.

Clients need to be HEARD
This raises another fear we often hear in workshops: "What if the client expresses a concern I can't do anything about? What if the client says 'It costs too much money,' and the solution can't be made less expensive? I can't put money in the client's budget." If you hear a client express a reservation you cannot deal with, your best bet is to hear the client out. Clients want to be heard, their 'real world' concerns listened to. Summarize the client's concern, then be honest and say you cannot do anything about it. Most clients will understand your dilemma and will often let you 'off the hook.'

66 **Quotable Quotes** 99
"Sometimes the reservations surface issues you hadn't considered—that are so serious your project or recommendations will not be approved. Your job as a professional is to help the client make the best business decision."
– George Campbell

A CHECKLIST OF TYPICAL CLIENT RESERVATIONS

It helps to anticipate your clients' reservations and concerns. Below is a checklist of typical client reservations. Remember these principles as you use the list:
- Reservations are usually specific to a particular client group.
- Clarify vague reservations. The more specific the reservation, the more specific the solution.
- All these reservations can be short or long term.

Financial:
- ❑ Costs too much
- ❑ Not in the budget
- ❑ Poor Return on Investment (ROI)
- ❑ Payout period too long
- ❑ Corporate 'hurdle rates' not met

People Resources:
- ❑ Not enough people to implement or operate
- ❑ People not skilled enough
- ❑ People don't know enough
- ❑ Need more training
- ❑ No buy-in by front line workers
- ❑ Change will upset people

Planning:
- ❑ Not enough implementation planning
- ❑ See problems with the plans

Time and Energy:
- ❑ Will take too long
- ❑ Bad timing
- ❑ Not a priority
- ❑ Will take too much time

Change:
- ❑ Will disrupt smooth running of operations
- ❑ Resistance to change on behalf of others

Risks:
- ❑ Exposure to failure
- ❑ Hidden problems
- ❑ Lots of roadblocks

Logical/Technical:
- ❑ Won't work as stated
- ❑ Too little research
- ❑ Needs more work
- ❑ No clear plan
- ❑ Needs a more strategic approach

Political:
- ❑ Senior managers won't buy-in
- ❑ Need to sell to others
- ❑ Someone who is not present makes the final decision
- ❑ May upset other peer managers
- ❑ May invade others' 'turf'
- ❑ Doesn't mesh with corporate direction

Listen to distinguish between 'What?' 'Why?' and 'How?' client questions.

WHAT? WHY? HOW? - TAKE 2

A very successful consultant, Norm Smallwood, suggests it's important to distinguish between 'What'? 'Why?' and 'How?' client questions.
- 'What' questions are looking for more information.
- 'Why' questions mean that you haven't addressed the client's need. You need to supply more logic and stress the benefits.
- 'How' questions mean that the client has already bought in and is wondering how to implement the recommendation.

Norm's observation (and ours) is that inexperienced professionals often confuse these. Taking a 'How' question as a 'Why' question can make the professional appear defensive and condescending and may even produce defensiveness in a client who was simply pondering how to implement.

THE COMMITMENT BALANCE

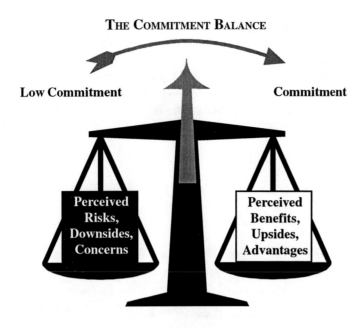

Low Commitment   Commitment

Perceived Risks, Downsides, Concerns

Perceived Benefits, Upsides, Advantages

Client commitment means the benefits, upsides and advantages outweigh the risks, downsides and concerns—as seen by the client.

6

If it has not been dealt with earlier, resistance will rear its head when you try to clarify the Change Plan and Close, manifested by your clients being unwilling to make commitment.

See Chapter 4, Clarifying Commitments, for Confirming Documents.

6. Change Plans and Close

'Change Plan,' the sixth and final spoke of the Selling Wheel, emphasizes that a professional's job is not done until successful implementation takes place—a most challenging part of the process.

The goal here is to effectively close the presentation meeting. This is the stage where agreements and actions are finalized and summarized. In external professional sales, commentators often talk about 'Closing the Sale.' This is usually unrealistic in an internal situation, since the nature of organizational change often requires multiple approvals. It is better to think in terms of verbal commitments and plans. In sales literature these are called:
   i. 'Advance'—planning specific actions to be taken by professionals and their clients to bring recommendations forward, or
   ii. 'Continuation'—planning how to continue the decision making process.

Tips for Closing a Presentation
   ❏ Ask for commitment to action.
   ❏ Summarize and make visible the major agreements.
   ❏ Clearly restate the next steps for you and your clients.
   ❏ Write a Confirming Document immediately after the meeting, especially if an important agreement or a fair amount of work is involved,
   ❏ Express support for your clients.
   ❏ Thank your clients for their time and effort.

Relieving the 'Pane' of Change—The Change Window

So far, we have emphasized the 'Recommendations' half of the *Recommending Change* stage of the Expertise Delivery Model. The rest of this chapter is devoted to the 'Change' half, by:
- visualizing the connection between recommendations and change
- pulling all the major concepts of this chapter into one straightforward model
- helping you understand why recommending significant change is rarely a one step process
- helping you present balanced, 'real world' recommendations in your clients' eyes (and hearts).

Our way of doing all of this is by looking at the 'Recommending Change Window.'

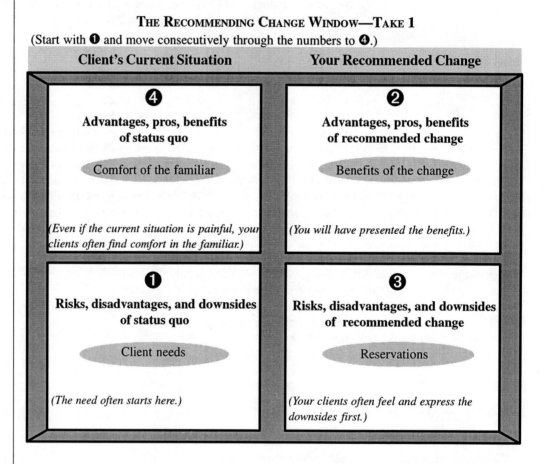

THE RECOMMENDING CHANGE WINDOW—TAKE 1

(Start with ❶ and move consecutively through the numbers to ❹.)

Client's Current Situation	Your Recommended Change
❹ **Advantages, pros, benefits of status quo** Comfort of the familiar *(Even if the current situation is painful, your clients often find comfort in the familiar.)*	❷ **Advantages, pros, benefits of recommended change** Benefits of the change *(You will have presented the benefits.)*
❶ **Risks, disadvantages, and downsides of status quo** Client needs *(The need often starts here.)*	❸ **Risks, disadvantages, and downsides of recommended change** Reservations *(Your clients often feel and express the downsides first.)*

Relating the Change Window to the Selling Wheel

According to the Selling Wheel, we ask you to cycle through the quadrants as follows:

❶ Risks, disadvantages, and downsides of the way things are. Change usually starts with a problem—a client need—usually the inadequacy of the way things are—equivalent to spoke 2, Re-establishing the Need.

❷ Advantages, pros, benefits of recommended change—equivalent to spoke 4, Selling the Best Option(s) using features and benefits of change.

❸ & ❹ Risks of recommended change and advantages of the status quo—equivalent to spoke 5, Dealing with Reservations & Resistance. Keep in mind the natural tendency for clients to think of quadrants ❸ and ❹—the reservations about your recommended change and the solace of the way things are.

This Change Window says clients need to go around this ❶ to ❹ sequence a few times before they get comfortable with the change (hence the client questions in each quadrant of the Change Window, Take 2, below). Keep in mind that the 'natural' thought pattern for a professional is to present ❶ and ❷. The natural thought pattern for your clients is to feel and think in quadrants ❸ and ❹.

So now we go into the next cycle around the window …

THE RECOMMENDING CHANGE WINDOW—TAKE 2

(Start with ❶ and cycle to ❹)

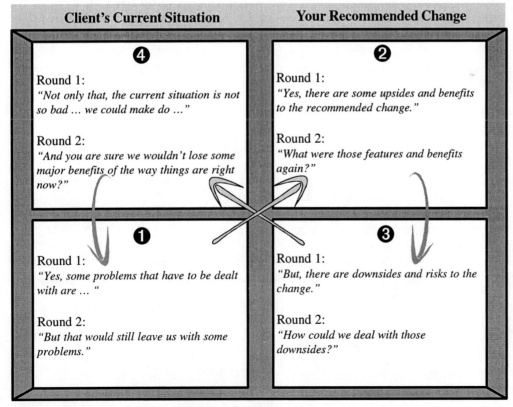

Client's Current Situation	Your Recommended Change
❹ Round 1: *"Not only that, the current situation is not so bad … we could make do …"* Round 2: *"And you are sure we wouldn't lose some major benefits of the way things are right now?"*	❷ Round 1: *"Yes, there are some upsides and benefits to the recommended change."* Round 2: *"What were those features and benefits again?"*
❶ Round 1: *"Yes, some problems that have to be dealt with are … "* Round 2: *"But that would still leave us with some problems."*	❸ Round 1: *"But, there are downsides and risks to the change."* Round 2: *"How could we deal with those downsides?"*

… and perhaps a third cycle around the window!

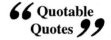

❝ Quotable Quotes ❞

"The devil you know is better than the devil you don't."

EYE WITNESS REPORT

Workshop participants have said that when making recommendations, they can tell by the clients' questions or remarks which quadrant the clients' heads and hearts are in. Categorizing the clients' questions by placing them in the appropriate quadrant, can help the professional frame a more appropriate response—which may be to let the clients 'talk through' the change for themselves.

"Where is this real world everybody keeps talking about?"
© *Ashleigh Brilliant*

It's much easier to be a 'pull' professional than a 'push' professional.

If this chapter has piqued your interest in the skills of selling your recommendations in a professional manner, or if you are recommending large scale change, we strongly recommend you read Neil Rackman's books on SPIN Selling or SPIN Selling Fieldbook. Although written from the external perspective, they have wonderful research and insights on large scale recommendations. (See Selected Further Reading at the end of the book for specifics.)

Being a 'Real World' Professional

On occasion, we have found that clients have accused many professionals (including the authors!) of "not living in the real world." Where is this 'real world' anyway? For client perception of the 'real world,' see the Change Window, Take 3, below.

THE RECOMMENDING CHANGE WINDOW—TAKE 3

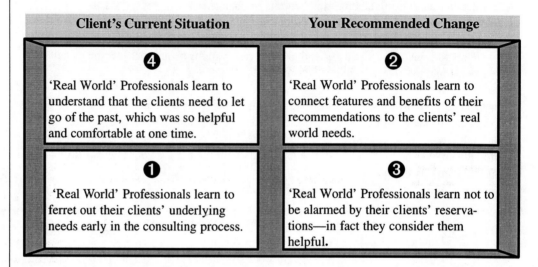

Client's Current Situation	Your Recommended Change
❹ 'Real World' Professionals learn to understand that the clients need to let go of the past, which was so helpful and comfortable at one time.	**❷** 'Real World' Professionals learn to connect features and benefits of their recommendations to the clients' real world needs.
❶ 'Real World' Professionals learn to ferret out their clients' underlying needs early in the consulting process.	**❸** 'Real World' Professionals learn not to be alarmed by their clients' reservations—in fact they consider them helpful.

If you wish to know more about ensuring that your recommended change sticks, read Chapter 9, *Sustaining Change*. Depending on your needs, you may wish to go directly to the *Recommending Change* worksheets, starting on page 103. If you wish to try out a fun experiential example of the Selling Wheel, read on …

Now For Your Real World Application

If you use this model and actually write your own data in each quadrant, you will benefit by:
- presenting a more balanced view of the change.
- having more empathy with a client's point of view.
- being more professional; not perceived as pushing (if you use quadrants ❶ and ❷ alone), but partnering in the change.
- having a better chance of commitment. In fact, if your clients don't go around the sequence a few times, they may not understand the change and may be surprised and disappointed later.

Why not try out the Change Window for yourself by jotting some notes in the matrix on page 101?

ON-JOB APPLICATION: THE RECOMMENDING CHANGE 'WINDOW'

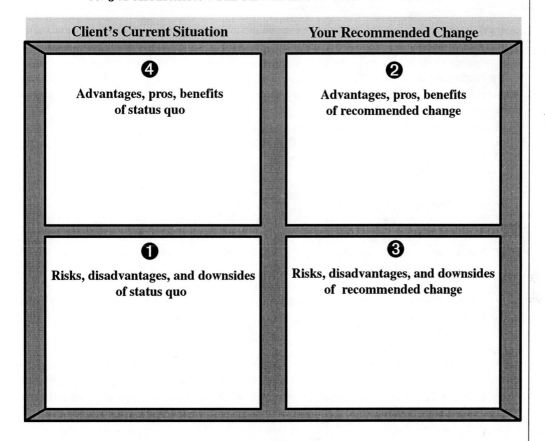

Much more information on the challenging subject of change is presented in Chapter 9, Sustaining Change.

6

A Working Example (Tongue-in-Cheek!)

One of the principles of effective consulting is to model the behavior you expect in others. By 'selling' you on the idea of recommending this book to others in your organization or profession, this example treats you as a client and you get to feel like a client would feel. (Don't take this example too seriously!)

Since you are not present, this is an even more difficult job than presenting to someone you know and can see.

RECURSION PRESS SELLING THIS *POWERFUL PROFESSIONALS* BOOK

Step 1: Establishing Rapport and Credibility
We hope you are enjoying and applying the ideas of this book to your professional role and that they are helping you become a more powerful professional in your organization. We bring much experience and research to the book, manifest in practical applications designed to help you in your 'real world,' to design your own models for effective delivery of expertise inside your organization. Our book models the business partner consulting role, in our view the only long-term satisfying professional role.

Recursion is a mathematical term meaning using an idea back on itself. Some versions of this idea are:
– practice what you preach.
– model the behavior you expect in others.
– do unto clients what you want done unto you.

Step 2. Establishing the Need

Since you have read this far, you must have reasons for reading it. If you are benefiting from this book, your professional colleagues would probably benefit from it as well.

Step 3. Presenting Data and Analysis

This book is designed to cover all the major skills of being a powerful professional inside your organization.
1. The 'What' and 'Why' of high performing professionals
2. A practical internal Expertise Delivery Model
3. How to *Explore the Need* with a client

(and the rest of the Table of Contents).

Step 4: Selling the Best Option(s)

1. The book is designed to be an on-the-job, on-the-desk reference; a book you could read from cover-to-cover, but is more likely to be used on an as-needed basis.
2. The models, skills, assessments, checklists, dos and don'ts, and worksheets are designed to be practical and helpful on-the-job.
3. The book is not telling you how to manage your job, but practising what it preaches, presenting lots of options and tools, giving you the opportunity to adapt those most useful to you.

Step 5: Dealing With Reservations

1. *"Maybe unlike me, other professionals understand and use this stuff already."*
   It's likely these skills and models will resonate with your professional colleagues as well. Distilled from work with thousands of professionals across many organizations and across cultures, this book is based on the world's largest database of what clients value in professionals.
2. *"Maybe they won't like the book and I'll look dumb for having recommended it."*
   Perhaps the best time to recommend the book is when fellow professionals express concerns resembling those in the book. At such a time, they would probably it is likely they would find the book most helpful.

Step 6: Change Plans and Close

We'll bet that as you've read this book, you've thought of others who could use its insights and models to improve their professional skills.
Who are they? List them below:

When I recommend—or better still, present them with—the book, what will I say to them that will raise the chances of their reading it?

If it is your boss or the manager of a professional group, how could you use the Selling Wheel to present the need for the book and its benefits in a powerful way? The next section of this chapter is in the form of a worksheet, to help you plan this, or plan an alternative recommendation.

How did we do? Did we sell you on the idea of selling the book (through our tongue-in-cheek example)?

Recommending Change: A Presentation Worksheet

Before the Presentation:

- Selling must start well before the meeting where you present your recommendations. Selling is done in every part of the project and doesn't end until the product or service is thoroughly owned by the client.
- Prepare your presentation with your clients' needs in mind, not your needs. The best persuaders sell completely from their clients' perspective. You are not selling professional or technical solutions; you are selling business solutions to client needs.
- Ferret out your client's needs. If you can present your recommendations as solutions to your clients' problems, you will make it easier all around.
- Ferret out your clients' probable reservations and resistance—the sooner the better. What can you do to anticipate your clients' reservations and build in solutions to their concerns?
- Discuss your presentation with a number of 'reality coaches.' If the presentation is crucial, get feedback and improvement suggestions from a number of diverse sources who are in touch with your clients' thinking and feelings. (Strangely, the least helpful coaches will often come from people you are in closest contact with—your professional colleagues. This is because they tend to look at your recommendations similarly to the way you do.)

*No need—
no problem,
no hurt—
no buy.*

What do you need to do to <u>before</u> the presentation?
-
-
-

At The Presentation Meeting:

1. Establishing Rapport & Credibility

- A basic issue is trust. Trust is based in your clients' emotions. You need to sell yourself—establish human-to-human contact—before you can sell your recommendation.
- Participant analysis: (Note the word *'participant,'* not the passive *'audience.'*)
    - Who will be participating? Who needs to participate for commitment?
    - What do they know about the project and your recommendations?
    - What do they expect?
- How will you get the meeting started:
    - Secure your clients' participation?
    - Get off the mark quickly?
    - Establish whether you want participation throughout the presentation or at specific points.
- How will you (re)establish trust and rapport:
    - Establish and maintain eye contact.
    - How will you quickly establish credibility?

*No trust—
no buy.*

What do you need to do to get the presentation off to a strong start?
-
-
-

"WIIFM?
(What's in it for me?)"
Robin Sober

Strutting Your
Professional Stuff ...
A professional actuary,
with a Ph.D. in
Statistics, came up to
the author during a
workshop break and
volunteered this
anecdote. "... About
what you said on
overdoing the data and
analysis, underusing
the other steps of the
Selling Wheel ... It
reminded me of when I
was in Graduate
School. A particular
professor would fill a
blackboard with proof
of an arcane statistical
theorem. Since he
wasn't exactly Arnold
Schwarzenegger, I now
can't help wondering if
this was his only way
of being macho!"

2. Establishing or Re-establishing Need

- From your clients' perspective, they must see how your recommendation will solve *their* problems. Clients must see how your recommendations connect to *their* business needs.
- You need to establish or re-establish the business need. If you have thoroughly clarified the expectations and commitments, it may merely be a matter of reminding participants of your agreement.
- Think of the multiple clients in the room. What would each client group see as the business need?

> How will you establish or re-establish the business need <u>in your clients' eyes</u>?
> •
> •
> •

3. Presenting Your Data and Analysis

- You must establish a logical basis for your recommendations from your clients' perspective.
- Professionals like to show off their professional stuff, making this the centerpiece of their presentations. If this part of your presentation takes more than 1/6 of the presentation time, you may be overdoing it.

> How will you briefly present your data and analysis so that it helps your clients to buy your recommendation?
> •
> •
> •

4. Selling the Best Option(s)

- How will your recommendations solve your clients' needs? You must show how your solution will benefit your clients within *their own frame of reference*.
- Present not only the features of your recommendation, but also the benefits.
- If you have multiple clients, keep in mind that a benefit for one client group may not resonate for another.

> How will you present the features and benefits of your recommendation *within your clients' frame of reference*?
> •
> •
> •
> •

5. Dealing with Reservations and Resistance

- Clients will naturally sense the risks and downsides to buying your recommendation. In fact, if they don't see any, you may have a problem.
- Expect your clients to feel resistant. It is natural and OK. Don't resist the resistance.
- These risks and downsides will either be directly expressed openly as reservations, or indirectly expressed as stalling or runarounds.
- You need to support your clients by actively listening to their reservations and helping them surface their resistance.
- You need to support your clients by showing them how you can help them implement your recommendations in their 'real world.'

> What will you do to help your clients express their risk concerns and resistance?
> •
>
> •
>
> •

6. Change Plans and Close

- The most common reason your recommendation is 'left hanging' is that you didn't ask for action. As sales books put it 'The most common reason for no sale is that it wasn't asked for.'
- Be a 'full cycle' consultant. Follow-through is extremely important. Lead the most challenging process—change.
- What are the next steps for you and your clients?
- How will you ensure transfer of ownership? Think of personal transitions for your clients as much as technical changes.
- How will you follow through?
- How will you support your client with the change?
- Remember that the closing tone of the presentation determines the feelings your clients will have about the entire presentation.

> How will you ask for action and encourage follow-through?
> •
>
> •
>
> •

This Worksheet is on the Web Site: www.consultskills.com.

WHAT YOU HAVE LEARNED SO FAR ...

IN BRIEF →

- The professional's job is not over until sustained change has taken place.

- Doing excellent professional work will come to naught if you cannot persuasively present your recommendations and take an appropriate hand in the change.

- Contrary to popular practice, the presentation of data and analysis should only take up 1/6 of your time and effort.

- The Selling Wheel will help you shift from this mindset. Its two crucial 'spokes' are: Selling the Best Option (benefits, not features, sell) and Dealing with Reservations. (Only when you get your clients' reservations out in the open can you do anything about them.)

- The Change Window is an effective tool for working with your clients to present 'real world' recommendations—balancing positives and negatives.

THE EXPERTISE DELIVERY MODEL

Taking Stock or Closing · Exploring the Need · Clarifying Commitments · Gathering Information · RECOMMENDING CHANGE · Client Commitment

"It ain't over till it's over."
– Yogi Berra

STAGE 5:
TAKING STOCK/CLOSING

Quick Snapshot

Did You Know?
- this stage is generally poorly done by professionals?
- you need a 'Taking Stock' meeting with your clients at the most unlikely time?
- the briefer the consultation, the more need for an Expertise Delivery Model?

How-to:
- use Closing and Taking Stock meetings to enhance your professional practice.
- establish an agenda for these meetings.
- adapt the Expertise Delivery Model for your personal use.
- use the Expertise Delivery Model for very brief consultations, for example, a telephone call.

The Bottom Line:
- You will get the feedback and recognition you need to improve your professional services, effectively using the ideas and checklists in this chapter.

7

Fizzling Out?

The purpose of this chapter is to underline the need to wrap up projects, or periodically take stock, so that both professionals and their organizations can learn from the past and improve for the future.

When asked how projects usually end, professionals give such responses as:
- "They don't end, they fizzle out."
- "When they are beaten to death."
- "They never end."
- "When people stop calling you."
- "When you start the fifth project after the current one."

In an extreme example, it was three years since a Fortune 500 company engineer had worked as an Operations Engineer at one of the company's manufacturing plants. This now Head-Office engineer told us "I received a call just the other day from a shift supervisor at the plant I worked at three years ago. The supervisor asked me about the status of a project I had worked on during that time. I had to tell him I hadn't been there or worked on the project for three years!"

On an economic note, a group of project engineers for a construction company estimated they could save the company hundreds of thousands of dollars annually, if only they could expedite the drawn-out closure of large construction projects. The pressure to start new projects inhibited closure of current projects, resulting in millions of dollars tied up in withheld funds.

Closing is not well done. Cited as the major culprits are time pressures and low priority of closing for both client and professional. With flattening hierarchies and responsibility diffusion in many organizations, many professionals and their managers express concerns about Taking Stock/Closing: "How are we going to share our project learnings so we don't keep making the same mistakes?" or more positively, "How are we going to pass on what we have learned and celebrate our successes?" Some organizations are remedying this by establishing processes to tie up loose ends and by promoting organizational learning through 'Look-Back Meetings,' 'Client Feedback Reports,' and 'Close-Out Discussions.'

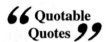

"Quotable Quotes"

"Most projects fizzle out or are delivered late. Make clear that your projects end on time and are successful and you will stand out as a consultant."
– George Campbell

Double Barreled Moniker

This last stage of the Expertise Delivery Model has two parts to its name, 'Taking Stock' and 'Closing.' Other authors refer to this stage as Closure, Review, Termination or Exiting. These terms seemed to us to imply walking away from clients. Most internal professionals supply expertise on a continuing basis to internal clients, managers and colleagues. A solution to our wording dilemma came by way of a bright workshop participant, who said, "Internally, closure is the right word if you are the kind of professional that works on discrete projects. But more often than not, professionals are doing a series of overlapping tasks for the same clients. What they need to do, periodically, is take stock."

Our distinction is:
- *Taking Stock*

  If your professional work is ongoing with the same clients, you need to take stock on a regular basis. Periodically, you need to meet with your clients to monitor results, priorities and working relationships, and to plan improvements in your working arrangements.

- *Closing*

  If your professional work is project oriented, where you move on to a new group of clients, you need the skills of wrapping up projects. You need to meet with your clients to assess results, evaluate the project's processes, receive and give feedback and recognition, and plan how to turn over the project to your clients.

Skills applicable to both *Taking Stock and Closing*:
- Review what has been done and the results achieved.
- Tidy up loose ends.
- Give and receive feedback.
- Talk about the working relationship.
- Propose, discuss and plan improvements.

For many organizations, project evaluations are becoming a fact of life. Besides being experts in their field, powerful professionals have become experts at delivering their expertise. They do not drop the ball at this last stage. They set up and manage *Taking Stock and Closing*.

Some Principles for Taking Stock/Closing

❑ Do not wait until this stage to think about *Taking Stock/Closing*. Negotiate this stage up front.

❑ Build in checkpoints along the way. Chunk your projects and build in informal close-offs, or progress review discussions, during your projects.

❑ Continually ask yourself "Is this the best use of my time and effort?" Read Chapter 13, *Your Strategy: Yes or No* and be ready to discuss your role and contributions in strategic terms.

❑ Don't assume that your clients will ask for these kinds of meetings. Take responsibility for the consulting process, including this final stage.

❑ Assume that your clients will find it much easier to talk about technical and business issues than relationship and performance issues.

❑ Don't be defensive. One of the reasons many professionals and clients avoid *Taking Stock/Closing* meetings is that they may get feedback they are afraid to hear.

❑ If you have needs, ask for them. If you want recognition for your good work to be sent to your manager, ask for it. The most common reason nothing happens is because no-one was asked to do anything.

❑ Be sure to think of all the stakeholders when planning *Taking Stock/Closing* activities. Just because you informed a manager, do not assume the whole department is informed.

❑ Try not to make this stage an 'add-on.' *Taking Stock/Closing* should be a logical and integral part of a successful relationship.

7

In this chapter ...

- *Why Taking Stock and Closing are important*
- *Typical problems with this stage*
- *Benefits of this stage*
- *What to discuss at Taking Stock or Closing meetings*
- *Brief consultations*

109

Take Stock When Least Expected

You need to initiate a Taking Stock meeting when your clients are least likely to see the need for it—when things are going well! Yet Taking Stock meetings usually occur only when problems crop up. This is the worst possible time to talk about improvements, when you and your client are focused on what has gone wrong and how to get things back on track. Like a baseball player in the midst of a great season, you have most leverage when things are going well.

Neither do you want this stage to be an 'add-on.' *Taking Stock/Closing* needs to be discussed as an integral and important part of the professional-client relationship. The reason many Taking Stock/Closing meetings don't have priority is because they are only an afterthought. Professionals have remarked that these meetings just don't happen unless these two conditions are met:

1. The *Closing/Taking Stock* stage was anticipated early in the Expertise Delivery process.
2. Clear project criteria were set up in the *Clarifying Commitments* stage. The clearer the expected outcomes and processes at the beginning, the clearer the review at the end.

Why Closing and Taking Stock are Important

Although often overlooked by professionals, Taking Stock at appropriate times is a vital element of the consulting process, avoiding many potential pitfalls or problems which may otherwise arise. Closing is crucial for powerful professionals. How the project wraps up greatly influences the clients' feeling about the overall success of a project and about your professional effectiveness. As projects wind down, clients frequently lose sight of key factors that contributed to the completion of the project. Your job is to clearly and effectively bring the project to closure by:

a. planning how to deal with follow-through issues

b. reviewing how results were met

c. looking at commitments made during the *Clarifying Commitments* stage, then evaluating how well they were carried out.

Benefits of Taking Stock/Closing

You will:
* *Be more appreciated by your clients.*
  Professionals often cite 'lack of recognition' as a concern. Ensure that your clients are aware of your ongoing contribution. Raise new, more strategic business needs that your clients may not be aware of. Celebrate success.
* *Carve out an effective role for yourself.*
  Clients can easily 'pigeon hole' professionals as only having limited skills or expertise. Often professionals limit themselves by staying in a comfortable, safe role (and complaining about it!) Negotiate how to let go of low value or nonessential work and propose more value-added work.
* *Negotiate more powerful consulting relationships.*
  Professionals can recognize an ineffective role but don't know how to extricate themselves. Taking Stock or Closing meetings, particularly at times of success, can be a natural time to discuss more powerful roles. Make sure to offer and negotiate higher impact work and roles for yourself. Offer new, more strategic professional services.

The aphorism 'No news is good news' is totally inappropriate for professionals. In fact, a more useful saying would be 'No news is bad news.' Only by Taking Stock or Closing will you know where you stand and how to improve.

Quotable Quotes
"Don't miss this opportunity to document and sell the impact of your work."
– Mark Thomas & Sam Elbeik
Supercharge Your Management Role

- *Make sure you cover important issues.*
  How often have you heard the phrase 'It fell between the cracks.' Follow through and follow up on tasks and responsibilities.
- *Ensure a service improvement process.*
  We have known professionals who have literally been fired and didn't understand why, because they never asked for feedback from their clients.
- *Avoid mutual or one-sided dependency.*
  Over time, continuously working comfortably with a client can lead to dependency. If for some reason a dependency relationship is challenged or changed, the impact of breaking dependency can be traumatic. Make sure to give your clients feedback and propose client actions which would produce better results.
  A professional cannot have it both ways—the security of dependencies and the thrill of new and strategic work. One definition of success as an internal consultant is 'leaving your clients in a better position to be self-sufficient from you.' Strong medicine! We have heard professionals say "My job security depends on my getting continuing work with my clients. Making myself dispensable is not a good strategy around here." We discuss this 'tender trap' more thoroughly in Chapter 12, *Enhancing Your Role & Career.*

More information on roles is in Chapter 12; more information on professional strategies is in Chapter 13.

How to Make Closing/Taking Stock Natural and Easy

Here are some ways of making this stage integral to your consulting practice:

❏ Schedule brief project and relationship discussions—talk about building these in, early and often.

❏ Break projects into natural 'sign-off' points. Schedule *Closing/Taking Stock* meetings at these points. Use the Checklists on the following page to discuss openly the future as well as the past; relationship issues as well as logical issues.

❏ Keep the reviews informal and short, and give these meetings informal names like 'Check-Offs,' 'Results Updates,' 'Keeping on Track' or 'Meeting Targets' meetings.

❏ If you use a written project evaluation/feedback form:
  – keep it brief—if possible one page or less, to encourage use
  – use check off questions to ease the most common complaint—'takes too much time.'
  – Remember someone has to read and summarize feedback. Only ask questions you are prepared to do something about.

❏ Many professional groups use brief, informal written updates (no more than one page) with, for example:
  – what has been achieved in the past two weeks
  – priorities for the next two weeks.

7

"We [professionals] have difficulty exiting when we have made the customer dependent on us. We can set up the situation so that the customer cannot get along without our close support. It requires a mature internal consultant to help a customer in such a way that the customer becomes self-sufficient and no longer needs the client's help ... Too many of us derive our sense of importance from making others dependent on us and then hanging around doing the work they should be doing."
– Geoff Bellman

TRANSFERRING OWNERSHIP

The client doesn't always know when or how to end the project, and the professional in turn may be reluctant to initiate the ending. It takes courage and maturity on the part of the professional to take the plunge and declare an end. This step is all about transferring ownership and supporting the client towards independence. Clarify that your final meeting is to wrap up any outstanding items and prepare the client to carry on independently. Be prepared that you, as well as your client, may feel a sense of loss from this ending.

– Ursula Wohlfarth

66 Quotable
Quotes **99**
*"We often struggle to
measure our impact
on the larger
organization; [Taking
Stock/Closing] is an
opportunity to do just
that, and in a way
that fully involves the
customer, which gives
credibility to the
results."*

– Geoff Bellman

How To Measure Your Impact

Try at every opportunity to put a value on the contribution that your project or your role is making to the success of the client. But be careful. Many clients are turned off by unsubstantiated claims. If possible, do this exercise with your client or a credible representative in the client group. It is much more powerful (and easier!) to have your clients trumpeting your value. This valuation is made much easier if measures of success were predetermined in the Clarifying Commitments stage.

Which of these measures below would be good indicators of your success? These measure are more powerful if:

1. They are agreed-to upfront.
2. They are specific, measurable and observable.
3. They are measured in partnership with your clients.

CHECKLIST OF POTENTIAL SUCCESS MEASURES

- ❏ Measuring against documented commitments or service agreement.
- ❏ Measuring agreed-to results accomplished.
- ❏ Measuring quality of service:
    - professional/technical
    - process
    - relationship/interpersonal.
- ❏ Measuring by speed, turnaround or cycle time.
- ❏ Measuring decreased rework/error rate.
- ❏ Measuring cost effectiveness compared to competitors'/benchmarking against others.
- ❏ Evaluating follow up, follow through and completion.
- ❏ Evaluating problems solved.
- ❏ Evaluating recommendations implemented.
- ❏ Tracking repeat business or referrals.
- ❏ Evaluating how well the client will be able to do this work without you in future.
- ❏ Counting the decreasing number of client contact hours.
- ❏ Counting work days against expected.
- ❏ Using client/customer feedback surveys.
- ❏ Using project completion/progress questionnaires.
- ❏ Calculating revenue generated, net profit of professional business unit.
- ❏ Calculating dollars saved by professional work.
- ❏ Calculating return on consulting investment.
- ❏ Calculating the cost of professional services against an organizational success indicator.

CHECKLIST OF TAKING STOCK/CLOSING
FOR PROJECT FEEDBACK AND/OR CLIENT MEETINGS

Use the checklist below to highlight those items most helpful to you. Some professionals say they are much more adept at the first group, Logical Review Items, than they are at the second group, Relationship Review Items.

Logical Review Items:
- ☐ Results and objectives achieved?
- ☐ Any loose ends?
- ☐ Are the changes 'sticking'?
- ☐ Follow up needed?
  - – ongoing support?
  - – training?
- ☐ Long-term cost-benefit analysis needed?
- ☐ Documentation needed?
- ☐ Final report or final presentation needed?
- ☐ Action plans clear?
- ☐ Authorizations completed?
- ☐ Longer-term systemic changes which must take place to support the changes discussed and planned?
- ☐ What new technology will improve your clients' productivity?
- ☐ Are there any other areas of the organization needing a similar project?
- ☐ Offer future high impact and strategic professional work.
- ☐ Talk about new or uncovered client needs which may require professional support.
- ☐ Discuss changes and strategies in your organization and their impact on professional services.
- ☐ If an ongoing relationship, recontract for services.

The Relationship Review Items:
- ☐ What worked well in the relationship?
- ☐ What could be improved in the future?
- ☐ Ask for feedback on your personal performance.
- ☐ Ask for feedback to your manager and for your performance appraisal.
- ☐ Give feedback and recognition for client performance.
- ☐ Communication—who needs to know this project is wrapping up?
- ☐ In the complex stakeholder system, who else needs this kind of wrap up/review discussion?
- ☐ Discuss the level of ownership and commitment in the clients' organization.
- ☐ Discuss concerns, if any, about the people side of change.
- ☐ Wrap up any people transition issues regarding the change.
- ☐ Discuss and plan how your client needs to support the change.
- ☐ Discuss the direction of your professional group and its implications for future relationships.
- ☐ Discuss and negotiate higher impact roles.
- ☐ Discuss learning—what did we learn that we could use on future projects?
- ☐ Discuss longer-term relationship strategies.
- ☐ Nostalgia—is there anything we want to remember—the highs and lows?
- ☐ How will we celebrate?

❝ Quotable Quotes ❞

"You will usually have to initiate a progress review. Customers don't seem to do this much, except when you or they are in deep trouble."
– Geoff Bellman

7

This Checklist is on the Web Site:
www.consultskills.com

Some Wrap-Up Items for You

We will use the last chapter, *Putting It All Together*, as this book's Closing. To close the Five Stage Expertise Delivery Model, there are two 'loose ends' to tidy up.

On-Job Application: Very Brief Consultations

The shorter the consultation, the clearer you need your process to be.

Some professionals' consultations are brief, often 20 minutes or less. Strange as it may seem, the shorter the consultation, the more planned it must be. Consultations spanning days or months can afford to go down a few dead ends. With short consultations, there is no time to make mistakes. Preparation is the key. Even in 10 minutes, you will probably follow all five stages of the Expertise Delivery Model from *Exploring the Need* to *Closing*.

THE BRIEF CONSULTATION CHECKLIST

The following Checklist suggestions were designed for professionals who do most of their consulting work in very short time frames, for example:
- A Systems Help Desk Advisor who does many consultations per day, mostly over the telephone.
- An Employee Benefits Advisor who counsels many employees during the day.
- A Librarian who receives research requests, both in person and over the telephone.
- A Medical Specialist who has numerous brief consultations face-to-face.
- An Operations Engineer who consults on numerous production problems.

Pick the items that would be most helpful for you and your consulting practice. Add any additional items you have found from your experience to be helpful.

1. Exploring the Need

The Issue	The Relationship
❏ Always summarize the presenting request: "So what you are asking for is …" ❏ Resist the temptation to ask "Why?" thereby putting your client on the defensive. Ask, "What led you to …?" ❏ If the concern is too fuzzy, ask for examples: "Can you give me an example of …?" ❏ If the request is not strategic and you need to say "no," always summarize the request. Say why you cannot fulfill the request. Give any options you can for getting the need met.	❏ Always smile (even over a telephone it shows). ❏ Over time, learn something personal about your most frequent clients. ❏ Summarize and paraphrase often. Listening is 'your ticket to talk.' ❏ Understand the pressures on your client to present a symptom or a solution rather than the underlying problem. Take time to surface the underlying issues. ❏ If your client is angry, allow your client to let off steam. Stick to the facts. Don't personalize the problem.

2. Clarifying Commitments

The Issue	The Relationship
❏ Be sure to do this stage. There is a strong temptation to jump from the problem to the recommendations and solutions. ❏ Always summarize at this point: "Just to be sure that we are on the same wavelength, what you need is … and what you want from me is …"	❏ If you cannot fulfill the request, always tell your client why, and where—if possible—they can get what they need. ❏ Remember, at every stage of the process, you are building commitment to your recommendations. Consultations which are not 'we' at the beginning are not 'we' at the end.

3. Gathering Information

The Issue	The Relationship
❏ Have a questioning strategy. Know when you are increasing the scope of the problem and when you are narrowing the scope. ❏ Be aware that the types of questions you ask determine your role. Ask big picture questions if you want a big picture role.	❏ Avoid closed-ended questions too early. Your client will feel interrogated. ❏ Remember rational, logical questions can easily be threatening to your client.

4. Recommending Change

The Issue	The Relationship
❏ Always re-establish the need. You must position any change in terms of client needs. ❏ Present the benefits of your recommendation in terms of client needs. ❏ Ask for your clients' concerns and reservations. ❏ Most changes fail, not because they are not good recommendations, but because they are not supported by clients' 'real world' systems. ❏ Ask your clients how they feel about the recommended change. An apparently 'simple' recommendation may be stressful to clients.	❏ Remember commitment is a matter of the heart as well as the head. ❏ Remember a benefit for one client can be a turnoff for another. ❏ Remember getting resistance out in the open is helpful. Don't resist resistance. ❏ Be a 'full cycle' consultant. Help the client deal with the stress of change. ❏ You don't have to 'fix' your client's feelings about change. Just ask, then listen.

5. Taking Stock/Closing

The Issue	The Relationship
❏ Do summarize your agreements. ❏ 'Begin with the end in mind.' Set up the success of this last stage early.	❏ Ask for feedback. ❏ For ongoing clients, close on a personal note.

7

You may wish to see how other authors have described their models. See the Web Site at www.consultskills.com for model comparisons.

On-Job Application:
Designing Your Own Expertise Delivery Model

One principle of this book is that besides being content experts, powerful professionals are also experts at how to deliver their expertise, that is, how to consult. We believe in the effectiveness of our Expertise Delivery Model, from pragmatic as well as from research perspectives. We emphasize, however, that our Five Stage Expertise Delivery Model is not the only way. We therefore encourage you to personalize it to your own situation, or to design your own model.

WHAT YOU HAVE LEARNED SO FAR ...

- Taking Stock/Closing are often not done well, or not done at all.

- Make sure this stage is not an 'add on.' Set it up early in the consulting process.

- The best time for Taking Stock meetings is when your clients are least likely to ask for it—when things are going well.

- The briefer your consultations, the better prepared you must be.

THE EXPERTISE DELIVERY MODEL

"Now that we've reached agreement, all we need is to get everybody else to agree with us."
© Ashleigh Brilliant

CHAPTER 8

MAPPING CLIENT SYSTEMS

Quick Snapshot

Did You Know?

- most professionals, by nature, tend to work best with one or two types of clients?
- different types of clients view your project differently?
- a group of 'hidden' clients can scuttle your projects?
- your career success is tied to handling increasingly complex client situations?

How-to:

- visualize a complex client or stakeholder system.
- balance your time and effort among groups of clients.
- ask the right questions to analyze client groups.
- prepare for, reduce and confront conflict.

The Bottom Line:

- You will be able to work more effectively with complex client systems, using the models, checklists, assessments and skills of this chapter.

8

Moving From One to Many

As in most consulting materials, up until now we have been writing as if consulting is one-on-one: you, a single consultant, consulting with a single client. Professionals yearn for clean and tidy relationships where all decisions are made by one manager sympathetic to the profession and its technology. Since this is rarely the case, we need to directly address more complex consulting situations. Rarely do recommendations impact only a single client; more often projects have multiple clients or stakeholders. To get ideas accepted and implemented, it is crucial to determine who the client groups are and what role each plays in the decision making process. Different groups of clients can have very different perspectives. Recognizing different types of clients who need to say "yes" leads to commitment at the implementation stage. Dealing with complex, conflicting wants and needs of various interest groups is often disparaged as 'politics.' Calling it names, however, doesn't make the complexity go away. The simple fact is that modern projects have complex client systems.

As in team sports, one-on-one skills are important, but team games are far more than a series of one-on-one interactions. One-on-one skills are helpful only if you can 'see' the whole game. Understanding and working with complex client systems are key to your success as a professional. Your ability to deal with increasingly complex and unstructured projects is a key indicator of professional career growth.

We will use interchangeably the words client and stakeholder, also multiple and complex. System is used to convey the complex ways in which client groups are interconnected.

Our goal here is to help you analyze complex client systems and deal with them successfully. The more significant the project, the more you will need the concepts and tools of this chapter.

We Regale You with More Sad Stories!

Guy Kawasaki, in his book *Selling the Dream*, tells of two large software companies, Lotus and Microsoft, vying for the support of Apple Computer in the 80s for a Macintosh spreadsheet application. One company negotiated exclusively with the executives of Apple. The second company, besides working with Apple executives, had their own managers contact peer Apple managers, analysts contact peer Apple analysts. Need we say whose spreadsheet is the best seller today? The second company succeeded by recognizing and working with the complex client system.

Another story comes from a large electrical utility. For safety reasons, the utility wanted to improve its tree trimming near electrical wires. The first plan, designed by a small head office engineering group, mandated Operations to carry out the work—with nobody in Operations involved in its design. The resulting tree trimming project was disastrous. Severe accidents occurred, including a tragic fatality. A new plan was devised right away, this time involving many more members of the client system.

- *The district operating managers.* Specific tree problems, including the types of trees, were quite different in each district.

- *The operating staff who actually performed the task.* Some procedures worked better in some areas than in others.

EYE WITNESS REPORT

- *The regulatory group of the utility.* The minimum legal requirements were clearly specified.
- *Local municipalities* were involved to deal with specific concerns.
- *Additional clients,* like the corporate environmental group, were involved for advice, information and commitment.

Understanding and involving the complex client system was key to a successful second plan.

We often hear of commitment failures caused by dealing with only one type of client during the design stage, expecting other clients to 'come on board' during the implementation stage. People buy into what they have had a hand in creating. If you want clients to be on board at project end, you need to involve them early, then continuously throughout the project.

The professional community is rife with sad stories—having management approval at every project stage, yet, in the end, professionals' recommendations sit gathering dust. Project failure often occurs when only one or two of the client categories (described on pages 121-122) are committed to the consulting project.

The Plot Thickens ...

Client systems are becoming more complex because:
- **Participative and consensual decision making is the rising norm.** More and more people are involved in decision making with the goal of enhancing both quality and acceptance of decisions.
- **Organizations are being organized in more complex ways**. No longer are organizations straightforward, hierarchical structures. Decision making is becoming increasingly diffused.
- **Consulting projects are becoming more complex**. For a project of even reasonable magnitude, a number of professional specialties need to work together because it is impossible for a single person to have all the required knowledge and skills.
- **Competitive pressures are forcing organizations to be more innovative**. The first solution is rarely the best solution. Participation by multiple stakeholders is necessary for innovation.
- **More people need to say "Yes."** While top management's commitment and approval is necessary, it is *not* a sufficient condition for consulting success.

8

In this chapter ...

- *Why map complex client systems?*
- *Who are the typical client types?*
- *How client groups view your project.*
- *Ways of visualizing your complex client systems.*
- *Questions to ask.*
- *How to reduce conflicting interests between groups.*
- *Worksheets for your use.*

Learn to 'Draw'

To help you look at clients in a new way, this chapter describes types of client groups which make up a multiple stakeholder system. They will help you work more successfully with them. Using our client categories and templates, you can 'draw' a diagram of your situation, using a structured format or a 'freehand' format. We will provide you with the key questions you need to ask.

We also include a how-to section on preparing for, reducing and confronting conflict between and among client groups.

Meet The Clients!

What follows is a helpful simplification of the real world. While applying the concept of visualizing and analyzing multiple client systems to your on-job situation, we suggest you practice the skill possessed by successful consultants—the skill of modifying the language and categories to suit your own reality and consulting needs.

We offer an encapsulation of five client types. More detailed profiles follow. As you read these, we are sure you will begin to identify them by name and face in a complex project relevant to you.

TYPES OF CLIENTS

1. Working/Contact Client(s)
➡ *the people you are actually working with face-to-face, often on a project team.*

The working client may be an individual or a group—a taskforce or committee, often representative of other client groups. A working client's typical question is:

"How can we successfully finish this project on time, within budget and get acceptance for implementation?"

Working clients are project-oriented, busy people who wish to minimize their time and energy with the project. A taskforce is usually set up to represent the diverse interests of other client types. Contrast these questions and benefits of your working clients with those of the remaining client types.

2. Financial/Sponsor/Funder/Decision Client(s)
➡ *the individual or group that actually has the authority to approve your project and proposals.*

Often senior managers or management committees, these clients approve the budget and free up resources for implementation. Their basic question is:

"Is this proposal organizationally and financially sound?"

Their perspective is much wider than your particular project. They are concerned about your project's impact on the organization. Beware the myth about this group, rampant among consultants—if you get the top dog's approval, the project is a shoo-in. Not true! Their commitment is certainly necessary, but not sufficient.

3. End User Client(s)
➡ *the group of clients who will actually use your recommendations and make them work on the job.*

Their basic question is:

"Will this really work under my practical conditions and make my job easier?"

Note how different this question is from that of the Financial/Sponsor/Funder/Decision Client. Internal consultants contend that *two different* project presentations may even be required because their perspectives are so different. Professionals, by nature, tend to be more comfortable working with one or two of the many kinds of clients. Those more oriented to needs of end users than needs of management can get themselves into difficulties, and vice versa. Who is your real client? They all are!

4. Indirect Client(s)
➡ *they exercise control by being able to say "No, your proposal does not fit our organizational policy or requirements."*

The least obvious clients, these are people who cannot directly approve your proposal but who can say "no," or can hold up your project. The basic question of Indirect Clients is:

"Does this proposal meet the professional standards and policies we control?"

Examples are people from groups such as: purchasing, legal, human resources, regulatory/governmental compliance groups, safety, systems, etc. Rather than considering these groups (of which many of our readers are members!) as roadblocks, you need to understand that they are rightfully trying to uphold the standards of the organization.

The inspiration for this model came from the book Strategic Selling by R Miller & S. Heiman .

8

❝ **Quotable Quotes** ❞

Who is your real client? "All my clients are unreal," jokes consultant Shaun Murphy.

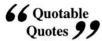
5. Coach Client(s)

➡ *help you understand and work within the informal client system.*

The most unusual clients, these coaches are needed for your consulting projects, particularly if you work at arm's length from your clients e.g. head office to field. They can come from any level of the organization, and be any person, from highly-placed executives who may coach you, right through to the office clerk! The role of coaches is to help you and your project get approval. The coach client's basic question is:

"How can we get the job done around here?"

These client-credible people will help you navigate around obstacles in the client system and help you understand unwritten rules—'how things work around here.' They will also give you blunt feedback—what is working and what isn't. The more complex the project, the more coaches you need.

6. Other Client Types

We have outlined five typical client types. Undoubtedly larger, more complex projects will have more. For example, there may be more than one group of Sponsor Clients. One sponsor group may need to take your proposal to a more senior sponsor group. There may be two sponsors, one line, the other functional, for your project. Approval from both may be necessary.

We encourage you to diagram freehand your multiple client system, grouping them by the similarity of questions they would ask. We give you an example of a complex client system map on page 132.

Double-Dipping

That's a thumb nail sketch of typical complex client types. Double-dipping, where a particular client is a member of two groups, happens frequently. For example, a particularly powerful coach is one who is also a sponsor client. A member of senior management will often take personal interest in professional employees as a coach or mentor. The best working clients are those who are also coaches. These ideal working clients (Kawasaki calls them 'angels'), will volunteer a 50/50 partnership with you. They will willingly give you insider information tips, feedback, and mentoring.

Next we will profile each client type in detail ...

Many professionals try to 'push through' change by concentrating on the professional and technical excellence of the change itself. Often, it is more effective and easier to concentrate your efforts on those stakeholders which may help or impede the change.

WORKING/CONTACT CLIENT(S)

Who Are They?
- The clients who actually work with you often as members of the project team.
- They often represent other client groups e.g. End User 'Reps.'

Their Role:
- To assist you directly with your project, usually as part of the project team.

Their Key Questions:
- "How can we finish this project on time, within budget and get acceptance for implementation?"
- "Will the project take much of my time and energy?"
- "Will it be interesting?"
- "Will we look good working with you on this project?"
- "How can we ensure the project will be successful?"

Perceived Benefits for Working Clients:
- I look good for having participated in a successful project.
- I learn a lot which helps my career development.
- I have a chance to interact with a wide range of employees.
- I enjoy the project.

Their Reservations:
- The project will take too much of my time.
- The project might fail.

HOT TIPS:
- Much of your success depends on a good relationship with your working clients. Individual project taskforce members should represent, have credibility with, and know what is going on within, their constituent group—so that you can take their understanding of constituent concerns as fact.
- Working Clients are:

Ideally	Realistically
– great coaches – help you understand the client system and personal needs of the clients' constituents.	– they often represent their own narrow perspective. – they do not communicate well with the people they represent. – some of the constituents' interests are not represented at all. – in the worst cases, the working client may bar access to the End User and Sponsor clients.

- As organizations become more complex, professionals increasingly work with people who represent other client groups. Our advice is to make these working clients look good. If you try to bypass them and go on to your 'real' clients, they will often impede or block your efforts. They often need coaching in how to deal with the client groups that they represent. High performing professionals can get their work done through others; see Chapter 12, *Enhancing Your Role and Career*. Guidelines for working through others will be presented later in this chapter.

Dealing with complex client systems is closely aligned with the topic Sustaining Change, the subject of Chapter 9, where you will find additional helpful models and checklists.

8

FINANCIAL/SPONSOR/FUNDER/DECISION CLIENT(S)

Who Are They?
- The clients who actually approve and sign off your proposal.
- Usually a management group, who sometimes need to report to a more senior group.

Their Role:
- To ensure the proposal meets organizational, strategic and economic specifications.

Their Key Questions:
- "How does this project enhance our organizational strategy?"
- "Does this project meet the organizational economic and financial specifications?"
- "Will this project 'fly' politically?" (Sponsors often must sell your projects to others in their stakeholder system.)

Perceived Benefits for Sponsor Clients:
- The business problem is solved.
- The project enhances the direction, strategy and economics of the organization.
- Financial results.

Their Reservations:
- The project and recommendations won't work as intended.
- The recommendations don't fit with other organizational systems and policies.
- The project runs over time or over budget.
- The recommendations are not financially sound
- The project doesn't meet either short or long term needs.
- How the risks will be managed.

HOT TIPS:
- Sometimes professionals have little direct contact with sponsor clients, therefore they need to influence sponsor clients through working clients. This can range from being easy, where the working client encourages access to the sponsors, through to being difficult, where the working client actually keeps you away from the sponsor client. In any case, you need to clearly identify Sponsor Clients, and their concerns and perspective on your project.
- Sponsor clients in Public Service organizations often have their own diffuse stakeholder systems. You may wish to extend your conceptualization of your client system to include the stakeholder systems of other client groups.
- Sponsor clients should take a comprehensive view of your project; in reality, they may be constrained by their own narrow focus. In North American industry, these clients are often accused of taking a very short term view, such as: 'How will this affect next quarter's economics?'
- Many consultants take the perspective that if senior management buys it, it's 'in the bag.' NOT TRUE! Although senior managers are extremely important clients, we have all heard stories of consulting projects which went nowhere, yet they had approval by senior managers.

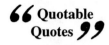

66 **Quotable**
Quotes 99

Guy Kawasaki tells us in Selling the Dream that "the right people" in an organization really means "the right levels." Traditionally one went right to the top level in an organization, a mistake, says Kawasaki, since "high-ranking people usually rely on staff when making decisions," and many staff "resent people who go over their heads."

END USER CLIENT(S)

Who Are They?
- The clients who will actually use your recommendations on-the-job.

Their Role:
- To put your recommendations to work under actual working conditions.

Their Key Questions:
- "Did you take into account my working constraints?"
- "Will this really work as well as you say, under our actual conditions?"
- "Will this really make my life easier, as claimed?"
- "How will I be trained?"
- "Will I look dumb as a result of the change?" or "Will I be able to learn the new procedures?" or "Will I lose my job?"
- Lots of questions that begin with "Why ...?," "But ...?" and "How ...?"

Perceived Benefits for End-User Clients:
- The project makes my job easier—ease of use.
- A change will relieve me of the unwanted parts of my job.
- The new skills will enhance my job or career.

Their Reservations:
- I am working to capacity already; I have no time to learn.
- Past history—I know things haven't performed as well as advertised.

HOT TIPS:
- End users are often the most skeptical of clients. They have experienced or heard of projects that didn't deliver as they should have. End users, from this perspective, are the ultimate 'devil's advocate.' You will need considerable involvement of and communication with, skeptical end users. They will continually ask "why?" and test your project against their reality.
- On the other hand, many internal consultants are too oriented to end users. Often these consultants get very frustrated when a project does not get final approval because they know the project will work 'in the trenches.'

TALK THE RIGHT LANGUAGE

"Senior management—justify with reasons, earnings before interest and tax
Middle management—cost savings, reductions in operating costs and efficiency
Operative staff—time savings and making the job easier."

– Robert Lanman quoted in
Supercharge Your Management Role
by Thomas & Elbeik

❝ Quotable Quotes ❞

Miller & Heiman point out in Strategic Selling the subjectivity of most client views because their jobs are affected. This very real factor needs to be acknowledged. As for getting them on your side, Miller & Heiman claim you have to answer for clients one simple question: "How will your product or service work for me?"

8

INDIRECT CLIENT(S)

Who Are They?

- Anyone who can hold up or veto a project because it does not meet some technical, legislative or policy standard. Typically, these kinds of people or groups are indirect clients:
  - regulatory compliance
  - environmental
  - purchasing
  - human resources
  - government agencies
  - systems

  - accounting
  - legal and taxes
  - safety and health
  - finance
  - public affairs

Change often fails, not because the identified change plan was inadequate, but because the change was not supported by some of the multiple clients/ stakeholders.

Their Role:

- To make sure this proposal fits with other existing organizational systems, policies, legislation and technical standards.

Their Key Question:

- "Does this proposal violate any technical standards or policies under our jurisdiction?"

Perceived Benefits for Indirect Clients:

- Policy or technical standards are upheld.

Their Reservations:

- Not consulted early enough.
- Not recognized by the consultant as important.

HOT TIPS:

- This group is the most difficult to identify because, in a typical large organization, there are potentially many indirect clients.

- Indirect clients may seem arbitrary and bureaucratic. For example, purchasing groups are charged with saving the organization money by requiring a number of competing bids. They will see their actions as not only justifiable, but as a service to the organization. The earlier in a project they are identified and involved, the better.

Remember that none of these individual client groups are sufficient for project success. *You need them all on board.*

INTERLINKED CLIENT SYSTEMS

"Think of your client system as a chain—with each client as a link. Your system is only as good as the weakest link. So it's important to pay attention to all, to ensure each is strong."

– Robin Sober
The Mutual Group

COACH CLIENT(S)

Who Are They?
- Any number of people who help you understand the informal systems, not evident to the naked eye, by telling you clearly 'how things really work around here' in their part of your organization. Often not part of any official client group, these people can come from any part or level of the organization. You need them to help get your project approved and implemented.

Their Role:
- To provide you with timely advice.
- To help you understand the informal system—'how things really work around here.'
- To provide you with blunt feedback on what is working, what to do or not to do, who to contact, and how key people are viewing your project.

Their Key Question:
- "How can we get our project ('our' because they often identify with you and the project) approved and working?"

Perceived Benefits for Coach Clients:
- I want to see this project succeed because it will benefit my group.
- Reciprocity: "I'll help you if you'll help me next time."
- Visibility with a successful project.
- Opportunity to work with you personally.

Their Reservations:
- Unrecognized by the consultant for their coaching efforts.

HOT TIPS:
- First, some values and ethics clarification. It would be easy to see this role as one where a couple of people team up to get something pushed through the hoops for personal benefit. Assuming your work is professional and of value to your organization, our ethical stance is that it would be tragic to see good professional and business projects sit gathering dust when a major barrier was lack of understanding of how things really worked in the client system.
- It may seem like coaches would be difficult to find. In fact, it is often easy to identify such people. After a meeting or two with the client group, find someone who seems to you to know what's going on—initially for feedback. If they give you some insights, you've got a coach. Be alert to this possibility at any level. Treating everyone with respect and attention is a sure way to attract excellent coaches. In many cases, a manager's secretary can provide vital information on those people to contact, timing of presentations, etc.

Treating everyone with human respect results in many coach volunteers!

8

Your On-Job Application

All these client categories come alive when you make a visual map of your client or stake-holder system. A visual diagram is easiest to create using the categories in this chapter. More difficult—and more beneficial—is to make a freehand diagram (p. 131).

HOW TO SKETCH OUT YOUR MAP

Our user-friendly diagram skeletons on the following pages will help you:

- Group people into client/stakeholder groups on the basis of whether they would generally see your project in the same way. Always go back over your groupings. Often an unexpected client group will surprise you by 'popping out,' and you think "How come I never thought of them before?"
- Consider the *stakeholders of your stakeholder groups*. They can often help or hinder your projects.
- Draw arrows showing the connections between client groups.

HOW TO FILL IN YOUR MAP

Ask these questions for each client group:

- Who are they? Give them a collective name which make sense in your organization.

- What is their priority compared to that of the other groups? How critical are they to the project's success?

- What is their current status?
    - Are they informed and up-to-date?
    - Are they supportive?
    - Are any offside?

- What benefits would they see in this project?

- What are current or potential problems with this group?
    - What reservations and risks would they see?
    - What are their major concerns about the project?
    - How might they be unsupportive of the project?

- Prioritize the client groups. Not all client groups are in need of equal attention.

- Are you giving each group of clients enough emphasis?

APPLICATION FORMAT #1:

If the client categories described fit for you, complete the following matrix:

Client Type	Who are they?	Key Benefits	Key Reservations	Next Steps
Working/ Contact Clients				
Financial/ Sponsor/ Funder/ Decision Clients				
End User Clients				
Indirect Clients				
Coach Clients				

8

APPLICATION FORMAT #2:
STAKEHOLDER ANALYSIS MODEL

In the client group boxes below, jot down answers to:
- Who, specifically, are the key client/stakeholder groups?
- How do these stakeholders support the recommended change?
- How could these stakeholders impede the recommended change?
- What do we need to do to work with stakeholders who may impede?

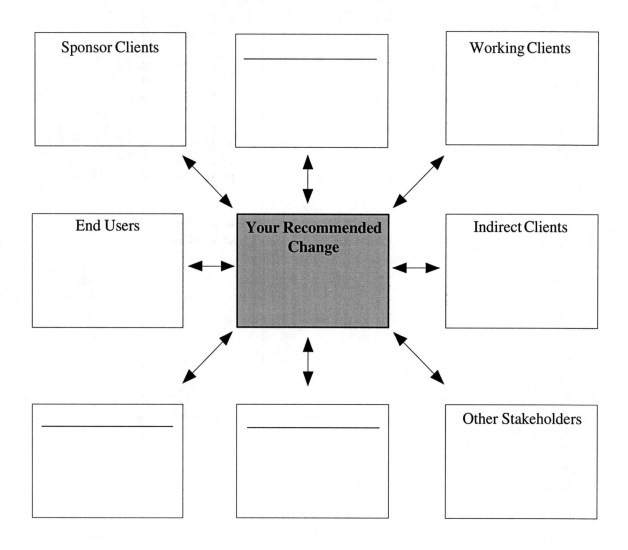

How to Design a Freehand Map

In most cases, client systems are unique to a project and a situation, and you are best served by drawing a freehand visual.

1. Visibility
➡ **Make your Stakeholder/Complex Client system visible.**
Take a large sheet of paper and make your complex stakeholder system visible. See the example of a partial freehand client system on the next page.
Ask these kinds of questions to surface client groups:
- Who are the project sponsors (approving funds and giving the go-ahead)?
- To whom do the project sponsors need to sell this project?
- Who are the end users of this project?
- Who is on the project team (working clients)? Whom do they represent?
- Which additional groups do we need to 'have on board' for this project to succeed?
- Which additional groups will see themselves negatively impacted?
- Which other groups in our organization will have an interest because it overlaps their functional or professional area?
- Are there special interest groups outside our organization (e.g. government agencies or customers)?
- Are there any additional groups which can expedite or hinder this project?

2. Benefits
➡ **For each group, list the benefits, *as each group would see them.***
- If people in this group said "Why?" or "So what?" or "What's in it for us?" what would you say? (Hint: be as specific as possible e.g. elaborate on 'save money.')
- List specific features which would appeal to this group, then the benefits.

3. The Three Rs
➡ **For each group list Reservations, Risks, Resistance *as each group would see them.***
If you are unsure of the downsides for a specific group, how will you find out their concerns? (Hints: Where, or to whom, would you go? Be specific about concerns!)
- How might this group suffer, or be negatively impacted by the change?
- What risks would this group see or feel?

4. Effort Priority
➡ **Determine where you need to expend effort for your project to succeed.**
- If you expend additional effort, where would it have the greatest leverage? (Hint: think 'add benefits' and/or 'reduce risks.')
- Circle the groups most critical for acceptance of this project. Are they on-board?
- Circle the groups who might be a barrier. How can you reduce the resistance?

For assistance, use the Benefits Checklist on page 91 and the Reservations Checklist on page 96.

8

131

APPLICATION FORMAT #3:
FREEHAND EXAMPLE

What a completed freehand stakeholder diagram might look like. Do not be constrained by this example.

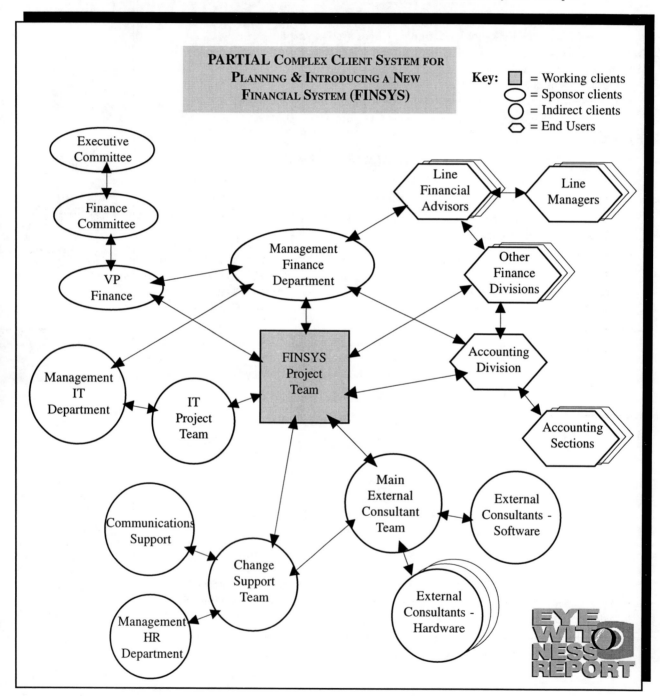

PARTIAL COMPLEX CLIENT SYSTEM FOR PLANNING & INTRODUCING A NEW FINANCIAL SYSTEM (FINSYS)

Key:
□ = Working clients
⬭ = Sponsor clients
◯ = Indirect clients
⬡ = End Users

Conflict How-tos

A common difficulty expressed by professionals is myriad conflicting goals, demands and expectations among stakeholders. Although no sure fire techniques are available, you can do a number of things to reduce the probability of conflict, or to resolve conflict when it does occur.

PREPARE:

❏ Diagram the complex client system. Identify where conflict may occur. Anticipating this is a powerful first step!

❏ Involve all stakeholders early and often.

❏ Clarify roles and responsibilities early. (Do you hear an echo? ... '80% of conflict arises from unclear expectations'?)

❏ Document agreements.

REDUCE:

❏ When you are planning a project, get the major stakeholders together face-to-face in a room so that they can personally hear others' needs and expectations. Facilitate agreements between the parties in the room.

❏ Do not cover up conflict. The best way to deal with most conflicts is to get them out in the open. Covered up conflict occurs anyway and is expressed indirectly in gossip, missed meetings, etc.

❏ Deal with conflict early before it has a chance to escalate!

❏ Do not assume others e.g. senior managers, deal with conflict better than you do.

❏ Communicate, communicate, communicate. Many studies show that leaders perceive themselves communicating about three times more than their followers perceive they hear!

❏ Do not avoid conflict. Conflict tends to get worse by avoidance. Your *own* avoidance will become part of the problem.

AND IF THE STEAM WHISTLES! ...

❏ Do not take sides. Stay objective.

❏ Allow your clients to vent—'let off steam.' Acknowledge the conflict. Summarize with a rational statement and issue an invitation to work on the underlying issues.

❏ A powerful technique taught to customer service representatives is 'don't take it personally!' Let the customer vent.

❏ If possible, get conflicting clients in the same room to work out their differences.

❏ If the conflict is severe, or if you feel you cannot facilitate such a meeting, engage a professional mediator or facilitator.

"Deal with conflict while it's a pinch, not a crunch."
– Bernie Novokowsky

8

A DO-NOT ...

Don't get in the middle. We have seen many professionals (with hero dreams?) shuttle between two groups, trying to placate each without having them talk to each other.
Often the professional ends up getting kicked by both groups!

WHAT YOU'VE LEARNED SO FAR ...

- Doing excellent professional work will come to naught if you cannot visualize and work with the increasing complexity of client systems.

- Picturing complex client systems is the first step to dealing effectively with them.

- Be careful not to spend undue energy on one client group, expecting the rest to 'come aboard' at the appropriate time.

- Involve the various client groups early and often. Involvement is the best way to secure commitment.

- Conflict of needs and expectations is common—almost inevitable—among client groups, simply because they do represent competing interests of your organization. Take steps to prepare for, reduce and resolve conflict.

THE EXPERTISE DELIVERY MODEL

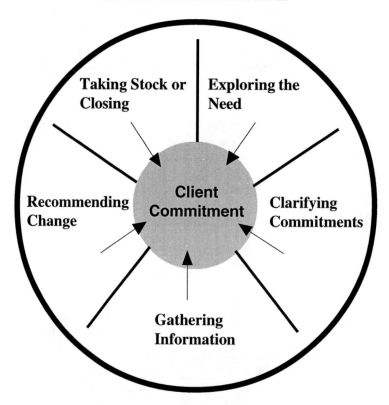

> *"I find it easier to be a result of the past than a cause of the future."*
> © Ashleigh Brilliant

CHAPTER 9

SUSTAINING CHANGE

Quick Snapshot

Did You Know?

- your professional success depends on your recommendations being implemented and sustained?
- professionally sound changes often fail because they conflict with some part of the larger system?
- clients rate professionals very low on 'helping people with change'?

How-to:

- determine an appropriate role in ensuring change.
- lead change as a professional.
- lead the 'people' side of change, which many professionals find difficult.

The Bottom Line:

- You will learn to successfully implement and sustain change. The purpose of this chapter is to present concepts, models, checklists and principles to achieve this.

9

Changing Directions?

Much has been written about change. In this chapter, we will focus on a number of approaches to *Sustaining Change*. This brief description of each section may help you choose which parts of this chapter will be most helpful to you.

❶ *Principles for Successful Change*
Successful change is based on sound principles and strategies. There is no recipe for change. Successful change is only *assisted* by techniques and tactics.

❷ *Assessment of Readiness for Change*
Introducing change is difficult at the best of times. This easy-to-use assessment will help the professional assess how easy or difficult a change will be.

❸ *Change Equation*
This 'Equation' will give professionals a concise, colorful, practical model of the change process, including a checklist of things to consider for successful change.

❹ *Systemic Approach to Change*
Many technically and professionally sound changes fail because they were not supported by the system into which they needed to fit. Successful professionals need to assess the relationship of their recommended change to the entire system—seeing the whole and understanding the processes by which the parts are linked together. This requires seeing how the change embeds itself into the broader system.

❺ *Leading People Through Change*
Many a rationally correct change plan has been impeded by 'resistance to change' or scuttled by lack of buy-in. Powerful professionals have learned how to lead people through change resulting from their recommendations. In addition to understanding their plan for change, professionals also need to know how to lead people through the natural stages of personal change.

This chapter is dedicated to change. Closely related topics:
- *Recommending and selling change is dealt with in Chapter 6, Recommending Change.*
- *Dealing with direct resistance is dealt with in Chapter 6 as well.*
- *Dealing with the more subtle indirect resistance is the topic of the next chapter, Dealing With Resistance.*

A Professional's Work Is Never Done?

As soon as recommendations are approved, the real work begins! You need your recommended changes to be smoothly implemented and you want them to stick. One of the biggest myths for professional specialists is that producing good technical recommendations is enough—enough to get you laid off, or outsourced, perhaps! Professional results are measured in *effective, implemented change*, that means in the real world, in real time.

Recommending change means you upset the status quo.

While some clients can't wait for change, for others, change seems like the worst nightmare that could happen in their work lives. Managing and leading change are crucial skills for internal professionals. The essence of being a powerful professional is helping your clients with effective change in your area of expertise.

There are two basic skill areas for leading change:
1. *Managing the rational side of change* :
   We will introduce a number of models to help you plan the logical side of change.
2. *Leading the people side of change:*
   Change inside people takes place much slower than the fast pace of external change. For example, installation of a new procedure or piece of equipment is usually fast, but 'people change' takes quite a while to follow. We call this people change 'transition,' presenting models and techniques which consider such transition. According to our database, helping people with change is a large skill deficiency for most professionals.

Change Isn't an Add-On

Change is an integral part of thinking about a project. Here are ways to think about change at every stage of the Expertise Delivery Model:

Expertise Delivery Model Stage	Some Change Elements
1. Exploring the Need	• Was there a clear and substantive need which set up the readiness and need for change? • Was the original issue framed to deal with underlying causes, setting up effective change? • Were stakeholders identified and involved early to ensure smooth acceptance?
2. Clarifying Commitments	• Who else has a stake in this problem and/or its solution? • Whose support is needed now, or in the future? • Who might be threatened or hurt when this problem is dealt with? • What is the role of the professional and clients in the anticipated change?
3. Gathering Information	• Who has information related to the problem and the practicality of potential solutions? • Where can you get 'real world' information about potential benefits and road blocks related to the problem or solutions?
4. Recommending Change	• Which organizational *systems* could inhibit the change? • Which stakeholders will see the benefits, and which may be hurt or threatened by the recommendation? • What reservations and objections to the change can be anticipated? • Is the recommended change supported by a logical plan?

9

Who's Involved in Change?

A crucial question arises at this point. What is the best role for professionals in the change process, in implementing their recommendations? Here are two quite different opinions for you to examine:

1. Ownership of the change must reside with the client. Thus clients should lead change implementation. The biggest professional issue is disengagement from the process.

2. Professionals are ultimately judged on enduring and effective change as a result of their work, therefore professionals should be thoroughly involved with facilitating the change.

Which opinion is right? Both are, depending on the circumstances. Sustainable change is what is at issue here—who needs to be involved and how should they be involved? To determine appropriate involvement, it is necessary to look at two areas: professional role and strategy.

i. Role clarification is crucial. It can be enticing and seductive for professionals to take on too large a role. On the other hand, professionals cannot wash their hands of change leadership.

ii. It is important to have thought through your professional strategy—"If this project is started, where is the best use of my professional effort?" Right from the first step, a professional needs to ask the question "When my client and I define the problem, who is best to support the process through to successful implementation?"

Change leadership is expected—a given. Many authors define consultants as change agents. Clients are increasingly asking for more than just technical advice and recommendations from professionals working inside an organization. Clients are looking for 'full cycle' consulting, beginning with clearly defined organizational need; ending when recommended changes are implemented. *Making professional recommendations which do not get implemented is a recipe for disaster.*

Professional roles are looked at in more detail in Chapter 12, Enhancing Your Role and Career; professional strategies in Chapter 13, Your Strategy: Saying Yes or No.

CONTINUUM OF PROFESSIONAL ROLES IN CHANGE

Professional **Hands Off**	Professional **Hands On**
←	→
Characteristics:	
• Clients drive the change	• Professionals drive the change
• Clients lead the change	• Professionals facilitate the change
• Clients own the change	• Shared ownership of the change
When Appropriate:	
• No need for long term professional support	• Need for long term professional support
• Client is capable of implementing the change	• Need for professional change advice

Cold Fish and Hot Potato: Two Examples

Here are two actual stories (both starting down the wrong road) of many we've heard from professionals in organizations undergoing substantive change.

Cold Fish—No Involvement

A Systems group was helping an expanding group of commodity marketing brokers (their clients) with on-line systems support for their increased worldwide commodity marketing efforts. Different brokers were striking conflicting deals because deals were poorly communicated among the brokers. The reason? Brokers monitored a number of separate information systems, passing on information to each other verbally, or on small pieces of paper. An in-house system was needed and recommended, where brokers could:
  – access common commodity information from one desktop computer monitor
  – get live updates on emerging deals and price negotiations
  – have access to completed agreements.
The highly regarded (to this point) Systems group took it upon themselves to assess broker needs, starting to design the new system. Brokers and managers had little involvement. Explained the Systems leader "The brokers were much too busy making money for the company to be involved in the details." A few months into the project, complaints began to surface on both sides about the other. The litany of broker complaints was long—the emerging system was much too slow, too complex, not 'real-time' because not everyone was using it—the list went on. Communication between clients and Systems professionals broke down, each blaming the other for problems.

A situation assessment revealed:
  – the Systems project team, with the best of intentions, had taken over ownership of the project.
  – the Marketing brokers had little involvement and didn't know what was going on.
The situation assessment resulted in the Marketing brokers getting much more involved and owning the project. Here was a case where *clients* needed to own much more of the change that was being inappropriately wholly owned, however generously, by the Systems group.

Hot Potato—Hands Off

A Systems group in another organization was assisting the Finance Department to design and introduce an integrated, on-line financial system. The VP of Finance admitted this would be the single largest change in how accounting and finance were done in the long and illustrious history of this organization. For this reason, a Project Task Force was struck, headed by two project leaders, one from Systems and one from Finance. Early in the project planning, complaints began to surface on both sides about the other. Communication between the Finance Department and Task Force professionals broke down, each blaming the other for problems at this early stage of the project.

A situation assessment meeting was held with Finance Department management, Systems Department management and the Project Task Force. At the meeting, the Systems manager made an impassioned plea. Unless Finance Department management saw themselves as the owners of the design, implementation and operation of the new system, the project would be mired in problems and would probably not succeed. "This is a Finance project, not a Systems project," emphasized the Systems manager. After hearing the Systems manager's impassioned plea, one senior Finance manager meekly admitted "This project is so far reaching, it's scary. I think we were hoping that we could be hands-off during the project, fully expecting to take credit if it worked and blaming Systems if it failed." Finance management decided to 'own the project.' Roles and responsibilities were clarified; things went much better for all parties after that point.

9

❶ Changing the Way You Lead Change—The Principles

How-tos and techniques don't work unless they are firmly grounded in sound principles of change. With human behavior, nothing works every time. Sometimes being tough and 'kicking butt' works, other times not. Sometimes high participation and 'attracting bees with honey' works, other times that fails. You do not have to agree to all items on this list of principles, but it should be a source of some good ideas for you. Your choice of change techniques and tactics needs a base in sound principles. Check off those which pertain to you, your situation and your organization.

The Big Picture:
- ❏ *Look at change systemically.* Research shows that technically sound change often fails because it is not supported by the larger system. See the chapter section on the *Systemic Side of Change,* page 148.
- ❏ *Know and communicate how this change fits* with the direction of the organization.
- ❏ *Know and communicate the client benefits* and manageable risks of the change.

The Stakeholders:
- ❏ *Ensure all stakeholders to your change are identified* and 'on board.' Staff your change task force with change leaders from each major stakeholder group. See Chapter 8, *Mapping Client Systems,* page 117, for models and assistance.
- ❏ *Look at change through the eyes of the various stakeholders* to the change. What are the benefits and risks from *their* specific perspectives?
- ❏ *Never assume you've 'got it made'* just because senior management has bought in. Their buy-in is necessary, but not sufficient for successful change. Assume even less that change will take place if the end users have bought-in, just 'because it works.'

Small Wins—Building Success on Success:
- ❏ *Work first in areas where you can already see a ground swell of support* for change:
    - ✓ Use a 'small gains' approach, if you can.
    - ✓ Phase-in the change, if possible. Choose the first steps carefully.
- ❏ *Change is more successful if it follows on successful change*:
    - ✓ Start with changes that have a high chance of success.
    - ✓ Bite off what you and your clients can chew: no more, no less.

Resistance:
- ❏ *Respect the past while leading change.* Things got to be the way they are for good reason in the past. Remember that those you are asking to change helped make things the way they are.
- ❏ *Resistance is natural and OK.* Don't ignore or suppress resistance and conflict. It will come back to haunt you later.
- ❏ *Don't be quick to blame people if change is sputtering.* It is more often the system than it is people at the root of change problems.
- ❏ *Change takes energy and persistence.* Like Newton's Law, things stay on their current course unless some energy is expended to take things in a different direction.

Change Leader's Field of Dreams
"If senior managers approve, the rest will come (on board)."

How do you eat an elephant?
One bite at the time.

"How we go about introducing possible change is often more important than the change itself. After all, what good is your great idea when you present it in a way that allows people to reject it?"
– Geoff Bellman

140

The 'People' Side:

❑ *Changing things is easier than changing people.* For example, when a head office manager exhorts professionals to be 'closer to your clients,' perhaps changing 'things,'—in this case physical environment, having professionals reside in their clients' location—is an easier way to get closer than to tackle relationships.

❑ *The best way to commitment is through involvement.* Involve early and often. (See the last section of this chapter, page 159 for specific suggestions.)

Communication:

❑ *Change is more acceptable when it's understood.* Early, frequent, ongoing communication is essential.

❑ *Leaders feel that they communicate two to three times as much as people feel* they are being communicated with.

❑ *Don't communicate to, communicate with.* Make communication a two-way process. When you are talking with clients and others involved in change, don't just talk *to* them and expect that you have communicated. Ask them for their reactions, concerns, feedback and suggestions.

❑ *Don't be surprised when you ask for feedback and initially get complaints.* See the section in this chapter on *Helping People with Personal Change*, page 152, for the natural transition that needs to take place in people as they come to terms with change.

Quotable Quotes

"Resist the urge to stop communicating. Just because you have said it a million times doesn't mean it's been heard that many times. You can get tired of your voice long before you're understood or believed."

– Ron George
CEO, Suncor Energy

CHECKLIST OF CHANGE BLOCKERS

In a typical organization, however, many well thought-out and well-planned improvements will not be implemented. Why? Because your clients and other stakeholders:

❑ don't think the change will work as well as you say.
❑ think your recommendations are faulty.
❑ think your change plan is inadequate.
❑ don't think that more senior management will support the change.
❑ don't think the end users will change.
❑ don't see the cost/benefit.
❑ won't want to make the effort.
❑ see too much risk.
❑ see too many potential problems.
❑ have other priorities.
❑ don't want to free up the resources for the change.
❑ are threatened in some way by the change.
❑ don't want to risk 'sticking their necks out.'
❑ see the change invading their 'turf.'
❑ feel/think that they will look dumb as a result of the new procedures and skills.
❑ are indecisive and just can't get started.
❑ are split: some agree, others don't.
❑ are satisfied with the current situation (even if it has many problems and many complaints).
❑ don't see how this fits into the bigger picture.

Avoid the Pitfalls

The following list, adapted for professionals, is inspired by John Kotter in his book, *Leading Change*. The most common errors with change efforts are:
* Insufficient urgency and need for change.
* Failure to visualize and deal with all the stakeholders involved in the change.
* Insufficient support by the most powerful stakeholder groups.
* Underestimating the need to understand and to communicate how this change fits into organizational direction.
* Undercommunicating by a 'factor of 10, 100, or even 1,000!'
* Failure to anticipate and deal with obstacles and barriers to the change.
* Failure to generate short-term wins to show progress and interim successes.
* Failure to understand how the change fits into, and meshes with, other existing organizational systems.

Sustaining Change: Small Wins or Full Systems?

Change is a complex topic, with no single model proving helpful over a wide range of change situations. Professionals need to consider and make a decision about the magnitude of change and whether it can be introduced in chunks. You may be able to strategize big picture, all-or-nothing change, but implement it in manageable pieces, reconciling the two approaches contrasted below, gaining the benefits of both while avoiding the problems of both.

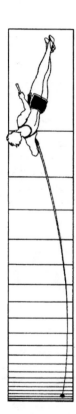

Small Wins Approach	Full Systems Approach
• Have an overall goal and strategy, then implement many small projects to attain the overall goal. • Start with subprojects which will almost certainly succeed. Build success on success. • Small changes allow the system to absorb the change. • Small changes allow people to absorb the changes. • It is easier to involve people in small specific changes.	• Look at the whole system. Assume most changes fail because the recommended change wasn't supported by the systems it needed to interact with. • Improvement is more than the sum of the parts. You can't tinker your way to 'breakthrough' change. • With a quantum leap change, no one can cling to the past. • Change is better introduced as one large change rather then 'death by a thousand cuts.'
In the 'Small Wins' Corner From *High-Impact Consulting* by Robert Schaffer: To avoid one of what Schaffer calls the "Five Fatal Flaws" of consulting: *"Instead of aiming for 'one big solution' that will require a long cycle time and huge upfront investment, high-impact consulting divides projects into increments, with rapid cycle times, for quicker results."*	In the 'All-or-Nothing' Corner From *Reengineering the Corporation* by Hammer and Champy: *"Reengineering, we are convinced, can't be carried out in small and cautious steps. It is an all-or-nothing proposition that produces dramatically impressive results. Most companies have no choice but to muster the courage to do it. For many, reengineering is the only hope for breaking away from the ineffective, antiquated ways of conducting business ..."*

❷ CHANGE READINESS ASSESSMENT

If you are wondering how easy or difficult a change will be, check the box in each row which best describes your change project; then use the score to assess readiness for change.

	'Low Hanging Fruit' System ready to change	*'Usual Hurdles.'* Change will require energy and effort	*'Brick Walls'* System entrenched against change
1. Nature of the Problem or Opportunity	❏ Problem is visible and hurting.	❏ Problem causes concern for some but not for others.	❏ Most can get along with the current system.
2. Cause of the Problem	❏ Underlying cause can be isolated and fixed.	❏ Multiple underlying causes or current talk is about symptoms.	❏ Underlying causes unknown, multiple or too threatening to surface.
3. Benefit/Risk	❏ Clear benefits and few risks and disadvantages.	❏ Good benefits with some risks.	❏ Benefits but with high risks.
4. Support of Primary Client Group	❏ Widespread support.	❏ Support by many in client group, but not by others.	❏ Change supported only by a few people or only by senior management.
5. Support of Outside Primary Client Group	❏ Other client groups have supportive management; does not threaten others.	❏ Change crosses a number of client groups; some benefit by the status quo, some threatened.	❏ Outside client groups benefit from the status quo; threatens other groups' reason for being.
6. Systemic Barriers	❏ No change needed in interlinking systems.	❏ Some straightforward changes needed in interlinking systems.	❏ Change would require many changes in a number of interlinked systems.
7. Funding	❏ Has funding or needs little extra budgeting.	❏ Needs some funding above the regular budget.	❏ Needs considerable or unbudgeted funding.
8. Payout or Return on Investment	❏ Quick payout.	❏ Medium term payout.	❏ Payoff is down the road; delayed benefits.
9. Speed of Implementation	❏ Can be implemented quickly, with little disruption.	❏ Implementation within a few weeks to a few months or can be phased in.	❏ Change takes months to years; or change is abrupt and severe.
10. Impact on End Users	❏ Little skill training or restructuring needed.	❏ Some retraining and restructuring needed.	❏ Considerable amount of training or restructuring needed.
11. Within your Span of Influence	❏ You can personally coach or troubleshoot the change.	❏ You need the leadership of a few others to implement; you cannot directly coach the change.	❏ You need the leadership of many managers and others; change is out of your hands.
Total Column Check Marks	**A =**	**B =**	**C =**

Your change's Difficulty Index = A ____ x 1 + B____ x 2 + C____ x 3 = ☐

- If the Difficulty Index is less than 13, go for it; it's a winner!
- If the Difficulty Index is 13 to 21, you will need to thoroughly plan and deal with difficulties.
- If the Difficulty Index is 22 or above, you will have considerable resistance to the change. For these kinds of projects, you need time to build a lot of support and reduce the risks.

❸ Sustainable Change Equation

Introducing change? We have just the tool for you, the Sustainable Change Equation:

Big Picture x **Buy-in** x **Skills & Tools** x **Managing Risks** x **Action** = Sustainable **CHANGE**

Some features of the equation:
- You will note the variables are *multiplied together*. For the mathematically challenged, when variables are multiplied together, if any variable is very small or zero, the product is very small or zero. In other words, if any variable is ignored, sustainable change is at peril!
- The equation can be modified to suit your project, your change and your organizational language. Details of the change equation are less important than the ideas behind the model. Do refine it to suit your needs and situation. We suggest alternative terms on page 146.
- Although straightforward, the equation is based on sound research. On the next page, we will make the case for considering each variable in the equation, showing why change sputters or fails if you fail to consider adequately every single variable.

The equation is a simple, effective tool with a number of benefits:
- It's easy to understand and explain to others. It will help you explain to clients or task force members the need to attend to some important aspects of change.
- If clients want to omit or gloss over some parts of the change equation, it will provide a tool to help you explain the need for the step.
- The Change Equation demonstrates why change is often a challenge. A number of conditions must be met concurrently for change to succeed.
- We propose the Change Equation as an effective tool to simplify the complex concept of change.

Still have reservations?
- "It's too simplistic for my change."
  Change leadership is a complex area. No one author or model has the answer. We encourage you to either modify the equation; to use more sophisticated tools described later in this chapter, or in the references in *Further Selected Readings* at the end of this book.
- "Does this Change Equation really describe the change process?"
  Not comprehensively. Our goal in this book is to provide internal professionals with practical, usable tools. We feel the equation is defensible from research, but somewhat simplistic to describe the complexities of change.

THE SUSTAINING CHANGE EQUATION

 X X X X =

Big Picture	Buy-In	Skills & Tools	Manage Risks	Action	Lasting Change
Most clients want to understand how this change fits into the larger organizational context. This understanding is a much bigger issue for some clients than for others. Change, lacking a fit with the big picture, results in misdirected energy—working at cross purposes.	The heart of the change must be attended to. Lack of buy-in results at best in complacency; at worst, in sabotage. If buy-in is high, however, clients will provide high energy assistance and go out of their way to make the change a success.	One of the most frustrating scenarios of change is where people are 'pumped up,' but lack the skills or tools necessary for the change.	When presented with change, it is natural for clients to think of its downsides and risks. Effective change leaders anticipate risk and plan to minimize it. If risks are not dealt with, clients will become pessimistic about the change. Openly exposing and dealing with the downsides is the best approach. Generally, clients reciprocate openness with openness.	This last variable of the Change Equation is in an appropriate place. Someone needs to lead the change and make sure that things get done.	

Examples:
In an organization introducing a new operating system for computing equipment, many clients will want to know how this change fits into the Information Technology strategy of the organization.

Sports psychologists work hard at helping high-performing athletes visualize the big picture—the winning process.

Example:
Buy-in is often reduced to 'communicating to.' Buy-in goes well beyond being told or informed. For commitment and support, two-way, substantive communication is required.

Example:
Even if a computer system upgrade clearly fits with organizational strategy and clients can see its benefits, if they don't have training or equipment to use the new or upgraded system, frustration quickly sets in.

Example:
In our operating system example, some computer systems may actually be slowed by the more elaborate software. Open and honest recognition of and plan for the downsides of change can go a long way to aid acceptance.

Example:
Sustained, successful action is most important in large scale projects. From an End User perspective, when change comes, it appears as long periods of inactivity interspersed by spurts of rapid action.

9

THE SUSTAINING CHANGE EQUATION

	Big Picture	Buy-In	Skills & Tools	Manage Risks	Action	= Change
Other Words Used:	Vision, direction Strategy, framework Overall purpose Why? Project Plan Inspiration, charisma Sense of urgency Transformation Environmental scan The business need	Commitment Incentives Rewards Recognition Engagement Empowerment Support Team development Leadership Pumping up Motivation	Skills Human capital Development Competencies Ergonomics Equipment Space Work design	Resistance Reservations Concerns Barriers Roadblocks Obstacles Uncertainty Apprehensions Objections Downsides	Leadership Tactics Doing it Action plans Next steps Small wins	Improvement Implementation Transition Performance Behavior change Results
Metaphors /Pictures:	Compass Framework Head Arrow & target Forest (compared to trees) Light bulb Systems models	Team sports 'Team player' Heart, gut Social system Multiple client system Alignment 'The best way to commitment is by involvement' Stakeholder analysis Benefits	Toolbox Toolkits Systems Quality circles Teamwork Training Process tools	Slow sign Yellow light Red light Tradition Comfort zone Status quo 'Pay me now or pay me later'	Trees (compared to forest) Perspiration Efficiency 'Take one step at a time' Action oriented	Quality ROI (Return on Investment) ROC (Return on Capital) Bottom line Satisfaction Victory
Why Needed?	Big picture inspires and aligns activity—ask Olympic athletes.	Lasting change must take place in the hearts and guts of real people. Change fails, not for technical reasons but for personal reasons.	Nothing is so frustrating as wanting to change, but lacking the skills or tools to do the job.	People find it very difficult to buy into change when they perceive the change leaders do not understand the risks.	Success breeds success and builds confidence.	
If Lacking:	Misdirection Short term results Shortsighted results Cross purposes Questioning need Feel manipulated No alignment Ineffective change Nonstrategic work	Complacency Compliance Undue politics Delay, inertia Push needed rather than pull Turf protection Grumbling Self-interest Skepticism	Frustration Anxiety Pain Safety problems Overruns Turf protection Alienation Backlash	Not 'real world' Pessimism Cynicism Overruns Uncaring feeling Blocking Turf protection Resistance Trauma Unexpected problems	Blue-sky syndrome 'All talk, no action' Rumors "What's wrong?"	

SUSTAINING CHANGE EQUATION—HOW-TO CHECKLIST

Here are a number of suggestions. Check and use those which will help you with your change.

Big Picture	Buy-In	Skills & Tools	Manage Risks	Action
❏ Prepare a vision—one that you can explain in simple words in less than five minutes.	❏ The best way to acceptance by others is through involvement—involve others early and often.	❏ Always provide for training in new skills.	❏ Treat reservations as normal—risks are a natural side effect of change.	❏ Prepare short term action plans which generate small wins.
❏ When you communicate, always place the change in a wider context; answer the question "Why?"	❏ Communicate, communicate, communicate. (Research shows that others feel we have communicated less than half as well as we think.)	❏ Understand that productivity often drops initially (just when you want gains).	❏ Ask for and listen to concerns and reservations.	❏ Recognize and celebrate successes.
❏ Enlist managers and others to talk about how your project fits with business direction.		❏ Although it seems overused, ensure your change is 'user friendly.'	❏ Don't resist resistance—use it!	❏ Always model the behavior you expect in others—walk your talk.
❏ Find and use good metaphors, stories and examples to illustrate— people need a good illustration to understand the change.	❏ Prepare a stakeholder analysis—often change has many client groups.	❏ Do not overlook the skills that managers will need to explain the change to their people—provide coaching.	❏ Learn how people need to transition internally.	❏ Minimize 'happy talk'—people can become cynical.
❏ Prepare an analysis of the system into which the change must fit.	❏ Always make communication two-way—giving information and receiving feedback.		❏ Never underestimate the power of the status quo.	❏ Undermine cynics with quick wins in the action phase.
❏ Prepare an interdependency analysis—often change has many interlinking systems which can foil change.	❏ Form support groups.	❏ Ensure end users have the right equipment at the right time.	❏ Own up to inconsistencies and problems and just say you're sorry—hiding gaffes rarely works.	❏ Keep your cool and sense of humor— introducing change is a challenge for everyone.
❏ Prepare a project plan.	❏ Form support early— often support is only asked for at the action phase.			
❏ Find and exploit synergies.	❏ Take time to garner support from all stakeholder groups.		❏ Anticipate as many risks and reservations as you can.	
❏ If the change is large enough, form a steering group to help you.	❏ Explain specific benefits to each stakeholder group.			
	❏ Recognize support when you get it.			
	❏ Use many types of communication.			

In contests between the existing system and your recommended change, the system will win unless you work the system.

❹ Systemic Side of Change

When recommendations are either (a) not implemented or (b) do not 'stick,' part of the solution is seeing recommended change in the context of the whole system. Professionals are generally good at the diagnosis of problems and design of solutions, but typically weak in thinking through implications of solutions on the larger system.

Systemic Principles

- Change often fails because it was not supported by other interacting systems.
- Many consultants try to 'push through' change by concentrating on the technical excellence of the change itself. More often, it is more effective and economical to concentrate effort on those subsystems which may impede or support the proposed change.
- For successful change, professionals need to identify those systems interacting with their change, asking:
  - Which interacting systems will support the change?
  - Which, specifically, will inhibit or be barriers to our recommended change?
  - What can we do to turn around or reduce the barriers?

In the coffee room you will often hear workers cited as the cause of problems. Peter Scholtes, in his The Team Handbook states: "… at least 85% of problems can be corrected by changing systems and less than 15% are under a worker's control."

Critical Systemic Variables

Below are subsystem variables which should be considered in almost any substantial change effort.

- *Capabilities:* Do end users currently possess skills and competencies required to (a) accomplish the new procedure and (b) work in the changed state? If not, what training and development plans need to be considered?
- *Roles and responsibilities:* Do managers and employees need to renegotiate new roles and responsibilities as a result of the change?
- *Information systems:* Do you and those involved in the change have appropriate tools and information to provide new ways to measure and support the change?
- *Work systems and design:* Is there a need to change the way in which the end users work?
- *Measures:* Does any activity, procedure, or result need to be measured differently than in the past to support the change?
- *Recognition and rewards:* Should performance be evaluated and rewarded differently to support the change?
- *Tie to strategy:* Can you link your recommendation to your organizational strategy, your clients' strategy and business needs?

SUSTAINING CHANGE: ALIGNING THE SUBSYSTEMS MODEL

Instructions: Place your change in the center box and, in the other boxes, list the interacting systems.

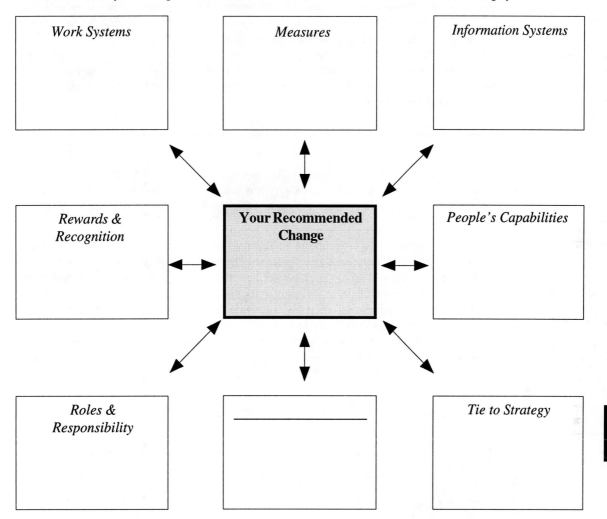

The 'Freehand' Approach to Mapping Systemic Change

You can use a structured model like the one just presented, or, better yet, use the ideas of the model to construct your own 'freehand' model specific to your situation. Let's show you how this is done, using a Career Development System example illustrated on the next page. We use this example because all readers can identify with the topic.

Let's say you are a member of a taskforce designing a new professional career development system for your organization. Here's how you would use the systemic change model in a meeting with the taskforce.

1. Explain the need to look at the systemic side of change.

2. In the center of a whiteboard or of a large piece of paper (four flipchart pages taped to a wall work well—forming a square), print the name of the system you are designing or redesigning. A sample completed Systemic Change Map is on the next page.

3. Around the system you are working on, draw systems with which your system needs to interact. We have often found task force participants can initially only see a few of the interacting systems. Throughout the meeting, print up interacting systems identified by the group. Leave the chart on the wall for the rest of the meeting, gradually adding any other interacting systems. To peoples' amazement, the paper will be full by the end of the meeting. Once people are attuned to interacting systems, they are often in awe of the number of interactions. They can then see why change might struggle if the interactions are not attended to.

4. When interacting systems have been identified, you may wish to make note of specific interactions in each area, as we have done in the example.

5. Now comes the payoff for your work. Go around the interacting systems and ask:
   • "Will this interacting system support or get in the way of our proposed changes?"
     (you may wish to circle support in green pen, barriers in red and unknown in yellow.)
   • For the supporters:
     "How can we enhance or use this support to ensure successful change?"
   • For the barriers:
     "How can we reduce this barrier to ensure successful change?"
     "How can we redesign our change to minimize the negative effect of the barrier?"
   • For the unknown:
     "How can we get information about this system, to ensure it doesn't get in the way of our   change?"

6. Use this information to redesign your changes so that they run into fewer barriers or get more support, to plan actions to minimize negative effects, or to enhance the positive. You can also use this Systemic Change diagram to explain your recommended changes to others.

SYSTEMIC CHANGE:
A FREEHAND EXAMPLE

Note: This example has been severely edited from an actual application to fit the space available.

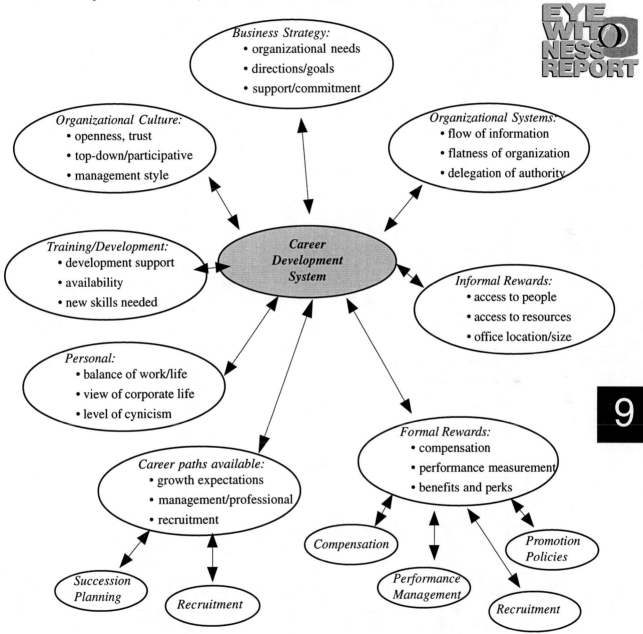

❺ Helping People With Personal Change

*Change Leaders
Field of Dreams:
"If the change is
logical, people will
'adjust' to it."*

Often, changes clearly beneficial from a technical, organizational, and business perspective are not accepted by clients. Why not? Our 35,000 survey database provides an insight. One of the lowest rated items by clients, professional peers, managers and others is the item 'Understands and helps others deal with the stress of changes resulting from his/her recommendations.' We have asked hundreds of workshop professionals "What is this low rating telling you?" Two main types of answers surface:

1. "It's not our job to deal with peoples' emotions and stress. We are hired to do a professional or technical job, that's all." This tends to dismiss the issue, doing nothing to assist people with change.

2. "We don't do a very good job at the people side of change," or "We don't like it when change is foisted on *us*, so it's easy to understand why people want more empathy when we ask *them* to change." (We often get professionals commenting that in modern organizations, change after change is occurring and even minor changes are seen as another stressful event in the work situation.)

*Our approach to the
'people side' of
change—transition—
is inspired by the
research and models
of William Bridges in
his book, Transitions:
Making Sense of
Life's Changes. We
have adapted it to the
professional role.*

Professionals often assume that if the change is logical from a professional and management perspective, people will adjust to it. Experience suggests, however, that the process of change is more like distress and disruption than it is like adjustment. Before they can accept change, people must frequently go through a transition period. Until this transition period is complete, low morale, stress and decreased productivity will occur.

Luckily, there is a very practical, straightforward model that can help professionals with some simple, yet effective, actions to minimize the increased stress of change as a result of their recommendations.

Difference Between Change and Transition

The noted author on personal change, William Bridges, made a critical distinction between change and transition:

Change:
The actual physical move, restructuring, placing, or replacing of equipment or procedures. This change takes place outside the person. This change often takes place quickly.

Transition:
The human re-orientation that people go through when coming to terms with the change. This inner transition often takes much longer than the outside physical change. The transition is internal and based on feelings, a new outlook, and a new way of looking at things. The human cost of change is usually unseen except by keen observers.

For example, an employee may have his or her desktop computing equipment upgraded. The switch over—the change—is brief, often less than an hour. The transition inside the person, getting proficient and at ease with the new equipment, may take a number of weeks.

Characteristics of a Transition

1. Transition occurs inside a person, not outside, and is often not observable.
2. Transition usually takes much longer than physical change.
3. Transition starts with an 'Ending.' Clients need to let go of the way things were, of the past.
4. Transition finishes with a 'New Beginning' where clients embrace the change, or at least come to terms with it.
5. In between is the 'Turmoil Period.' This period between 'Endings' and 'New Beginnings' is like a limbo where clients have to let go of the old and come to terms with the new. It is often characterized by confusion, uncertainty, waffling between the old and the new, chaos and ambiguity. Here clients often want the best of both the old and new worlds.

PEOPLE TRANSITIONS

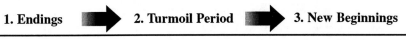

1. Endings	2. Turmoil Period	3. New Beginnings
• Letting go of the way things were.	• Waffling between old and new ways.	• Capturing the benefits of change.

Endings

This stage is identified by a feeling of loss or of having to give up something.

Typical perceived losses can be:
- loss of the familiar
- loss of security
- loss of identity
- loss of control
- loss of meaning
- loss of belonging
- loss of a future
- loss of the 'good old days.'

We have heard systems analysts tell of situations where end user clients have complained about their 'antiquated' desktop PCs. After considerable complaining, new, modern computers are purchased and the systems technician installs them. This 'change,' as defined by Bridges, takes less than an hour. Now the person starts using the new machine. The installer, if he or she hangs around—many want to disappear quickly because they don't want to deal with the feelings–hearing things like:

"I really got to like that old dinosaur machine. I'm going to miss it."
"The keyboard feels different. It's going to take some getting used to."
"Where is the access to the network on this new screen?" and so on.

The first thing the professional hears is complaints and expressions of affection for what, just yesterday, was a problem! The professional just wants to install the machine and get out of there thinking, "Those inconsiderate clients, they complain about everything. You can't please them."

9

The saying 'The devil you know is better than the devil you don't know' is often applicable to the Endings stage

What the systems technician is experiencing is Endings. Clients first of all need to let go of the familiar, let go of the past. And even if the familiar or the past has been painful, there is still a letting go. The impact of these losses on your clients can be reflected directly or indirectly through complaints, talking of the 'good old days,' or they may be as strong as hostility, anger, and inaction. Clients may go as far as hanging on to unproductive behaviors, even if they rationally agree the change would be beneficial.

What's the best thing you can do? Nothing! Well, a conscious sort of nothing—you must listen. The worst thing you can do is treat these normal expressions of letting go as aberrations, which must be corrected. Doing that has the effect of driving emotions underground and entrenching people in resistance. Most people, after the expressions of loss and complaints, will move on to the next phase, the Turmoil Period, which may sound even worse, but is actually progress! We will give a full checklist of possible actions to deal with this first stage later in this chapter.

For those of you who have read the chapters on *Recommending Change* and *Dealing With Resistance*, note the strong parallels. Resistance is natural and OK. The skill is to help clients vent their concerns, not suppress or run away from them. The benefits of getting out in the open these natural feelings about change are:
- Clients get their feelings off their chests so they can deal with the change more rationally.
- When you hear their resistance, you can actually deal with their legitimate concerns.
- Not only will you be considered a good professional, but clients will value you more as a caring human being. From our database, clients greatly value professionals who provide great professional advice, and do it in a very human way.

The Turmoil Period

The period between 'Endings' and 'New Beginnings' feels uncertain, uneasy, unproductive, stressed and often chaotic. Other authors have referred to this in-between period as:
- limbo
- the neutral zone
- uncertainty period
- chaos zone

Things Will Get Worse Before They Get Better!
Change researchers speak of this Turmoil Period as natural. People, faced with change, regularly regress to less productive behavior to recapture the status quo in their lives. Clients may have one foot in each camp: one moment talking about the benefits of change and trying to adapt to the changes, the next moment longing for the past; the following moment resisting again …

"We want it ALL!"
We have consulted with managers trying to change from a 'top-down' management style to a more participative, team-based management style. Employees are asking for the change. When the change is introduced, some interesting reactions take place in the group. During the Turmoil Period, employees often want the 'best of both worlds'—for example, to participate in every decision, yet still retain the right to blame failure of decisions on management!

Lower Productivity—At The Worst Time ...
Productivity will often go down at the very time you most want it to go up! From a consulting perspective, this is the least opportune time for low productivity, since you just presented productivity improvement as one of the benefits of change. One way you can use this Transition Model is to reassure and explain to your sponsors that in the transition process, you anticipate a period of lower productivity preceding the expected productivity gains; then stay calm during this period. Learning a new skill often results in decreased productivity for the transition period.

In the Productivity and Transitions diagram below, a typical transition is charted from a productivity perspective. In the productivity 'valley,' the natural temptation is to panic and make more changes on top of the recommended changes. If this happens, you set up new transition cycles where productivity may dip even lower. The danger is that if you double pressure on your end users, you may inadvertently entrench them in Endings.

PRODUCTIVITY AND TRANSITIONS

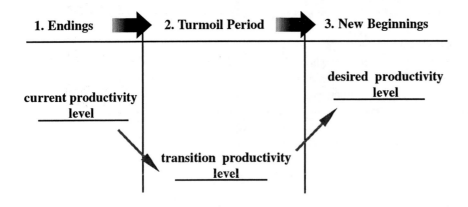

Productivity often decreases just when you have promised an increase. This effect happens in sports. A new technique in golf, for example, can result temporarily in a poorer score for the first few rounds while you adapt to the 'improvement.'

9

Honeymoon Period?
The Turmoil Period can also be a most creative period. The positive side of the turmoil is described as a 'Honeymoon Period.' Here, new norms and groundrules are established—which will again be difficult to change in the future. A closely related model of change describes the three stages of change as:
1. Frozen—the accepted way things are done before the change, the 'status quo.'
2. Unfrozen—when the change is introduced, the new ways are open to change.
3. Frozen—when the change takes hold—after the Turmoil Period—a new 'status quo' is established.

During the middle stage, the Unfrozen Stage, new, more productive ways of working can be established. Leadership is most needed at this stage. You must provide enough leadership so that people do not feel adrift, but not so much that people feel coerced. The balance between the two can be delicate. We will provide you with a checklist of things you might do to make good use of this Turmoil Period.

If encouraged, needed creativity can unexpectedly flourish during the Turmoil Period.

Group change is always more leveraged than one-at-a-time change.

New Beginnings

The end of the transition process is a new status quo called 'New Beginnings.' This is the goal of your consulting project recommended changes. Signs of New Beginnings are:

- smiles, at least acceptance
- enthusiasm for the change
- helping others accept the change
- productivity increase

Timing is important. Professionals and sponsor clients are apt to want to encourage New Beginnings too soon, with the hope that people will come along more quickly. End user clients are usually last to arrive because they have the most reason to be skeptical—will this change actually work under their practical working conditions?

Project closure and turnover are natural at the New Beginnings stage. You and your clients will want to move on to other priorities. Ironically, the more successfully you have led the transition, the less likely clients will have noticed your finesse and skill at leading the change. You may not get the recognition you deserve!

Group change is more powerful than individual change. When a critical mass of clients has reached New Beginnings, they will nearly always carry along the remainder of the group.

A Word of Warning to Professionals

Now that you have seen the whole Transitions Model, keep in mind that you, the professional, have worked long and hard on a project; *you, too, have gone through a transition.* You, your project team and your clients went through an Ending when you explored the need; through a Turmoil Period where you gathered information, debated options and recommended change. Now, introducing 'sweat and tears' change to the end user clients, you hear everything in the Transitions spectrum, from Endings—complaints, uncertainty, questioning of your competence, to Turmoil—uncertainties, uneasiness, through New Beginnings with 'early adopters' saying "It's about time. What took you so long!"

Our advice:

- You will probably hear reactions from the full Transitions spectrum. It's natural and OK. We have heard many professionals say you can actually chart different peoples' reactions, recording them against the Transitions sequence. This helps you respond in more effective ways.
- In particular, when you hear complaints from the Endings period, it is hard to avoid doing two dysfunctional things:
  1. Labelling your client's venting as an aberration that must be fixed or corrected. You may even bad mouth this venting and drive it underground where it can become entrenched, thereby extending acceptance of your recommendations.
  2. Talking 'New Beginnings talk,' reiterating the benefits and glories of the change when people just want to be heard and want you to understand their feelings. You will be labeled by end users as 'insensitive' at best; 'x?!*x' at worst.

Downsizing By One-Third in Three Weeks

A final example had considerably higher stakes and risks: a small company of about 150 employees, heavily in debt, was in imminent danger of being forced into bankruptcy by lending institutions. The only survival strategy was to downsize by one third—within a month. Senior management was greatly distressed because the company was closely knit; everyone knew one another personally. The HR manager used the Transitions Model to try to smooth the downsizing and lessen the pain. The managers planned and were trained in managing transitions. The transition would take place over three meetings.

1. The first—Endings—would announce the change and layoffs. The meeting would be focused on letting go of the past, listening and letting people express their feelings.
2. The next meeting, a week later, would be a Turmoil Period meeting with the downsized and reorganized groups. The focus would be on the transition between letting go and starting to plan the future.
3. The last meeting, a week later, would be around New Beginnings, making plans and setting goals for the future.

One manager expressed the feelings of most: "I've been through downsizing before and never want to go through one of these exercises again, but this was by far the least traumatic. Normally at the first meeting, managers, uneasy with the emotions of layoffs, would quickly shift the meeting agenda to the 'bright future' when people could only think of the traumatic present."

Downsizing is painful no matter how well it is handled. Using the Transitions Model can help minimize the pain.

LEADING THE PEOPLE SIDE OF CHANGE SUMMARY

- The physical change usually happens quickly.

- The changes inside people happen much more slowly.

- Coach clients through the three stages of personal transition:

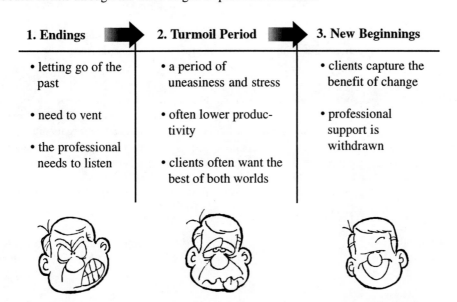

1. Endings	2. Turmoil Period	3. New Beginnings
• letting go of the past	• a period of uneasiness and stress	• clients capture the benefit of change
• need to vent	• often lower productivity	• professional support is withdrawn
• the professional needs to listen	• clients often want the best of both worlds	

9

TRANSITIONS GUIDELINES CHECKLIST

Endings

❑ Do not assume others have moved with you. Do not assume all people will be in the same phase of transition. Ask those who are in a more advanced stage of transition for patience. Often, you, as consultant, are at the New Beginnings stage and wonder why others are not there with you.

❑ It is OK for you and others to gripe, to wish for the 'good old days,' the past, the way things were.

❑ People need to vent and to express their feelings at Endings.

❑ Help people to express their feelings:
  – ask people about their feelings
  – protect persons who vent
  – express your own feelings, concerns.

❑ Your role is to listen:
  – summarize and paraphrase
  – empathize, not sympathize.

❑ Honor the past. Acknowledge what has worked in the past.

❑ Do not take the venting personally:
  – you don't have to solve the hurt
  – 'You can fix things, but you can't fix people.'

❑ Most Endings end naturally. After venting, most clients want to move on.

❑ Use the power of the group. Endings are much more powerful and quicker when they occur publicly and in a group session. Less powerful are Endings which occur one by one.

❑ Support is a key feature: listen and lead.

Turmoil Period

❑ It is natural and OK to be in turmoil:
  – **Emotionally:** confusion, stress, vacillation, blaming others
  – **Thinking:** wanting to understand, asking why, resisting suggestions, second guessing.
  – **Behaviorally:** going through the motions only, activity.

❑ Some will try to recapture the way things were; others will want to rush on. It's OK and natural to regress.

❑ Much of the Turmoil Period takes place internally. Tell your clients about this phase of transitions.

❑ Transitions can't be forced, but can be led. They take some time, but be definite about a time limit.

❑ Insist on the rational change while personally supporting your clients. Be tough on the problem but supportive of people. 'Tough Love' is an apt phrase.

❑ Focus on the here-and-now; on short term, familiar activities. Insist the day-to-day work gets done.

❑ Balance between individual and group work:
  – *Individual:* Dealing with individual issues; helping individuals through change
  – *Group:* Harnessing the power of the group; helping groups through change

New Beginnings

❑ Declare the transition over. Announce New Beginnings.

❑ Celebrate or otherwise symbolically mark the New Beginnings.

❑ How to recognize new beginnings:
  – **Emotionally:** new energy, new spirit, focus outward.
  – **Thinking:** setting new goals, looking ahead, focusing on results.
  – **Behaviorally:** talk of future, focus on productivity.

❑ Help the group members look beyond the day-to-day, which you encouraged during the Turmoil Period. Formulate expectations, state them clearly and follow up.

❑ Clarify longer range goals, results, vision, and strategy. Focus on a target and marshal work towards that target.

❑ A group will need to (re)consider:
  – Group Mission or Purpose
  – Goals
  – Roles and responsibilities
  – Groundrules

❑ Check for systems alignment. One of the major reasons for the failure of change to take hold is that other interacting organizational systems do not support the change. For example, the change may be great from a professional perspective but skills development, leadership skills or style, budgets, decision making groundrules or social bonds do not support the recommended change. Look beyond the change itself.

People Who Need People ...

A crucial skill for introducing change, and for managing transitions, is getting individual and large scale client participation and involvement:
- The best way to personal commitment and buy-in is through participation.
- Participation can lead to higher quality, more innovative solutions.
- 'Two heads are better than one.' Effective participation leads to synergy. Two or more people working well together can accomplish much more than the sum of these same people working separately.
- You want people's commitment, not their compliance. Ideally, you want clients' discretionary effort to support and advance the change, not impede it. The best way to get this discretionary effort is through involvement.

You need participation on at least two levels:
- Participation and involvement of the right people in the project. A stakeholder analysis is essential (like the one described on Page 130, Chapter 8, *Mapping Client Systems*).
- Participation and involvement of people in meetings and presentations. Some guidelines and how-tos for group participation are outlined below, followed by a Self-Assessment of your Skills.

How to Secure Participation in a Group

There is no one best way to elicit participation from a group. Here are some suggestions:
- ❏ Ask for participation. A direct and honest request for participation is very effective.
- ❏ Do not dominate 'air time' yourself. The most common reason for lack of participation is lack of opportunity provided by an overcontrolling or dominating leader.
- ❏ The earlier you give people the opportunity to participate, the more likely they are to participate. People are more likely to participate in what they have a chance to influence.
- ❏ Express appreciation and thank people who participate.
- ❏ Avoid evaluating ideas too early. Be careful of any implied evaluation of participant ideas. For example, inexperienced group leaders will often make visible only the items they agree with, or they will use terms like 'excellent idea' only when it supports their view.
- ❏ Protect the first few ideas. Participants often judge the safety of participation by how well the first couple of contributions are handled.
- ❏ Ask open-ended questions to get participation going.
- ❏ Asking for examples is a powerful way of getting participation. Participants often find it easier to tell a story about what they saw or heard than to state an abstract summary.
- ❏ Summarize verbally or, better yet, summarize by visibly recording the key points.
- ❏ Always summarize or make the ideas visible, so that the participants know you understand, before you make an evaluative or rebuttal response.

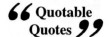

Quotable Quotes
"The challenge is to make 'have-to's' into 'want-to's'."
– Geoff Bellman

9

Most religions have a variant on the golden rule: "Do unto others as you would have others do unto you." Accordingly, "Consult unto clients as you would be consulted unto."

How to Handle Participation in a Group

- If the group is large (more than 12), and full group participation unwieldy, break the group into subgroups early and ask a subgroup spokesperson to lead the reporting on an issue. People who may be reluctant to speak up in a large group will often participate readily in a small group.
- If group members are hesitant to participate, put a safe agenda item at the beginning of the meeting. Leave contentious issues until the group has warmed up to participation.
- You cannot 'turn on' participation. Ask for it consistently. Support it consistently. Don't wait until you need participation to ask for it.
- The amount of participation in a group is proportional to the leader's listening skills. Always summarize or paraphrase participants' contributions, particularly if you have differing views.
- If you hear something you disagree with, make a strong listening response or make the idea visible before commenting. Participants are much more likely to hear you if you demonstrate that you heard them.
- Be careful how you handle contentious contributions outside a meeting. If you talk outside a meeting about how dumb the participants were inside the meeting, you can expect low participation at your next meeting.
- Call group members 'participants' if you want them active, rather than a passive 'audience.' Call sessions where you want participation 'workshops,' 'working sessions,' or 'bull sessions' rather than the more passive 'meetings,' 'presentations,' 'updates,' or 'seminars.'
- How you arrange room seating can assist or detract from participation. Arrange the room so participants can see and talk easily with each other.
- Observe other group leaders. What do they do which enhances or inhibits participation?

66 Quotable Quotes 99
Any fool can criticize an idea and most fools do.

Who, Me?

If you have read this far, you may be in the Turmoil Period around your previous ideas and models of change. Your feelings toward this chapter and its models may be a microcosm of personal transition. You may be thinking "Am I going to apply these models? How might I modify them? Will they work in my role and organization? How will my clients respond if I use these models? Should I get involved with the people side of change?" You have to sustain the change that your recommendation entails, planning and executing the rational and systemic sides of change. For most professionals, the challenge is the human side, the side where commitment to personal action resides.

Checklist: Group Participation Skills

Check those items you already use effectively. Highlight those items which require development. Ask for feedback from people who have seen you in the role of group leader or facilitator. You can easily be unaware of the impact of your behavior in this area.

1. At the Start of a Session:
- ❏ I ask directly and honestly for participation when I want it.
- ❏ I protect the first few ideas by asking people to postpone evaluation.
- ❏ I know how to establish rapport with a group so they are at ease with me and each other.
- ❏ I know how to arrange an agenda to have items with easiest participation first.
- ❏ I know how to use open-ended questions to help participants open up.
- ❏ I can make information visible as a means of helping people participate.

2. Logical Skills:
- ❏ I am conscious of both group content and process.
- ❏ I do not ask for participation when I really don't want it.
- ❏ I listen well by summarizing and paraphrasing.
- ❏ I don't discourage participation by dominating air time.
- ❏ I know how to ask for an example when an idea is confusing or abstract.
- ❏ I know how to close a topic without turning off participation.
- ❏ I know how to use both developmental and evaluative thinking to encourage participation.
- ❏ I can use meeting breaks to keep participation high.
- ❏ I am aware of nonparticipating members and ask for their ideas.
- ❏ I use humor to encourage participation.

3. Emotional Skills:
- ❏ I am able to separate the person from the problem.
- ❏ I am conscious that any implied evaluation can cut back on participation.
- ❏ I am able to ask for feelings on a topic just as easily as technical content.
- ❏ I am aware of my feelings when something is said which I do not like.
- ❏ I know how to be supportive to unexpected contributions.
- ❏ I know how to handle difficult participants, for example long winded participants, without losing the confidence of the group.
- ❏ I am careful with information gathered in a participative meeting, so that group members are not punished outside the meeting for being open.
- ❏ I am known as a participative group leader.

People remember:
- *20% of what they hear,*
- *40% of what they see and hear, and*
- *80% of what they hear, say and do.*

9

Participation skills are closely tied to the listening skills of Chapter 11 and the s questioning skills of Chapter 5.

WHAT YOU HAVE LEARNED SO FAR ...

- Be a 'full cycle consultant.' The best professional work is only valuable and complete when change takes place.

- Roles: You will want to stay involved enough to make sure the change takes place and is sustainable, but not to own the change.

- Systemic: The natural tendency is to look only to the professional excellence aspect of the change. Change more often fails because interacting systems are not supportive.

- On the personal side of change, helping people deal with the stress of your recommendations is one of the weakest skills of professionals.

- People naturally go through three stages in coming to grips with change—Endings, Turmoil and New Beginnings. You cannot avoid having people go through these stages; you can only help people through them.

THE EXPERTISE DELIVERY MODEL

10

"Whatever it is—I'm against it."
– Groucho Marx

CHAPTER 10

DEALING WITH RESISTANCE

Quick Snapshot

Did You Know?
- your challenge is to resist resisting resistance?
- resistance is natural and OK; in fact, no resistance may indicate a problem?
- direct resistance—clients directly stating their concerns—is preferable to indirect resistance?
- the skill of handling indirect resistance is crucial to your career growth?

How-to:
- distinguish between direct and indirect resistance.
- help clients 'come clean' and tell you their real concern.
- manage indirect resistance.

The Bottom Line:
- You will be able to recognize and use the skills for dealing with indirect resistance with the skills, models and techniques of this chapter.

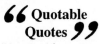

❝ Quotable Quotes ❞
"Agree with me now, it will save so much time."
© Ashleigh Brilliant

We gratefully acknowledge the inspiration and seminal thinking of Peter Block in the understanding and the skills of dealing with resistance.

Resistance to Change

Dealing with resistance is a challenge for professionals. Although cited over and over again as a cause for the failure of professional projects, resistance is not a valid scapegoat for failure. Most employees, if asked, can suggest a dozen ways of improving their work, aware that these ways would involve change.

In this chapter, we take a fresh, different look at resistance. If you consider resistance as natural and OK, you will prevent conflict and 'butting heads' with your clients.

Notes To Our Readers

1. If you have come to this chapter after reading Chapter 6, *Recommending Change*, bear with us. Since the first few sections of this chapter have similarities to the 'Dealing with Reservations and Resistance' spoke of the 'Selling Wheel,' you may wish to skim the next pages before turning to new material on page 167, starting with *A Wolf in Sheep's Clothing?—Understanding Indirect Resistance*.

2. *Dealing with Resistance* is closely related to four other topics:
   • Dealing with difficult clients (and people in general)
   • Dealing with conflict
   • Dealing with differences
   • Assertive behavior for professionals.

We touch only briefly on these topics. If any one of them is an issue for you, we suggest you see *Selected Further Reading* at the end of this book for more detailed coverage. However, we have chosen to cover comprehensively in Chapters 6 and 9 another closely related topic, recommending and sustaining change.

Resistance to Resistance

It is a natural impulse for most human beings to resist when significant change is proposed. In only a few cases where a mechanical law applies to human behavior, Newton's Law *for every action, there is an equal and opposite reaction,* holds true. Try this experiment with a colleague, friend or family member. Turn face-to-face and press the palms of your hands against his/hers. Gently begin pushing. The other person, without thinking, pushes back, resisting your force. Natural as this may seem, intuitive push-back behavior is rarely productive for professionals. Pushing matches, if won by anyone, are usually won by clients. Many professionals, when faced with fuzzy resistance, cannot understand what is happening, take it personally, and instinctively push back. Clients probably don't understand resistance any better and react in equally dysfunctional ways.

A better metaphor for dealing with resistance is martial arts. Using martial arts principles, rather than resisting the resistance of your clients, study the dynamics of their resistance, anticipate it and make it work for you! Client resistance can become positive energy in the hands of a skilful professional. This chapter will help you handle resistance so it works to your advantage.

No News Is Bad News!

When you ask clients to significantly change, *lack of resistance may mean you have a problem!* Perhaps your clients don't understand what you are asking them to do? Perhaps they are dismissing your recommendations without thinking of implementing them? Resistance is a clear sign that you *are* getting through to your client; that your recommendations are hitting home; that you are having an impact. You can learn to recognize what is happening and respond in a way that not does not escalate conflict. You can turn difficult situations into long-term relationship builders.

Credibility And Career Builder

Powerful professionals are required to have the skills of this chapter:
- Our comprehensive client database shows poor ratings of skills of dealing with conflict. Skills of dealing with resistance are closely related to the skills of dealing with conflict. Because they are rare, professionals with these skills are highly valued.
- Research on professional careers shows that high performing professionals must deal with increasingly complex projects over time. More complex projects mean more significant change on the part of clients, and mean dealing with more resistance.
- Stakeholders increasingly require involvement in professional projects. Few stakeholders now accept change without question.

Two Types of Resistance

In this chapter, we distinguish between two kinds of resistance. The methods for dealing with each kind are very different.

The first is *direct* resistance, where your clients tell you openly the difficulties they have with your consultation. At first, direct resistance may seem blunt and uncaring, but it is actually the easier form to deal with. If your problem is dealing with this 'upfront' form of resistance, better called 'client reservations,' you may wish to turn directly to Chapter 6, *Recommending Change*, since this present chapter deals with indirect resistance.

The second form of resistance, the subject of this chapter, is *indirect* resistance, where clients do not openly tell you what their concerns are. They substitute an apparently rational reason instead. In everyday language, you would say you are being stalled, 'getting the runaround,' a 'brush-off' or a 'put-off.' Your client is beating around the bush. The rest of this chapter will investigate *indirect* resistance—how you can test whether the resistance is indirect and how you can assist your client to come clean and surface the real reason for resistance.

Here is a real-life example of both kinds of resistance.
The Situation:
Assume you are considering interviewing all the members of your client's work group in an open session to gather data for a project. Because your client feels that group members may be critical of senior management, making the project politically sensitive, your client wants you to limit your interviewing to one or two selected members.

> **66 Quotable Quotes 99**
> *"The challenge is that what you perceive as indirect resistance may be the straight goods. In today's hurly burly world, a more important meeting could very well appear on someone's schedule; someone may think they have a better idea; the dog might really eat the homework."*
> *– George Campbell*

In this chapter ...

- *Why resistance is natural and expected.*
- *How to separate two types of resistance, direct and indirect.*
- *How to recognize indirect resistance.*
- *How to deal with indirect resistance, using a four step model.*
- *How to apply the model.*
- *How to minimize instances of indirect resistance.*

Directly Resisting Client:

Your client has two alternatives, the first is to resist directly: "You want to interview all the members of my work group in a group setting. I do not want you to do that because the group may be critical of management and I do not want them to get stuck in organizational politics. I think one or two people privately would be enough." You can now negotiate with your client how best to get the information. Although direct, straightforward resistance may be hard to take at times, at least you know where you stand and you can work on the real issue.

Indirectly Resisting Client:

Contrast this with indirect resistance, where your client, sensing the same personal political ramifications, may respond like this: "You want to interview everybody in our group in an open session. This will take too much time away from their work. It would be more cost effective to talk to just one or two in your office. We don't want to raise people's expectations about this project." Note that indirect resistance is stated in very rational terms. Cost effi- ciency, in most organizations, is a good reason for not taking too much employee time. This phony reason could get you off track, working side issues, and leave you with a sinking feeling of frustration. You have been given a runaround, a polite put-off. The client's real reason is not out in the open.

Family Example of Indirect Resistance:

Indirect resistance on the part of clients is not bad or unusual. Clients may not even realize what they are doing. Indirect resistance is common in everyday life. Take the example of a teenager asking a parent for keys to the family car on a Friday night. Most parents have a repertoire of runarounds, ranging from the family car needing maintenance, to a sudden need for parental transportation that evening. Rarely will the parent talk about the real reasons: fears of speeding, drinking, peer group pressure, or accident. Parents, like clients, 'protect' their children (and themselves!) from difficult realities. Similarly, many clients find it chal- lenging to face difficult situations. Indirect resistance is the natural result.

DIFFERENCE BETWEEN DIRECT AND INDIRECT CLIENT RESISTANCE

Direct	Indirect
• Resistance stated openly and honestly; the real concern stated.	• Resistance stated in apparently rational terms; is not the real concern.
• Usually the client maintains eye contact and uses 'I' statements.	• Usually the client does not maintain eye contact and uses third party 'we' or 'they' statements.
• May feel hurtful at the time because it may feel blunt but is actually the more honest and easier to deal with.	• A put-off or runaround.
• You know exactly where you stand, the issue is clear. ▼	• Feels out-of-focus, like foggy film. Hard to get a grip on what is happening. ▼
• Leads to honest negotiation or conflict resolution.	• Leads to misdirected energy and frustration.
• You can put your energy into the real issue.	• You will be led to put energy into side issues.

166

OR

A Wolf in Sheep's Clothing?—Understanding Indirect Resistance

To deal successfully with indirect resistance, you need to be able to recognize it and surface it. For many professionals, recognition itself is most challenging. Recognition of resistance takes place at two levels, rational and emotional. The characteristics of typical rational, indirect resistance statements are:

- They are stated in normal, rationally acceptable terms.
- They *could be* legitimate reasons and often are in your organization.
- They are often expressed using third party language. 'They' and 'We' are used in place of 'I.' For example "They wouldn't go for this," rather than "I won't go for this."
- Rational thinking usually lags behind emotional—the feeling in your gut. That's why frustration and emotion can quickly arise over apparently rational issues.

Stress Happens

You will feel resistance in your gut before you can rationally understand what is happening. When resistance is felt, many of the following may occur:

- the pitch of your voice becomes higher
- your speech becomes louder
- your rate of speaking becomes faster
- your palms become sweaty
- you tend to repeat yourself.

You, as the professional, must be able to spot your own emotional response to resistance so you can deal with it for yourself and your clients. When you put the rational together with the emotional, you have a potent combination for sniffing out and surfacing indirect resistance.

Emotions and feelings need the corroboration of nonverbal client behaviors like:

- minimal eye contact
- fidgeting
- turning away
- getting up to move away.

What You See Is NOT What You Are Getting

Expression of indirect resistance, by definition, is subtle. It is a phoney reason clad in legitimacy. The trouble is you can't be sure which is which. You try a couple of times to respond directly to the rational issue, because the reason could be legitimate. We call these attempts to resolve the apparent resistance at the rational, expressed level as 'Good faith responses.' In the worst case, you sense your emotions rising in response to vague clues given out by your client. You respond emotionally and inappropriately.

This process of responding to vague emotions leads to counterproductive behavior by both client and consultant. The professional, sensing something is wrong, pushes harder and the client, sensing the professional's resistance pushes back harder. The point is that without anyone realizing it, the resistance is escalating! Someone, preferably you, the consultant, must break the cycle early before it escalates into conflict.

> **❝ Quotable Quotes ❞**
>
> *"For technically oriented consultants —like engineers, accountants, computer and systems people— resistance can be very hard to identify. Our technical backgrounds so orient us to data, facts, and logic that when we are asked to perceive an emotional or interpersonal process, it is like trying to see the picture on a badly out-of-focus piece of movie film."*
>
> *– Peter Block*
> *Flawless Consulting*

TYPICAL FORMS OF INDIRECT RESISTANCE

Which forms of indirect resistance are used most frequently in your organization? *Which have you used?*

"Your recommendations (or proposals) are good, BUT …
- ❏ The time is not right:

  – vacation time   – planning time
  – budgeting cycle   – performance appraisal.
- ❏ Too little information.
- ❏ Too much information.
- ❏ Didn't interview the right people.
- ❏ Need to take it to a committee.
- ❏ Need to "kick it upstairs."
- ❏ Not in the budget.
- ❏ Doesn't fit with policy.
- ❏ Someone—staff, managers, end users … "can't handle this."
- ❏ That amorphous group, 'they,' who make so many decisions, "wouldn't go for this."
- ❏ Operations (or some other department) wouldn't go for this.
- ❏ 'Resistance to change' on the part of someone else.
- ❏ Takes too much time.
- ❏ You don't live in the client's 'real world.'
- ❏ Not enough documentation.
- ❏ Not enough research.
- ❏ What are other organizations doing?
- ❏ It will be done after some other event has occurred, e.g. reorganization is complete, budget has been approved, strategic planning is done, etc.
- ❏ "Give me a few days to think it over."
- ❏ Silence

The last, silence, is difficult to deal with. As one professional said "For professionals, no news is NOT good news."

SURFACING INDIRECT RESISTANCE

Here is our four-step process for surfacing indirect resistance:
1. *Give two good faith responses to your client's request for information.*
2. *Check your gut feeling and the client's nonverbal behavior.*
3. *State what you see happening, in as non-punishing a way as possible.*
4. *Be quiet; let the client respond.*

Surfacing Indirect Resistance

10

1. Give two good faith responses to your client's request for information.
Remember the request could be legitimate. If possible, respond at the level of the request. For example, if the time is not right, propose another time. Because indirect resistance is clad in the guise of a legitimate reason, you cannot be sure it is indirect resistance at this point. In some circumstances, you may not have the opportunity to give two good faith responses. You may need to move directly to Step #2.

There is no point in confronting the client over the wrong issue. For example, we often hear professionals suggest a more assertive response when they sense a stall on the basis of time. They ask "If your proposed time is not right, why not press the client to provide you with a time to do it?" We strongly counsel that you do *not* take this approach. Your client will almost certainly give you a meeting time—in the distant future. Almost certainly you will receive a message shortly before the meeting date, saying the client regrets not being able to make it to the meeting. *There is no point in pressing the client for a time when time is not the real issue.*

2. Check your gut feeling and the client's nonverbal behavior.
Check inside yourself to satisfy three critical specifications:
  • Your rational answers aren't working.
  • You are feeling there is something wrong here.
  • Your client's nonverbal behavior is out of sync with the rational message.

If all three data points lead you to confirm indirect resistance, then you move to Step #3 of the process. For professionals, the skills of Step #3 are crucial to your effectiveness.

3. State what you see happening, in as non-punishing a way as possible.
You want your client to come clean and state the real reason for resistance. You need to clearly confront and state the apparent resistance in a non-punishing way, to call the bluff without punishing your client's natural, intuitive behavior. The characteristics of an effective, non-punishing confrontation are:
  • It is challenging enough to demonstrate to your client that you know what is happening.
  • It does not push the client into a corner by attacking the client's self esteem.

For instance, assume the client is resisting on the basis of time and you have twice tried to schedule an implementation meeting. "Twice we have tried to find a time to schedule an implementation meeting for these recommendations. Perhaps there is something else that is concerning you about these recommendations?" The trick is to push just hard enough to show you know what is happening. Confronting too harshly can lead to one of two directions:
  i. The client will shift the field of resistance e.g. from that of time to needing more data. For example, "Well I suppose we could start at the end of the month, but we would need a lot more data on the cost/benefit to take it upstairs for fast-tracking approval."

  ii. Clients dig in their heels at the level of resistance they have expressed. For example, "You staff people don't live in the real world and don't understand the time pressures on us."

In their delightful book, Dinosaur Brains: Dealing with All Those Impossible People at Work, A. Bernstein and S. Rosen name the unconscious response to threatening situations the 'Reptilian Response,' adding that it happens outside the conscious mind, with the result that people aren't even aware of it, "... but it has left countless careers dead in the water," they say.

4. Be quiet. Let the client respond.

A strange step indeed—be quiet, do nothing! The natural tendency, after making what is an uncomfortable statement, is to talk on and let your client off the hook. The client needs quiet time to assess the situation—clients may not even know that they are resisting indirectly. The client needs to 'stew' a little. Going through the client's head are questions like:

- "Am I going to come clean and state my real reason?"
- "Am I going to shift ground to another type of indirect resistance?"
- "Am I going to dig in my heels and maintain the bogus reason?"
- "Will I lose face if I come clean?"
- "Will this professional be able to handle the real reason?"
- "Will this professional be able to keep confidences if the real reason is politically sensitive?"

The client needs time to think.

Here's hoping the client comes clean and gives you the real reason! We present more alternatives a little later.

Now for a brief example and a full scenario of naming indirect resistance.

NAMING THE RESISTANCE

Here are some typical expressions of indirect resistance and a potential non-punishing statement. As always, please modify these examples for your own situation, and remember that what is non-punishing in one organization may be very punishing in the next.

Form of Resistance	*Non-Punishing Statement*
• Need to take your proposal up to the steering committee.	• "You are planning to take my proposal to the steering committee. Will you support the recommendations?"
• Attack or anger.	• "You seem to be getting upset. Is something bothering you about how we're handling this?"
• Delay until after some other event.	• "You say you like the recommendation, yet you appear to be putting off implementation. Do you have concerns about this recommendation?"

❝ Quotable Quotes ❞

"Silence is (can be) golden."
– Robin Sober

Most people have learned indirect resistance as part of survival in organizations and are not even conscious of its use.

A Classic Example of Naming the Resistance

A professional, leading a data feedback session with the executive group of a large corporation, had led a taskforce which designed, then administered an organizational diagnostic survey to every employee. Presenting the survey results to the executive group, the professional noticed that the executives kept on referring to the survey results as "your data" and "your survey." The professional remarked on this, saying "I want to remind you that you asked me to gather data from your organization. This data is from your people. As long as you refer to the data as if it is my data, you're not going to do anything about it." After a few tense seconds, one executive spoke up meekly. "We don't like what you are presenting because it means we have problems here. It makes us feel very uncomfortable." Disliking what they were hearing, the executives were resisting by pushing back the data to the professional. Subsequently, the meeting went much smoother, as the executives started talking first of all about "the data"— still keeping it at arm's length—then gradually shifting to "our data."

What If Your Client Doesn't Come Clean?

A natural objection to this model of dealing with indirect resistance is "What if the client doesn't name the real issue?" One could imagine a range of client responses from no reaction to anger. The most common response is to switch to a new form of indirect resistance. If this happens, you could try again to call the client's bluff. This is a low probability option because clients practised in runarounds can have a large repertoire.

What if your client ignores your naming the resistance? First, perhaps you weren't clear or forceful enough when you named the resistance. If this is the case, try again more clearly and forcefully. A second reason for not responding may be that your client is choosing to ignore your call to come clean. An example is the client who switches the form of indirect resistance.

What about the client who reacts in anger to your gall of calling a bluff? If you feel that you haven't been too punishing, you may have inadvertently tripped into a very difficult client. Read on about the reasons for resistance. Be careful and do not prejudge. You may have misinterpreted the resistance as indirect. One reason for the client not coming clean is that the original resistance was legitimate. In some situations, your best consulting skills won't work. If you have given it your best shot and your client takes it like water off the back of an otter, you can at least know you've done your personal best.

What if Your Client Does Come Clean?

If your client names the real, underlying resistance, you must actively listen to your client's response. You must, at minimum, summarize what your client said. Better yet, you might use an empathic response to the emotion of the situation. A range of listening responses is discussed in Chapter 11, *Listening Skills for Professionals*. Depending on the nature of the new concern, your consultation could go in various directions. Remember, you must *not* let your clients lose face or self esteem when they come clean; carefully handle the client's real resistance.

An interesting variant (on the next page) is where the client was protecting the professional from a difficult reality. The client may not like your work! In this case, you need to handle both the unexpected feedback *and* the direct resistance.

SCENARIO OF INDIRECT RESISTANCE

Now we can pull the whole model into a full example. This scenario takes place in a large organization. A Systems Analyst has just presented a report to the Accounts Receivable Manager. The Analyst and Manager have agreed that the new system, when implemented, will have a benefit of about a $10,000 per month, since accounts will be tracked and followed up more thoroughly. The Analyst is anxious to start work soon, because the project is high profile.

Manager: Thanks. This is a good report. *(Stands up and looks at watch and schedule.)* I must get to my next meeting. Thanks again. We'll get back to you.

Analyst: Before you go, can we set a time to meet and discuss implementation? If we get started next month, you will begin seeing the benefits within a couple of months.

Manager: (Looking at watch and not into the eyes of the Analyst.) Gee, I've got to get going. Next month would be pretty difficult for us because we'll be tied up in Performance Appraisals. Thanks, it's a good report and we'll get back to you.

Analyst: (Getting a little anxious sensing that something is wrong and feeling an important project might be slipping away.) Well, if next month is no good, I could get started the month after, in July. I'd like to see you capture the $10,000 per month benefit as soon as possible.

Manager: (Starting to finger through some file folders on the desk and again looking at the watch) I've really got to go. Summer's not a good time to do something like this, vacations and all. Don't worry, we'll get back to you.

(At this point you can imagine what is going through the Analyst's head. "If it is such a good report, how come I can't pin my client down?" The Analyst feels uneasy, alternating between self doubt for having blown it and a distinct feeling that the client is stalling. In either case, emotions are rising and it is difficult not to take what is happening personally. Let us assume the Analyst, sensing the nonverbal cues, pulls his/her thoughts together and intervenes according to the model.)

Analyst: You say this is a good report and agree it will save you $10,000 per month, yet you are having difficulty finding a time to implement the recommendations. Perhaps there is something else that is bothering you about this report?

Manager: (Shuffling the files even more, alternating glances between the files and his watch. A few seconds pass, feeling like an eternity to the Analyst. It is tempting to talk because the tension is high; the situation is crying out for resolution. The Manager is quietly considering two choices, giving the real reason or stalling once more.) Well ... er, yes. The report is good. *(Another few seconds pass and the manager briefly meets the Analyst's eyes a few times.)* Actually, there is something that bothers me. You do produce great reports. It's implementation that bothers me. I have somebody else in mind to implement the project. You have been late and over budget on the last two projects.

(At this point it's the Analyst who is fidgeting. The client was protecting the Analyst from some difficult feedback. We will end the scenario here because the indirect resistance is now in the open.)

10

Why Do Clients Resist?

To look at resistance in a larger context, what are its roots? Why is it natural to resist?
The most powerful sources of indirect resistance are:

1. Client vulnerability

2. Client need to keep control

3. Client need to avoid risk.

Clients have come by these fears honestly—and of necessity. Fears need not even be real; they
only need to be perceived to be real. For instance, you may have inadvertently:

a. challenged client control of the situation, or

b. your proposal will put the client at risk.

Either of these will cause clients to protect themselves.

Keeping control and avoiding risk continue to be two practices valued and rewarded in most
organizations—despite the fact that studies consistently show that both practices, when done
well, lead to more productive organizations.

Clients won't buy anything for which they cannot see clear benefits. It is more natural for
them to think of the upsides of staying with the status quo than it is to face the risks of
changing.

- Clients can often see a wide range of implications for your proposal. These potential
  problems can be frightening. As a professional, you may have a more limited view of the
  impact of your recommendations.
- Clients have learned organizational survival techniques. Some clients are so risk adverse
  that *any* recommendation meets a stall.
- Some organizational cultures discourage risk-taking. Having 'experts' study a problem
  and make impotent recommendations can actually be a strategy for delaying dealing with
  difficult issues.
- Many clients are too polite to tell you the shortcomings of your proposals. In many
  organizations, some clients are too polite for effectiveness.
- Clients may not be able to face up to their own inadequacies. They are afraid to change
  the way they manage.

Generally, professionals are strong at explaining the technical features, but less skilled at
presenting the benefits of their proposals. A thorough explanation of the benefits of your
proposal must take place before you can ask for commitment from the client.
(A specific process for doing this is discussed in Chapter 6, *Recommending Change*).

Zip Your Lip!

Knowing when to maintain the confidences gained from your clients is a major, sensitive issue
throughout a consultation, but particularly at this stage, with fears of loss of control or too
much risk. You put clients doubly at risk if you misuse sensitive information you have gained.
Breaking a confidence will make it very difficult for you or for the next professional to get to
the real issues.

> 66 **Quotable
> Quotes** 99
> "When managers are
> being defensive, they
> are defending their
> own managerial
> adequacy—a natural
> thing to defend ... A
> resistant manager is
> much more
> concerned about his
> or her esteem and
> competence than
> about our skills as
> consultants."
> – Peter Block
> Flawless Consulting

> "Resistance is an
> emotional process,
> not a rational or
> intellectual process."
> – Peter Block

What may have been a little 'burr in the saddle' reservation for a client at the early stages of a project can become a 'pain in the butt' in the last stages.

An Ounce Of Prevention Is Worth a Pound of Cure

Given this challenge of helping your clients express indirect resistance, it's easy to see that developing skills for a long term problem prevention strategy, is much better than the skills of the cure—although you need both! You want to be known as a professional who is a straight shooter and will name any indirect resistance, making it less likely that your clients will try to give you a runaround in the future. Your treatment as a consultant will mirror the way you treat your clients. Perhaps the golden rule for professionals should read "Treat your clients as you want to be treated as a professional."

Clients respond assertively to assertive behavior.

CHECKLIST FOR MINIMIZING RESISTANCE

❑ Be open and straightforward yourself. The best way to get superior client behavior is to model the behavior you want. Clients will come clean with consultants who come clean. Act in an assertive manner.

❑ Think the best of your clients. 'Dumb clients' are assisted by dumb professionals. Powerful professionals take on the job of making their clients better.

❑ Always work in a win-win, 50-50 mode. If clients feel you are winning at their expense, they will naturally protect themselves.

❑ Involve people early and often.

❑ Be as sensitive to the process as the content. By training, most professionals are exquisitely attuned to the professional or technical content of a situation. They are less attuned to the process of the situation—how the problem is being worked.

❑ Make it easy for people to tell you where they stand. Ask for feedback from clients. Clients are more willing to accept feedback from professionals who accept feedback.

❑ Do not ever, ever break confidences. Bragging about 'getting a client' or about ferreting out risky information is death to your career. The reason many clients use runarounds is because they have been burnt in the past by learning that someone bragged about what was expected to be held in confidence.

Clients play games with professionals who play games.

Dealing with resistance is a professional career builder. Do it well and you will be presented with core issues, not side issues—you will see indirect resistance less often.

Fine Tuning

Powerful professionals have developed a delicate sense of timing—the kind of timing that great comedians and actors have mastered. Sometimes—not always—the most elegant way to deal with resistance is to let it resolve itself. The first few statements from your client often express natural resistance. If you are patient and actively listen, you will often see your client call his or her own stall. For example, if you propose that a client totally revamp a system at considerable effort and cost, the client, even if he/she knows the change needs to be made, will usually protest. After a few patient minutes, the client will often say "I know we need to do this, but it is really going to stretch us. Are you sure we can't do this in a simpler way?" Timing is of the essence.

Inexperienced or unskilled consultants can create resistance by their own behavior. If resistance occurs regularly, deficiency in consulting skills could be the problem, not just client deficiency. Powerful professionals have learned when to consider the question 'Who has the problem?'

Powerful professional projects will become over time more complex and involve more clients. In your growth as an internal professional, you will be asking clients to change in more significant ways; consequently you can expect to meet more resistance. The skills of preventing and finessing resistance in complex client systems is crucial. In this chapter, we treated your client as a single individual. For insights into dealing with multiple clients, read Chapter 8, *Mapping Client Systems*.

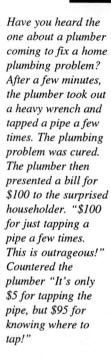

Have you heard the one about a plumber coming to fix a home plumbing problem? After a few minutes, the plumber took out a heavy wrench and tapped a pipe a few times. The plumbing problem was cured. The plumber then presented a bill for $100 to the surprised householder. "$100 for just tapping a pipe a few times. This is outrageous!" Countered the plumber "It's only $5 for tapping the pipe, but $95 for knowing where to tap!"

Ultimately, the only behavior over which you have direct control is your own.

SURFACING INDIRECT RESISTANCE

1. Give two good faith responses to your client's request for information.

2. Check your gut feeling and the client's nonverbal behavior.

3. State what you see happening, in as non-punishing a way as possible.

4. Be quiet; let the client respond.

WHAT YOU HAVE LEARNED SO FAR ...

- Why resistance is natural and expected.

- How to separate two types of resistance, direct and indirect.

- How to recognize indirect resistance.

- How to deal with indirect resistance, using a four-step model.

- How to apply the model, using an example of resistance.

- How to use long-term strategies to prevent this kind of difficulty.

THE EXPERTISE DELIVERY MODEL

11

*"If you think communication is all
talk, you haven't been listening."*
© *Ashleigh Brilliant*

CHAPTER 11

LISTENING SKILLS
FOR PROFESSIONALS

Quick Snapshot

Did You Know?

- many professionals are poor listeners?
- lack of listening skills is at the root of many consulting problems?
- there is a human process for error correction, similar to digital electronics?
- listening takes place at many levels—mechanical, active, empathic …?

How-to:

- understand and use listening as a professional performance enhancer.
- assess your own listening skills.
- listen at many levels, for many nuances.
- learn effective techniques to increase your listening skills.

The Bottom Line:

- You will have more influence and power as a professional by making effective use of the models, checklists, principles and skills of this chapter.

Listen to Me!

Listening skills are crucial to your consulting success. Listening is a key part of every consulting and interpersonal skill. Effective listening skills are required at every step of the consulting model. Our worldwide database tells us, however, that consultants, like most people, are not great listeners.

In this book, we make a distinction between listening and hearing. Hearing is hearing the actual words your clients are speaking, then making sense of those words. Listening is far more than hearing. Hearing and silent understanding—difficult enough for many—are only the first steps to listening. Listening is where you can demonstrate to your clients that *you have heard*, by a 'loopback technique' such as summarizing or paraphrasing.

Communication is not the message sent; it is the message received. Most of us assume that what is spoken is what is received. Listening ensures adequate congruence between the message sent by your clients and the message received.

Communication is a two-way process. The more clients and consultants feel they listen to each other, the stronger the relationship. *Active listening* involves making appropriate responses to client messages, clearly demonstrating you have understood. Active listening means actively checking that what you have heard is what the client meant. Active listening takes energy. The energy input can range from a nonverbal nod or brief "uh-huh," to helping clients identify and express emotion in a consulting situation.

Human Need for Listening
Listening is central to your success as an internal consultant and as a participant in human relationships.
- Listening is a crucial step of every interpersonal and communication skill.
- Listening is a powerful skill for building relationships; it's the basis of great relationships. Poor listening destroys relationships. Family counselors spend hours learning how to listen to their clients. They then spend additional hours helping their clients listen to each other!
- Clients are more likely to listen to consultants who listen to them.
- Listening is a powerful tool for reducing conflict. How often have we heard someone say *"If you would only listen ..."* in conflict situations. The simple act of listening can defuse many conflict situations.

Logical Need for Listening
- From a logical perspective, you cannot have an effective consultation without thoroughly understanding the problem and its data. Listening is the basis of rational problem solving.
- Ineffective consultants jump from what they think they have heard, to formulating solutions! Jumping to solutions is dangerous to your consulting career. Countless gaffes in organizations, worth thousands of dollars, are debriefed starting with words *"I thought you said ..."* or *"I thought you meant ..."* Listening means rarely having to say you're sorry. Effective consultants make sure that they thoroughly understand their clients' wants and points of view before giving advice or taking action.
- Listening is the other side of the coin to powerful questioning skills. In other chapters of this book, we discuss the need for consultants to ask good questions. There is no point in having excellent questioning skills unless you listen to the answers!
- Listening is the foundation for effective, win-win negotiation techniques. Any negotiation book will thoroughly reinforce this statement.

178

Electronic Need for 'Listening'

Listening means clearly demonstrating to your clients that you thoroughly understand their messages. The power of listening has close analogies to information processing. Communication protocols for computer modems have checksum procedures, which compare the number of bits of information received with what was sent. If the checksum numbers differ, the receiving computer requests that the block of misunderstood information be repeated. As you will see, one important listening competency is like a checksum procedure.

Electronic communication theory is built around how to effectively ensure that the message sent is the same as the message received, within an acceptable threshold of error. Human communication is built around a similar technique—active listening. Communication is a high energy state that requires continual energy to prevent disintegration into noise. A constant input of energy is required to reconstruct your client's message. The greater the complexity of the communication with your client, the more energy, in the form of listening, is needed from the consultant.

Just as a computer screen is redrawn hundreds of times per minute, powerful communications need continuous redrawing in the various forms of listening we will describe. A sharp computer screen image is produced by adjusting the brightness and contrast. Listening skills are the equivalent of brightness—clearly understanding your client's message—and contrast—helping your client sort out important information from background data.

If electronic systems, with precise bits, bytes and protocols, require multiple forms of 'listening,' how many more forms are required by human beings, who are prone to biases, unstated agendas, and have an imprecise language?

Consultant Need for Listening

Effective listening skills are required to execute every stage of the consulting model. A few examples for each stage are:
❑ Exploring the Need:
  • Listening to build rapport with clients.
  • Listening to understand clients' presenting problem.
  • Listening to help clients surface difficult underlying issues.
❑ Clarifying Commitments:
  • Listening to client wants.
  • Listening to build a win-win agreement.
  • Listening to negotiate effectively.
❑ Gathering Information:
  • Listening to clients during interviews.
  • Listening to help information sources relax and open up.
  • Listening to help clients express emotional or threatening data.
  • Listening to help clarify garbled data.
❑ Recommending Change:
  • Listening to client reservations and concerns with your proposal.
  • Listening as part of dealing with resistance.

11

Jumping to solutions without understanding the problem is like an eyesight professional, after hearing your eyesight concerns, saying "Here, take my glasses; they've helped me for years."

In this chapter ...

• *The benefits of listening.*
• *A seven-level model for listening, starting with the mechanics of listening, progressing to deeper listening.*
• *Many how-tos, hints and techniques for listening more effectively.*
• *The principles underlying the techniques of good listening.*

Listening is a powerful conflict prevention and reduction tool.

Information Theory shows that any communication is subject to error and degradation by entropy. Active listening is the simplest error correction algorithm ever produced for human interaction.

Why Is Active Listening So Powerful for Professionals?

- One of the strongest compliments you can give your clients is to show that you understand their message and point-of-view. Even if you disagree, most clients will respect differences if you demonstrate that you can understand what they are saying.

- Most consultants (and people in general) are poor listeners. From thousands of internal clients, peers, and managers who completed our *Consulting Skills Profile* survey for internal professionals, one more negative survey item is *'talks to others more than listens to them.'* Most consultants are more concerned about their own message than their clients' messages! That's why most clients respond so well to consultants with good listening skills.

- Most clients are also poor listeners. They expect from you what they may not give to you—active listening. They often don't feel listened to. One of the principles of effective consulting is the concept of modeling the behaviors you expect in your clients. You tend to get more effective listening by modeling effective listening skills. Conversely, clients will generally not listen to you unless you listen to them.

- The more clients and consultants thoroughly understand what they expect from each other, the greater the chance of commitment to consulting projects and their success, and the less chance of conflict.

Some professionals are loath to practice active listening because they fear that clients may take their paraphrase as acceptance. If this happens, you may wish to preface your paraphrase with "I'm not sure I agree, but let me first understand what you are saying."

Three Disclaimers

1. Listening is certainly powerful, but it cannot make recalcitrant clients fall to their knees! Your clients can range from those who are ideal, helping you consult more effectively, to those for whom no known (legal!) human behavior is helpful. At one end of the spectrum, your best clients model many skills—including listening—by example and by coaching. At the other end are the ogres. Ogres take listening responses as signs of weakness! If you are faced with these kinds of clients, you may wish to pursue some references in the *Selected Further Reading* at the back of this book on *Dealing with Difficult People.*
   Concentrate on the vast majority of clients, who try to communicate more effectively, responding to your improved consulting techniques. We are assuming a reasonable amount of goodwill on the part of your clients.

   One principle of effective consulting is that most clients will respond to effective consulting behaviors. You cannot directly control the behavior of your clients, but you can master effective behaviors for yourself.

2. Our second disclaimer is that this 'Listening Skills for Professionals' is a short chapter on a complex topic. Many books have been written on human communications, including listening skills. See the *Selected Further Reading* for reference suggestions on the wider issues of verbal communication. We are not asking you to be a psychologist or counselor. We are assuming that you are a professional wishing to improve your understanding and skills of the basics of listening.

3. Our last disclaimer is that many communication skills are culturally dependent. The techniques we are about to describe are based upon typical North American organizational life at the time of writing. These concepts and skills may not work well with people from other parts of the world. As organizations worldwide become increasingly multi-cultural, some of these techniques may not be appropriate. Later in this chapter, we will examine the principles underlying these listening techniques; these principles are less culturally dependent. See the *Selected Further Reading* for cross-cultural references.

Levels of Listening

Levels of active listening (listed beside the ladder below) range from the basic mechanics of listening, right through to listening for emotion. Each level builds on the previous one. You can enhance your listening at the most basic level by practicing some physical and mental mechanics. The highest level of listening is empathic listening—understanding and responding appropriately to the emotions of clients.

Cross-Cultural Listening Eight to ten seconds is the average pause before a response in many North American Aboriginal conversations (and in many other cultures), while two to five seconds is normal consulting time response.

STEPPING UP THE LEVELS OF LISTENING EFFECTIVENESS

7. **Actively listening for emotion.**

6. **Actively listening to the process.**

5. **Actively listening to the content.**

4. **Asking good questions.**

3. **Using appropriate silence.**

2. **Listening with your eyes and ears.**

1. **Using good mechanics for listening.**

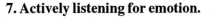

This seven-level listening model was inspired by David Godfrey.

LEVELS OF LISTENING SELF ASSESSMENT

Rate yourself from 1 = needs much improvement to 5 = a strength. If you are serious about improving your listening skills, after you've completed this self-assessment, ask a few clients and coworkers to rate you on your listening skills; then compare their ratings with your own.

1. Mechanics:

1 2 3 4 5 I do not allow the telephone to interfere with listening.

1 2 3 4 5 I know I can think faster than clients can speak. I use this time to understand and find patterns in my clients' words—not to prepare my response.

1 2 3 4 5 I make brief notes of what I want to say before the meeting so that I can concentrate on what my clients are saying.

1 2 3 4 5 I make brief notes during the meeting of how I want to respond, so I can keep my mind on my clients' words.

1 2 3 4 5 I seat myself in a way that encourages listening.

1 2 3 4 5 I keep a 'To Do' list on my note pad where I can list things to do, so I can keep my mind free to concentrate on my clients' words.

1 2 3 4 5 I realize most people can only keep about seven items in their short term memory.

2. Listening with my eyes:

1 2 3 4 5 I make eye contact early.

1 2 3 4 5 I maintain an appropriate level of eye contact.

1 2 3 4 5 I am conscious of my clients' nonverbal behaviors.

1 2 3 4 5 I use my clients' nonverbal clues to help me assess appropriate replies.

1 2 3 4 5 I am conscious of cultural differences in nonverbal behavior, particularly eye contact.

3. Appropriate silence:

1 2 3 4 5 I give my clients time to complete their thoughts.

1 2 3 4 5 I give my clients 'air time.'

1 2 3 4 5 I am conscious of, and OK with, silence periods.

1 2 3 4 5 I can remain silent to help clients formulate and state deeper thoughts and feelings.

4. Asking good questions:

1 2 3 4 5 I know how to use questions to show that I am listening.

1 2 3 4 5 I know how to use questions to help clients 'talk through' issues.

1 2 3 4 5 I am aware of a range of questions from closed-ended to open-ended, and know when to use them.

1 2 3 4 5 I formulate a questioning strategy rather than ask whatever pops into my head.

1 2 3 4 5 I am aware that I can ask questions anticipating answers which keep me in my 'comfort zone.'

1 2 3 4 5 I can use questions to help clients surface reservations or resistance to my ideas.

5. Actively listening to content:

1 2 3 4 5 I consciously use summarizing, and paraphrasing before I give my point of view.

1 2 3 4 5 I consciously ask for clarification if I do not understand my client.

1 2 3 4 5 I am aware of the difference between stating an observation and an evaluation.

1 2 3 4 5 I am able to name problems in a way that does not make them personal.

1 2 3 4 5 I can ask for clarification if I am uncertain.

1 2 3 4 5 I am aware of the difference between listening to content and listening to process.

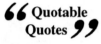
Quotable Quotes

"We have two ears and only one mouth, so we should listen twice as much as we speak."

– a common saying quoted by Robin Sober

"One pair of ears draws dry a hundred tongues."

– George Herbert

6. Listening for process:

1 2 3 4 5 I understand when to respond to process, that is, how my clients deal with concern (rather than content), and what the concern is about.

1 2 3 4 5 I have a repertoire of process tools for suggesting more powerful ways of dealing with consulting situations.

1 2 3 4 5 I am able to meta-communicate, that is, talk about what we are talking about.

1 2 3 4 5 I understand the power of framing and reframing.

1 2 3 4 5 I can help clients reframe when appropriate.

7. Listening for emotions:

1 2 3 4 5 I can 'hear' the emotion in my clients' words, voice, tone and other nonverbals.

1 2 3 4 5 I can listen by reflecting the emotion I hear.

1 2 3 4 5 I know when it is appropriate to make a listening response to my clients' emotion.

1 2 3 4 5 I know I cannot fix emotions, I can only help clients express them.

1 2 3 4 5 I do not suppress conflict or anger by changing the subject.

8. Listening as a whole:

1 2 3 4 5 I often ask for feedback on my listening skills.

1 2 3 4 5 I understand my own 'comfort zone' for dealing with ambiguity and conflict—at what point I feel the need to change the subject when my client's problem becomes complex or emotional.

1 2 3 4 5 I understand that all client behavior makes sense in my clients' frame of reference.

1 2 3 4 5 I use a wide range of listening skills.

1 2 3 4 5 I can give equal air time to myself and others.

1 2 3 4 5 I am considered an effective listener by others.

Any language where 'fat chance' and 'slim chance' mean the same thing, requires excellent listening skills!

LISTENING EFFECTIVENESS: ON-JOB APPLICATION PLAN

1. What are my listening strengths?

2. What are my listening needs for improvement?

3. Who can give me confirmation of my strengths and need for improvement by completing this Levels of Listening Self Assessment for me?

4. Who could give me day-to-day feedback or coach me with my listening skills?

This Assessment is on the Web Site: www.consultskills.com.

1. Using good mechanics for listening:

Active listening begins with good mechanics. Physical and mental techniques, easy to use and practice, are an essential foundation for the deeper level listening skills that follow. Let's start with these straightforward techniques.

a) Physical Mechanics
- *Where to meet?*
  If you meet in your own office or in a meeting room, you should think of the atmosphere. Where can you physically create a 50-50 atmosphere that is so important to consulting success? Below are some things you can do to create this atmosphere.

- *Desk, room arrangement*
  Sitting across a desk is certainly not conducive to a 50-50 relationship. Get out from behind your desk. A round table with similar chairs is best. Sit at an angle where you can keep eye contact with your client. Examine your meeting spaces:
  – Do they reflect the partnership you are trying to establish with your clients, neither one-up nor one-down?
  – Do your meeting spaces encourage your clients to relax and open up?
  – Do you know of convenient private meeting spaces where you can meet with clients to discuss difficult issues?

- *Distractions—telephones and computer displays*
  Distractions are easy to succumb to. Put your phone on *Automatic Answer*. Taking a call in the presence of clients is discourteous; many people consider it rude. Moving objects attract eyes and are distracting. Turn down, off or away your computer monitor. Check whether technical wizardry in your meeting space may intimidate clients, detracting from listening.

Listening intently is difficult at the best of times.

- *Distance*
  The comfort zone for most North Americans is arm's length when sitting, two arm's lengths when standing. Encroaching on these privacy zones, or distancing yourself beyond these guidelines, can be disconcerting to your clients.

Keep in mind that different cultures have different comfort distances.

b) Mental mechanics
- *Speed of listening vs. talking*
  A typical person can talk at about 150–200 words per minute. Your brain can process information at many times that rate. This makes the opportunity for mental distraction very high! The following items have some suggestions for capitalizing on the difference in rate between talking and listening.

- *Pattern recognition*
  Given differences in rates of speaking and hearing, you can profitably keep your mind occupied and on topic by listening for patterns. Listening for patterns means listening for the overall, macro communication pattern as well as for the micro detail of your clients' words. For example, do clients describe solutions more than problems? If your clients are continually focusing on solutions before clarifying the problem, you may intervene at a micro or a macro level.

- micro: help your clients express the underlying problem for the proposed solution.
- macro: discuss your clients' pattern of presenting solutions, explaining the benefits of first examining the underlying problem. Macro intervention has added potential benefit of more effective behavior in the future.

There are two benefits to micro and macro pattern recognition:
1. you keep your mental processes occupied on at least two levels
2. you create opportunities for more powerful interventions.

- *Short-term memory limitations*
Your clients will have difficulty listening to you if they are trying to remember even a few things they want to say. You can help your consultation by having clients do a data dump —saying aloud everything on their mind about the issue. Afterwards, your clients are more likely to have their short term memory available to listen to you. During the data dump you will want to briefly summarize to show you are listening. Use open-ended questions. Leave probing questions until the end. Probing questions may sidetrack you at this point. This technique is particularly powerful and appropriate when your clients are emotional.

This data dump technique is further enhanced when your clients' information is made visible. Use a white board or note pad, visible to both of you, to keep track of the items your clients raise. Don't worry about priorities or where to go with the information. The first stage is to get the information out in the open. Of course you, as a professional, can only keep a limited amount of data in your short term memory as well. Here are some techniques for you, the professional.

- *Note taking*
One way of clearing your mind for listening is to make notes of what is on your mind and what you want to say during the meeting. Make a few quick notes in point form about the consultation and any other priorities for the meeting. You want your short term memory clear for your clients' information. If anything pops into your mind during the consultation, jot a few key words in the margin of your notebook. The same goes for anything you want to say about your clients' views during the interview. Without note taking, when a few ideas pop into your mind, you will have a powerful urge to speak, just so you won't forget your ideas. Your needs and ideas can thus become more important than your clients'. Jot down your thoughts and reactions and let your clients continue talking so they clear their minds to listen to you.

If you anticipate that making notes may be annoying to your clients, tell them what you are doing and why. *"I would like to take notes so I am able to listen to your ideas when you are speaking."* Making your notes visible to your clients can be a helpful way of easing any tension about note taking. *One final hint, stop taking notes during emotional parts of the conversation.*

The average person can only hold about five to seven items in short term memory. Think of seven digits in a phone number.

You will remember particularly emotional issues. Don't worry about documenting them at the time. But do make notes soon after, if needed. (Average retention is 20 - 30 minutes.)

185

BENEFITS OF & TIPS FOR
MAKING INFORMATION VISIBLE

'A picture is worth a thousand words.'

A powerful form of listening is making information visible on a white board or a flipchart. Most experienced, effective consultants practise this.

✓ It cuts down on repetition. Clients know you've grasped the key points.

✓ It shows you've listened by what you've written.

✓ People will remember more. Written words and pictures increase retention.

✓ It helps people put otherwise unrelated things together.

✓ It is a memory aid.

✓ It is documentation for the meeting.

Some tips for making information visible are:

❏ Use short phrases, three to five words— key points only.

❏ Write just enough to be able to reconstruct the idea. *Do not try to write long sentences.*

❏ Use client's words wherever possible.

❏ Flipcharts are ideal because you can tear off the page and tape it to the wall so that all have the full range of ideas in view.

❏ If you are sitting with one or two clients, use a note pad to make information visible.

❏ If you are brainstorming, write up the idea first; later ask for clarification or discussion.

❏ If you are in a closure mode, let the participants discuss how to close *first*. Then write up the consensus and action plan.

❏ If spelling is a problem for you, abbreviate or put (sp?) next to the word.

2. Listening with your eyes and ears:

Research on human communication tells us that the actual words spoken by clients contain only about 10 -15% of the information conveyed. Much valuable information is contained in nonverbal aspects of the communication—tone of voice, rate of speech, eye contact, body posture and gestures. Much of this information is captured through your eyes.

• *Make eye contact, but how much?*
In the corporate world, eye contact is very important. In North American society, too little eye contact is often interpreted as unassertive at best; untrustworthy at worst. Most people are comfortable with eye contact spans of a few seconds. Much more than a few seconds may be interpreted as staring and uncomfortable. Less than a few seconds may be interpreted as furtive and can be distracting. But do keep eye contact when someone is speaking directly to you.

The norms for eye contact are culture-specific.

• *Cultural aspects of eye contact*
Eye contact is culturally dependent. In some societies, casting the eyes down is a sign of respect. Reciprocation of eye contact is helpful to establish a 50–50 relationship. Use approximately the same span and kind of eye contact that your client uses.

• *Body posture*
Body posture is often a good place for insight into a client's emotional disposition. But be careful with your interpretations. Arms crossed is often interpreted as aloofness or a closed

mind. Arms crossed can also mean *"I'm comfortable with you"* or even *"I'm cold."* Here are some things to look for and their common interpretations:
- not facing you—not wanting personal involvement, unable to face the situation.
- leaning back in chair—comfortable and feeling at ease.
- leaning forward—interested and engaged with you.

- *Gestures*
Gestures are an additional source of information. Wide, sweeping gestures are often a sign of openness and emotional engagement. Abrupt gestures or lack of gestures are often signs of discomfort.

- *Vocal cues*
The tone of voice is a rich source of information. If you can pick up the base line tone for your client's normal speech, you can assess differences against it. Increasing speed and raising the pitch of the voice often indicates stress or emotion. Lowering the voice against the base line tone often indicates the person is making a significant point.

- *Minimal listening responses*
Your minimal listening responses are the typical *'uh-huhs,"* *"I see,"* *"I understand,"* and nods. They are minimal but important. Particularly when a client is doing a data dump, you will want to show, with little interruption and minimal response, that you are tracking your client.

As we have stated, all nonverbal cues must be interpreted with care. They are only indicators of your client's disposition. Nonverbal cues are easier to interpret when you combine them with other cues like rational cues and the feeling in your gut. The principle here is not to outsmart your client, but to use all the observational techniques you can muster to assist your client in a 50-50 manner.

Tone of voice is a rich source of information

Overused, minimal responses like 'uh-huh' or 'I see' can be seen as mechanical, even a sign that you are not making a substantial effort to listen.

NONVERBAL CLUES: A SELF ASSESSMENT

Check off those non verbal clues you are usually aware of. Highlight those you need to be more conscious of:

Eye contact:
- ❑ Your own eye contact.
- ❑ Your client's eye contact.
- ❑ Amount of eye contact.
- ❑ Duration of eye contact.
- ❑ Cultural differences in eye contact.

Voice:
- ❑ Your own voice.
- ❑ Your client's voice.
- ❑ Pitch of voice.
- ❑ Rate of speaking.
- ❑ Inflection of voice.
- ❑ Variance in pitch or rate.

Body:
- ❑ Your own body position.
- ❑ Your client's body position.
- ❑ Leaning forward or back.
- ❑ Redness in the face.
- ❑ Tense or relaxed.
- ❑ Changes in body position.

Gestures:
- ❑ Your own gestures.
- ❑ Your client's gestures.
- ❑ Amount of gestures.
- ❑ Open/closed gestures.
- ❑ Change in amount or type of gesture.

3. Using appropriate silence:

Silence is Golden. Silence can give 'permission'—to elaborate, to process thoughts, to reiterate ...

Strangely enough, keeping quiet is a powerful form of listening— particularly if the client knows that you have something significant to contribute. Give your clients about 50% of the air time during a consultation. It's an excellent way of modeling a 50-50 relationship.

- *Typical silence times for normal consultations*
  Silent breaks between the time the client completes a thought and you start to speak are typically very brief. Many consultants break in, not allowing sufficient time for clients to complete their thoughts. For normal consulting communications, we recommend a two to five second break.

- *Typical silence times for emotional consultations*
  If your consultation has a lot of emotional content, longer breaks are appropriate. Why? First, longer breaks allow you to gather your thoughts to make a more thoughtful reply, as well as giving your clients time to express any further, often deeper, thoughts. Second, typical of emotional communications, your clients will not express all their emotional content at first pass. Allowing a substantial break before you reply allows clients to say more, to summarize, or to reiterate important points. The principle here is the greater the emotion in the communication, the more you will want your clients to talk it out— consequently the more you need to stay quiet and listen.

Equal to knowing what to say and when to say it is knowing when to keep silent and let the client think and speak. Another principle here is that silence can be powerful, especially if the client knows you have something to contribute. We are not advocating that you use silence as a weapon. We are advocating that you use silence to enhance your consulting skills for the mutual benefit of yourself, your clients and your organization.

4. Asking good questions:

Listening and questioning are two sides of the same coin.

A particularly powerful form of consultation is the *'Socratic method,'* honed to perfection by the ancient Greeks. It consists of asking questions of your clients in such a way that they come to their own analysis and solutions. Thoughtful questions convey to your clients that you are listening well. Besides demonstrating that you have heard and understood, a good question shows that you have thought through the impact of what your client is saying.

Questioning techniques outlined below are an abbreviated form of a more detailed discussion in Chapter 5, *Gathering Information*.

- *Question types*
  Questions can range from closed-ended questions to open-ended questions. The ultimate closed-end question elicits either a "yes" or a "no" response. We recommend you do not overuse closed-end questions because your clients will feel interrogated rather than interviewed. At the other end of the scale are open-ended questions. Typical open-ended questions are: *"Can you tell me some more?"* or *"Can you help me understand the big picture here?"* These kinds of questions are particularly powerful when you want to get your client to open up. Open-ended questions are also very helpful in emotional or conflict situations.

- *Questioning strategies*

  Both order and type of questions make a difference. Asking a closed-end question too early in a conversation can cause a client to clam up, yet asking closed-end questions to clarify a crucial point can be appropriate. In general, a good strategy is to ask open-ended questions at the beginning of a consultation to get your client to open up. At the point where you feel you have the big picture, turn the corner and ask closed-end questions to narrow problem scope and plan specific action. Open-ended questions are particularity helpful in emotional or conflict situations.

- *Questioning outside your comfort zone*

  One of the most subtle forms of *not* listening is to restrict your questions to your personal comfort zone. If your expertise is in personal computer systems, your tendency will be to ask questions which assume personal computers are the solution to client problems.

  Especially as an inexperienced professional, you will feel very uncomfortable when you realize that your set of expert solutions isn't going to solve a particular client's problem. For example, if there are personality problems embedded in the client's presented concern, not many professionals feel comfortable questioning about personal conflict which lies outside their comfort zone.

  We don't mean to pick on technical specialists here. Most professionals—most people—only listen to what they want to hear. As a consultant, you may be unaware of this tendency. We tend to ask questions that get the answers we prefer. To listen to all aspects of the situation equally is rare and the sign of a powerful professional.

  Most consultants find it difficult to listen to reservations that a client may have to proposals or recommendations. After you have helped clients express their reservations, make a listening response before responding to the concern. The rationale for surfacing conflict, resistance, and concerns is dealt with in Chapter 10, *Dealing with Resistance*.

The next three levels describe how you can effectively listen to client responses.

It is fair to say that most consultations fail not because of what consultants know, but of what they don't know!

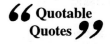

"... a man hears what he wants to hear and disregards the rest."
– Simon & Garfunkel song 'The Boxer.'

MORE CROSS-CULTURAL CONSIDERATIONS

"In the West professional/technical competence comes first, trust and relationship, maybe later. In the East trust and relationship is the major priority, with technical or professional competence coming later. ... [Also] business is carried out through lines of connectedness, relationship and influence."
– Mel Blitzer
Consultant
Bangkok, Thailand

LEVELS OF LISTENING SUMMARY

1. Using good mechanics of listening:

a) physical:
- Distance
- Desk, room arrangement
- Which office?
- Distractions: telephones, computer terminals, etc.

b) mental:
- Clearing the mind for listening
- Speed of listening vs. talking
- Pattern recognition
- Short-term memory limitations
- Making notes of what you want to say both before and during the meeting.

2. Listening with your eyes and ears:
- Body posture: the talker and listener
- Gestures: yours and your client's
- Vocal cues
- How much eye contact?
- Cultural aspects of eye contact.

3. Using appropriate silence:
- Typical silence times for normal consultations
- Typical silence times for consultations with emotion.

4. Asking good questions:
- Question types
- Questioning strategy
- Questioning outside your comfort zone.

5. Listening to the content:
- Restating
- Summarizing
- Parroting
- Paraphrasing
- Asking for clarification
- Solving the problem vs. 'naming to blame'.

6. Listening to the process:
- Listening to how the issue is being dealt with
- Naming the process
- Proposing a process to deal with the content
- Framing/reframing.

7. Listening for emotion:
- Listening to the emotion of how the content is being presented
- Listening with empathy
- Defusing anger and conflict in order to move to rational discussion
- Solving the problem versus emotional reactions
- Empathy is a key to influence.

66 Quotable Quotes 99

Management guru Stephen Covey, in his book The 7 Habits of Highly Effective People, advises us to understand first, then seek to be understood.

'To be understood as to understand'
— line from hymn

5. Actively listening to the content:

The content is the *what* of the problem, the process is the *how*. By *content* we mean the technical or business part of the problem, the facts; distinct from the *process*—how the problem is being solved. The bread-and-butter technique for professionals is actively listening at the content level.

- *Restatement or parroting*
  Restatement is the simplest form of active listening—repeating back to your client what was said, using the client's words: *"So what you're saying is ..."* The more significant the statement of your client, the more you need to restate, to show you have heard the words.

- *Paraphrasing*
  Paraphrasing is a more powerful form of active listening than restatement because you *do not use the client's words*. Paraphrasing is restating, this time in your own words, what your client just said. Clients are reassured their core messages got across and were processed when they hear their ideas expressed in new words.

- *Summarizing*
  Summarizing means formulating a summary of your client's major points. A notch up in the listening scale, this form of active listening is a must when making commitments; also at the end of any meeting. You can approach this technique in a straightforward manner: "In summary, we have agreed to ..."

Restatement, paraphrasing and summarizing techniques have two powerful benefits:
  i. Clients are assured that their message has reached you
  ii. They give clients a chance to check their own messages.
Sometimes, after a consultant has paraphrased, clients will say something like *"When you put it that way, I'm not so sure ..."*

- *Asking for clarification*
  Asking for clarification has benefits as well. In helping clients express themselves more clearly, you will be clearer on your client's point-of-view. Clients will know you are listening, if you ask for clarification of unclear points. Often professionals have unrealistic expectations that clients, especially senior managers, should be totally clear and understandable at all times.

- *Asking for a summary*
  If your clients have presented very complex or convoluted information, ask them for a summary. You will usually benefit by getting a clearer and more concise statement; your clients will benefit by clarifying their own thoughts. If you see your consultation as a 50-50 project, you do not have to take 100% of the responsibility for communication.

- *Naming the problem vs. naming to blame*
  In organizations, we often hear what we call 'name-to-blame.' Typical groups named with generalized problems are: *Management, The Engineering Problem, The Maintenance Problem, Personnel Issue, The Systems Problem*, or just *THEY*. Help your clients and help yourself by asking for specifics of the problem. Specific statements lead to specific solutions. A great question for professionals under many circumstances is "Can you give me an example of ...?"

Understanding does not mean agreement.

In an elevator, a senior executive of a large manufacturing company chatted with a Human Resource professional. The executive asked "How's it looking for the summer jobs program?" Without further clarification, the HR professional sent a brief report on the summer jobs program to the executive. Seeing the work that had gone into the report, the executive reacted with angry surprise, "I didn't want a report. I was just wondering whether there would be a job for my son!"

Content Bound!
Many professionals think and talk mainly in terms of their own expertise. They are content bound. As someone said "I don't know who invented water, but it probably wasn't a fish."

- *Observation vs. evaluation*

  An annoying habit of many professionals is to reply to clients in an evaluative way. It's important to listen in an observational way before making any evaluative responses. Read between the arrows below for the difference between evaluation and observation.

Listening to content is the stock in trade of professionals. Consultants are naturally inclined to pay attention to content, through their professional training, knowledge, skills, methods and language. In fact, most professionals and clients are blinded by content—they are content bound. Professionals often get so immersed in the content of the problem that they forget about the next two levels of listening—how the problem is being solved, and the emotions of their clients. Read on for assistance in these two areas.

DIFFERENCE BETWEEN OBSERVATION AND EVALUATION

Evaluating with a listening response creates difficulties with clients. Clients do not like to be evaluated; they like to be heard and understood. This does not mean you cannot be evaluative with your clients. In fact, we encourage you to clearly and directly state your evaluations. *But only after your have made a non-evaluative, observational response.*

Look around your location right now.
1. Note the nuances of color, textures, angles, levels of light and shadows around you.
2. Now ask yourself whether you like those shades of color, textures, angles and level of light and shadows, as you are experiencing them in this location.

#1 asked you to observe your environment. #2 asked you to evaluate your environment. It is extremely important that you first listen by observation before you make any remark which evaluates what your client is saying. Clients are much more willing to hear evaluative comments when you have demonstrated that you understand what they are saying.

LEVELS OF LISTENING
ICEBERG

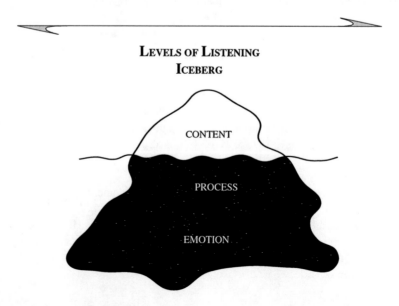

6. Listening to the process:

Listening to process means listening to *how* a client is solving the problem—steps being taken to encourage a solution to emerge. Many technical specialists find even short process discussions uneasy, preferring to stay in comfortable content, showing professional prowess—by jumping to causes, solutions and action. Actively listening to *client process* as well as to content, however, allows the professional two ways to intervene: (i) by providing good content advice, and (ii) by providing effective process suggestions.

- *Listening to how the issue is being dealt with*
  At the early stages, processes to solve a problem are often vague or not yet identified; that is, clients have either thought little about *how* to solve their problem or have assumed a single method for solving it. If you listen, then summarize the implied process as you hear it, you are in a better position to discuss process alternatives.

- *Naming the process*
  When the process is breaking down or going around in circles, a powerful listening intervention is to name what is happening and, if possible, some process alternatives. For example, if clients are repeating themselves and getting worked up emotionally, you might intervene with "It seems like we are going around in circles and getting upset with each other. Can I suggest we … ?"

  This form of listening is called meta-communication—communication about how a group is communicating. It is particularly effective when you and your clients are moving toward conflict. By making a process intervention, you can lead a discussion one level up from the content and then move back down. "I don't want to lock horns here. Is there a way of recognizing and resolving our differences before we move on?"

- *Framing/reframing*
  A particularly creative form of active listening is to acknowledge client response, then suggest a reframe; that is, put the situation in a different context. In a reframing mode your active listening response might be "So you are looking for solutions in the area of … can I suggest we also look for solutions in … ?"

FRAMING & NAMING TO BLAME

Framing the concern incorrectly can result in failure to solve the right problem, as we see in this example of a problem presented to a team learning Process Improvement Team Leadership Skills. A problem was initially framed as 'Hourly Worker Attendance,' implying hourly workers were the problem ('naming to blame' the hourly workers).

After much confusion, frustration and wasted time in the Process Improvement Team, the problem was reframed to: (i) shoddy attendance record keeping, and (ii) poor supervisory skills for dealing with attendance problems. The frustration of the team stemmed from the original problem frame. One can only speculate how much grief and expense organizations have gone through when incorrect problem frames sent people off 'to fix the problem' in the wrong area.

*Please can you listen to what I am **not** saying?*

More information on the powerful skill of reframing is contained in Chapter 3, Exploring the Need.

7. Listening for emotion:

At this level you listen for emotion, implicit or explicit.

No matter how bizarre their words or behaviors may appear to you, clients will always have a rational explanation for those words and behavior

- *Listening for emotion of how the content is being presented*
  No matter the concern—accounting problems, systems difficulties, maintenance concerns— clients will have emotions about the situation. A typical client will have difficulty expressing the emotions of the situation, while most professional specialists, when they sense anger and conflict, want to avoid it. This makes for an awkward situation on both sides. Since you can process information at a faster rate than your clients can speak, another way to use this extra processing time is to listen to the emotion of the situation. For this, you need to tune your ear to emotions. A way to encourage expression of emotion is to name them: "It *seems that you get frustrated when ...*" It is difficult to problem solve rationally before emotions have been vented.

When emotions do come out:
1. Do not fix! Professionals are inclined to want to fix. Normally this disposition is very helpful. With emotions, it is not. If a client is angry because your staff group has gone over budget, you cannot fix the anger. Clients must own and come to terms with their own emotions themselves.

2. You *can* help your clients vent their anger and get on with a rational process for solving the concern. You do this by: (i) helping your client express emotion, and (ii) reflecting *back* the emotions you hear: *"You appear angry about the budget problem ..."*

Empathy is not sympathy. Empathy means understanding the client's underlying emotions. You do not have to agree. Sympathy is agreement and can lead to dependencies.

- *Listening with empathy*
  Empathy is the skill of seeing a situation from a client perspective. It *does not* mean you have to agree with client's point-of-view. It is *not* sympathy. It does mean you can understand why your client would feel that way, given the assumptions your client is making. Metaphorically, professionals must be able to walk in their clients' shoes.

Skills of listening with empathy and helping your clients express emotion are the culmination of the seven levels.

INTENTION AND EFFECTIVE LISTENING

Effective listening assumes these elements of intention:
- *You have to want to hear.*
- *When you listen, you are changed. Are you willing to be changed?*
- *You must start from a position of respect for the other person's opinion or you will only go through the motions.*
- *Most of all what you really want is to be listened to. The currency for this is to listen to the other first.*

– George Campbell

ACTIVE LISTENING TECHNIQUES

Listening occurs at many levels, from mechanics to emotions. You, as consultant, need a wide repertoire of listening responses. Powerful professionals have acquired a wide range of listening skills and have learned when to use them. Here are some examples:

11

Technique	Purposes	Typical lead-ins
Neutral	• To show you are interested. • To encourage your client to continue talking.	✓ "mmm …" ✓ "That's interesting." ✓ "I understand; I see."
Restatement & Paraphrasing	• To check your meaning and interpretation against that of your client. • To demonstrate that you are listening and that you understand what your client is saying. • To encourage your client to analyze other aspects of the situation and to discuss them with you.	✓ "As I understand it, your plan is …" ✓ "You have appear to have decided to …" ✓ "So your reasons for favoring this option are …"
Summarizing	• To bring the discussion into focus. • To clarify priorities. • To help you and your client agree on major points.	✓ "The key ideas you have expressed are …" ✓ "If I understand how you see the situation, your major points are …" ✓ "In summary, we have agreed to …"
Clarifying	• To get at additional information. • To help your client explore a problem.	✓ "I'm not sure I understand, could you clarify what you think about … ?" ✓ "Do you mean … ?" ✓ "I don't understand, give me an example …"
Naming the Process	• To understand how the situation will be dealt with. • To formulate a different method for dealing with the issue. • To propose a method for dealing with the issue.	✓ "As I understand it, you are proposing that we first gather data …" ✓ "You have proposed I gather information on the issue, can we clarify the issue first?" ✓ "You have given me a lot of data about the problem; can we now talk about how we can go about solving the problem?"
Empathic	• To show that you understand how your client feels about the situation. • To help your client vent feelings.	✓ "You appear to feel that …" ✓ "You seemed shocked when you heard …" ✓ "You seemed let down when …"

Listening is More Than Techniques

We have presented a wide range of listening skills. These skills must be based on sound principles. Unless you have sound principles, your listening techniques will seem stilted and awkward at best; manipulative at worst. The principles of effective communication that relate to effective listening are:

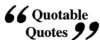

Quotable Quotes

"When rational, intelligent people that you respect seem to be taking irrational, illogical positions, it's time to ask yourself whether you have heard what was said correctly."
– Bob Ratay

Active listening has the dual benefits of keeping you out of trouble and helping you do the right thing.

To be able to assist your clients, you must understand their point of view.

- Communication is not the message sent. Communication is the message received. Always check that what you have heard is what your client meant to say. This principle is career enhancing.

- Only a fraction of communication is conveyed by words. The rest is conveyed by voice tones, body language, etc. Listening is more than listening to words.

- The best way for you to get your clients to use more effective behaviors with you is for you to model the behaviors you expect in others. If you want to be listened to, you must develop and demonstrate that you, yourself can listen effectively.

- The best consulting relationships are 50-50, a win-win, a partnership. Your techniques must be based on achieving and maintaining a 50-50, win-win atmosphere. Techniques used to manipulate clients into saying "yes" to something they don't need, will ultimately lead to other problems. Techniques which lead to one-upmanship and games are counter-productive in the long term.

- Listening is so powerful that you can use these techniques to win the trust of clients. What you do with this trust is crucial. Often, clients are distrustful of professionals because they have been burned in the past by opening up. To misuse client confidence will ultimately lead to problems both for you and for any other professionals who try to work with your clients in the future.

- No technique of human behavior works 100% of the time. Most clients will respond to effective consulting techniques. A few will see your listening skills as a weakness. We recommend you 'take the high ground' here. Good principles and techniques will be effective in the long term for most clients in most organizations. Don't let the few who use your empathy dissuade you from using this skill with most people who deeply appreciate it.

- Every client behavior, no matter how bizarre it may appear to you, has a rational basis in your clients' minds. If you can get your clients to speak 'off the record,' they will always have a rationale for their behavior.

Recursion: The Touch of Powerful Professionals

Finally, all communication skills, including listening, are recursive. The concept of recursion comes from mathematics and computer science. Recursion involves self-reference: for example, if you want your clients to listen to you, you must effectively listen to them; and you must listen to them listening to you, and so on. Recursion makes human communication a particularly rich area for continuous and deep learning. If you have used recursive functions, you know there are no limits to their depth, except the ones you impose. We wish you well in launching a particularly rich and unending search around the skill of listening.

Completing the Loop

You may wish to reassess your listening skills by redoing the *Levels of Listening Self Assessment*, page 182.

Recursive functions are those which call upon themselves as part of their solution!
For example, we are now communicating about communication. We could not write a good chapter about listening without having listened to professionals like you—our clients!

WHAT YOU HAVE LEARNED SO FAR ...

- Listening is vital to your professional success.

- Listening is more than hearing.

- Listening can be done at many levels:
    1. Using good mechanics for listening.
    2. Listening with your eyes and ears.
    3. Using appropriate silence.
    4. Asking good questions.
    5. Actively listening to content.
    6. Actively listening to process.
    7. Actively listening for emotion.

THE EXPERTISE DELIVERY MODEL

> *"Even if you're on the right track, you'll get run over if you just sit there."*
> *– Will Rogers*

CHAPTER 12

ENHANCING YOUR ROLE AND CAREER

Quick Snapshot

Did You Know?
- you can enhance your role by asking your clients better questions?
- starting roles may later become limiting roles?
- professional career growth is nonlinear, with need for dramatic changes?

How-to:
- assess which role is most appropriate for a situation, not getting trapped in any role.
- choose and adapt your role from a range of roles.
- understand how professional careers grow in influence, power and satisfaction.

The Bottom Line:
- You will be a much more powerful and satisfied contributor to your organization's success by using effectively the models, research, and checklists of this chapter.

Role, Role, Role Your Boat?

In this chapter we will deal with role issues first, then careers—although they are connected. Should you wish to bypass discussion on roles and go to a discussion of professional careers, turn to the section 'Key Career Questions' on page 205.

A crucial issue for professionals is role. If you want to be a powerful professional, you need to have a powerful role. These principles and examples are sprinkled throughout this book:

Role Principle	Further Information
There are natural times to explicitly negotiate roles: • one is during the *Clarifying Commitments* step, where you clarify many elements of a consultation.	Chapter 4, page 47
• another is at *Recommending Change,* where you make recommendations, and propose how you can best be involved in the change.	Chapter 6, page 81
• another powerful time is, strangely, at *Closing/Taking Stock.* Particularly if the work has gone well, you have much leverage to propose role improvements.	Chapter 7, page 107
You have most power over your role at the very inception of a project. Taking a narrow definition of a client's problem results in a narrow role for the professional. Offered a complex problem definition, trying to simplify it too quickly also results in a narrow role.	Chapter 3, page 23
A role is assumed in every question you ask and every statement you make. For example, if you ask a series of narrow questions, you are telescoping to your client that you are narrowing your role and vice versa. Powerful professionals do not necessarily need to negotiate roles. As the word 'role' implies, they just act them out.	Chapter 5, page 65
Professionals often blame their clients for what they do to themselves, saying "They won't give me those kinds of roles." While certain kinds of managers and clients may be threatened by powerful professionals, we challenge you to look first to yourself to change before looking to others to change.	Chapter 15, page 257
The most successful and enduring long-term role is that of business partner, a 50-50 relationship in your area of expertise. Long term, you neither want to be one-up nor one-down to management and clients, but considered a business partner in your area of expertise.	Chapter 1, page 6

A professional role derives from the problem frame:
large frame, large role;
narrow frame, narrow role.

In this chapter, we will propose these additional professional role principles:
- The role best suited for a starting professional—often a pair of hands role—is a tender trap. From research, we will show that what it takes to be successful at a certain role level often entraps you there.
- Role flexibility is important. Sometimes you will need to be a pair of hands and do what you are told. At other times you will need to push hard to establish an advocacy role. Powerful professionals have developed a strong role strategy, and role flexibility within it.

In the next chapter, *Your Strategy: Saying Yes or No*? we will look at roles from another important perspective—connecting your valuable knowledge and skills to the success of your organization.

12

... Gently Down the Stream: The Tender Trap?

The best way to initiate a new relationship may, over time, create relationship problems. (This is true of consulting, and of life. Anyone married for more than a few years has experienced this!) Here are two examples:
1. The New Professional
   A neophyte professional, new to an organization or a position, needs to begin in a pair of hands role, working under the guidance of others. For that period of time, the need to be dependent can be frustrating for many professionals. Even as an experienced professional, if you switch organizations or departments within your organization, there will be a start-up period where you'll need lots of coaching from people around you. Dependence on this guidance, however, should not deter you from shaping a future, more powerful role.

2. The New Client
   Professionals can unwittingly collude with their clients by deferring discussion of a more powerful role. Experienced professionals have asked "Isn't the best way to get started with a new client to do what you are asked and not rock the boat? As I become more experienced, I will question more and ask for what I want." Yes and no. Often this strategy is a trap. Without any challenge, even at the very first meeting, clients will tend to pigeonhole professionals into a pair of hands role.

Taker, Maker or Shaper?

Strategically, professional roles can range from:
- 'Role Taker,' where professionals accept, or even expect, client-determined roles, through to
- 'Role Maker,' where professionals tell their clients what their role is—take it or leave it.
- 'Role Shaper' is where the role is negotiated in the spirit of partnership, considering what's best to accomplish the task at hand.

We strongly recommend the Role Shaper role as the only long-term, satisfying one for both professionals and clients. While some professionals never move beyond a pair of hands, Role Taker orientation, others may choose the 'expert consultant' Role Maker orientation as a frustrated response to a one-down feeling to line management. On occasion, professionals need to take a role as offered. In other situations, they need to be authoritative and tell the client exactly what needs to be done. This is the best long-term and most satisfying role—that of a strategic professional partner with your clients—the Role Shaper.

In this chapter ...

- *Why a broader context is needed for your skills*
- *Roles and role strategies*
- *The four levels of professional career development*
- *Implications for a professional*

201

ROLE STRATEGY:
TAKER, SHAPER OR MAKER

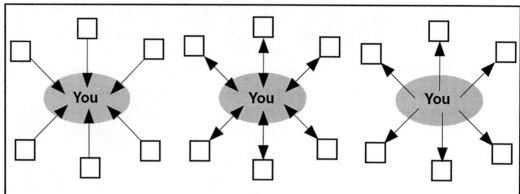

The role that is easier to get started is often the role that causes a professional difficulty.

Role Taker	Role Shaper	Role Maker
• Professionals expect clients to determine their role.	• Professionals work with clients to determine the best role for the situation.	• Professionals tell clients their role.
• Pair of hands role: "You know best."	• Partnership role: "Together we know best."	• Expert role: "I know best."
• Dependency.	• Interdependency.	• Independence.
• Usually difficult to change once the norm is established.	• Best long-term role.	• Often leads to client resentment.
• Basic stance: "Tell me ..."	• Basic stance: "Let's work together..."	• Basic stance: "I'll tell you ..."
• Appropriate for new professionals.	• Best long-term strategy.	• Can be very efficient.
• May be helpful with new clients, but be cautious.	• Takes time to establish and maintain.	• Necessary in emergencies or in dangerous situations.
• Clients often blamed for limiting professional role.	• Both parties feel reasonably equal and satisfied.	• May be a reaction to feeling one-down.

Two Concrete Examples: Taker, Maker or Shaper?

A Regional Manager of a large retail chain said of Information Systems (IS) professionals from Head Office, "When a new IS professional comes into the region, either I myself, or one of my managers, is happy to spend some time helping the new analyst understand our operations. I am no IS expert and need advice on the best use of Information Technology (IT) systems. If, however, the professional continues to expect me to 'hold his/her hand' I get annoyed, because we need value-added advice. On the other hand, the real *problem* IS people are those who come in and try to tell me how to run my business. That's my job! I need to understand how IT can help us, but our own management needs to make the decisions and live with them. We need both inputs on the table—IS and Operations. The best IS professionals understand this give-and-take approach."

Safety Advisors is one example of a segment of professionals who have difficulty with the Role Shaper role. We choose this example because it is easy to understand the transition difficulty. Safety is not a matter of choice; it is legislated and can be a matter of life and death. In a new consultative or advisory role, Safety Advisors often retain their expert stance—crucial in emergencies—and frustratingly try to tell management and others how to run a safe organization, rather than being more consultative and helping them take shared responsibility for safety. The expert, Role Maker orientation does not accomplish many of the longer term goals for a safe operation, where managers and employees willingly and knowingly *themselves* take responsibility for the safety of their operation.

A Role on the Range?

Within the long term Role Shaper strategy, professionals can temporarily assume a variety of roles, depending upon the nature of the problem and the needs of the situation. The table on the next page summarizes a Range of Roles and when they might be best used. This is followed by an Application, giving you a chance to reflect on your role and how you might improve it.

> Powerful roles need to be put into two even wider and longer term contexts:
> 1. professional career—the subject of the balance of this chapter
> 2. professional strategy—the subject of Chapter 14, *Your Strategy: Yes or No.*

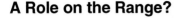

ROLES AND CONTROL

"When it comes to internal and external consultants, clients appear to have a perception barrier: the client expects to be in control when dealing with an internal professional, yet, in a parallel situation, expects an external consultant to take charge! As long as we, as internal professionals, allow the client to control the process, we will continue to play a pair of hands role. As soon as we take the initiative to control the process, we immediately define our own roles, where we can propose priorities and be most effective. By being in control of the process, we can benefit the client, no matter what the issue or problem."

Bill Sefcik, CPA
Consulting Skills for Professionals workshop instructor.

A RANGE OF ROLES

Non-Directive
- help clients help themselves
- help with the process, the 'how'
- facilitator of others

Directive
- help clients with expert answer
- help with the content. the 'what'
- expert advice

Sounding Board /Clarifier	Facilitator	Problem Solving Partner	Educator Trainer	Technical Expert	Challenger/ Advocate	Regulator/ Enforcer
Observes, gives feedback, raises questions, and helps reframe concerns.	Provides process suggestions to help clients find their own answers.	As a partner, participates in the problem solving process with clients.	Helps clients develop new knowledge and skills.	Provides expert information and solutions to clients.	Actively promotes and sells solutions to clients.	Provides 'governance,' protects integrity of the system in area of expertise.

This model is adapted, with assistance from Janet Mairs, from a model developed by Ronald and Gordon Lippitt.

ON-JOB APPLICATION: ROLE

1. In a typical month, which role(s) would you use most often?

   Least often?

2. In which role(s) do you feel most comfortable?

   Least comfortable?

3. Which role(s) are the best to provide value-added service for your clients? Why?

4. Which role(s) do your clients expect from you?

5. If there is a discrepancy between #3 and #4, how could you negotiate a more congruent role?

Key Career Questions

All the skills of this book are for naught unless they fit into the bigger context of your professional career.

Ask yourself: "Will the perspective and skills of a powerful professional presented in this book
    a. help me to be a more valued contributor over the long haul?"
    b. help me with a more satisfying career as a professional?"
Step back with us for a look at professional careers.

Four Levels: Management Elevator; Professional Stairs?

A general assumption is that professional career growth takes a linear path. Becoming more specialized and more efficient within a professional expertise is not enough. Gene Dalton and Paul Thompson in their landmark book, *Novations: Strategies for Career Management*, cite research showing highly productive (and personally satisfied) professionals progressing through four nonlinear, discrete levels. Each level is a quantum leap, requiring a new outlook and different skill sets. Specifically, high performing professionals widen perspectives of their role from that of specialist—where their success is personal success, to a more leveraged role—where their success is the success of others. Dalton and Thompson also found that high professional performance is strongly correlated with increasing project complexity. In other words, as you become a more powerful professional in your organization, you can expect to lead increasingly complex projects.

Most professionals peak in productivity around mid career (note the word 'most,' not 'all'), say Dalton and Thompson. They also present research data showing that some professionals can continue to increase leverage and productivity over their whole careers. What is their secret? Research is clear: as their experience increases, those professionals who continue to be productive fundamentally change the way they look at their role.

Many professionals decry the lack of good models for professional career development. We now present such a model for your use—straightforward and practical.

In this chapter, we will use an adaptation of Dalton and Thompson's research and combine it with our own database—what we have learned from working with over 6,500 professionals—to produce a practical, powerful way to look at your career as a professional.

Powerful professional careers move through four discrete levels of performance:

1. **Apprentice Professional**—learning how things work in the organization.
2. **Independent Professional**—contributing by individual professional work.
3. **Contributing Through Others**—levering professional contribution through others.
4. **Organizational Consultant**—leading the organization with a professional skill.

Many professionals are caught in Level 2 and, for a variety of reasons, do not move to Level 3. This book is about moving toward broader, more leveraged Levels 3 and 4 perspectives in your career. The purpose of this chapter is to help you position your consulting skills in a more powerful context, thereby developing a successful and satisfying career inside your organization.

12

Many of the ideas in this chapter are inspired by the work of Paul Thompson and the late Gene Dalton, and their book, Novations: Strategies for Career Management. See Selected Further Readings for a description of the book.

Career Levels and Professional Contribution

Why does professional value increase with levels? Because movement through the levels is synonymous with increasing leverage, influence, and impact on the organization.

Level 1—The Apprentice Professional: Depending on Others
- All professionals start their careers in Level I, the 'apprentice' level, where they do more of the detail and routine work of the organization, relying heavily on others for guidance and support. Professionals effective in Level 1 experience rapid personal and professional growth that enables them to make the quantum leap into Level 2.

Level 2—The Independent Professional: Contributing Through Expertise
- The minimum level expected of most professionals.
- In career Level 2, professionals become experts in their particular specialty or technical area and have earned the right to work independently. Working on professional problems without much supervision, they rely on their peer network if they do need help on a complex problem.

Level 3—The Master Professional: Contributing Through Others
- In Level 3, professionals start to contribute through others. No longer rated solely on what they can do individually, their value is now more determined by how well they help and coach others to contribute in their area of expertise.
- Professionals make more significant contributions here than in a Level 2 role, as they learn to leverage the work of others in making change happen.
- Often a difficult transition for professionals to make, Level 3 requires renegotiation of roles, in how professional projects are conceived and completed. In Level 2, professionals preferred to have projects structured, tidy and neat. Level 3 professionals, however, need a broader view of client problems and ways of solving them. One difficult characteristic of this level is that problems are often more ill-defined and complex, resulting in the need to deal with complexity and ambiguity not faced in Level 2.
- It is imperative that professionals understand the differences between Level 2 and Level 3 roles in order to successfully negotiate role expectations with clients. In Level 3, professionals look well beyond their personal expertise for resources. The difference between these two approaches to projects usually nets significantly greater results for clients, because of the breadth of viewpoint and leverage of resources involved at Level 3.

Level 4—The Organizational Consultant: Leading the Organization Professionally
- In Level 4, professionals have a broader and more substantial impact through their ability to lead an organization in their area of expertise. They influence organizational direction and impact major organizational decisions within their professional specialty, usually without having the direct control typical of executive positions.

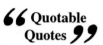

"All the professional expertise I have so painstakingly amassed needs to be given away in Level 3! It's one thing to be expert yourself, it's another to help others be expert."

– an engineer

Learning the skills of Level 3 can lead to considerable job satisfaction.

Discontinuous Career Progression Example

As an example of this discontinuous career progression, newly graduated Systems Analysts typically start careers as programmers in Level 1, responsible for parts of larger projects under the guidance of more senior professionals. After a period of time, which can vary from a few months to a couple of years, the more experienced professional will be expected to take over specific projects, e.g. database applications, and do professional quality work. Through Level 2, the person will probably become more specialized, more of an expert.

For the transition to Level 3, the *key change is from amassing expertise in Level 2, to giving it away in Level 3!* Now expected to be database project leaders, professionals in Level 3 are expected to coach others in database expertise. They are also expected to interact with multiple clients from problem definition to resourcing. Some professionals find difficulty with this transition from working independently to working interdependently. After a number of years in Level 3, however, some professionals become database 'gurus' in Level 4, helping the whole organization with database strategies.

What is rewarded at one level can be the problem at the next.
- Rewarded at Level 1 are dependency and asking "Tell-me-what-to-do-boss" questions.
- At Level 2, specialization and individual excellence is rewarded. Clients expect professionals to figure things out independently, requesting coaching as needed.
- The reward at Level 3 is not one's own success, but rather helping others be successful.
- The reward at Level 4 comes less from working with groups and clients, to working to influence strategy of the organization in one's area of expertise.

Good News, Bad News and Mixed News

We have selected three from our many stories to illustrate some professional career issues. Variants of these kinds of stories exist in every profession.

Terry
As a chemical engineer joining a multinational petrochemical company, Terry's first role was to help with the design of part of a new oil production facility. Rotated though a number of clearly Level 1 engineering functions for the first two years, Terry worked under the guidance of a number of senior engineers and project leaders. After 19 months, Terry joined the Facilities Engineering Section as a Facilities Engineer, performing specific projects, often as part of a project team and was told "ask for help when you need it."

Over the next five years, Terry worked as an individual contributor, typical of Level 2. Toward the end of this period, Terry became worried as first rate performance ratings dating back to engineering school began to plateau, then wane. Terry became uneasy about career choices and began to look around, thinking, "Although I like the work, do I want to do this for the next twenty years?" Terry's manager started asking for 'more leveraged work.' Reluctantly, Terry began to lead project teams, thinking "I don't like all this people stuff and meetings. I don't have time to do the engineering I was hired for." Terry was frustrated at the pressure of the transition from Level 2—the independent professional, to Level 3—the leveraged professional contribution.

We will deal with the issues of this very common transition problem later in this chapter.

Lee

After five years of previous experience with a competitor, and with an MBA in Finance from a prestigious business school, Lee was hired into a financial institution . Tension was evident from the beginning. Trying to apply management school theories, Lee was critical of the style and direction of management, saying "There are many improvements I would make if I were in charge around here. Management is back in the Dark Ages." Lee did not assume the Level 1 role of a dependent learner. Behind Lee's back, coworkers would say "Lee's a real pain in the butt— just doesn't understand how things work around here, always wanting to change everything." After a stormy six months, Lee settled down into Level 2 and became a great financial analyst.

The career model of this chapter will help you understand when and how to be dependent on others.

Pat

Hired into a management position by the forest regulatory agency of a national government, Pat had worked for nine years in a wide range of Level 2 roles, learning all there was to know about forestry, in a small consulting firm as a Forestry Consultant. Pat expressed frustration with the first few month in the government agency, saying "Between all these meetings, learning new government procedures and the like, I have no time to apply my expertise."

Hired as an excellent Level 2 professional contributor, Pat was nevertheless expected to contribute in the new position as a Level 3—Contributing through Others. Pat did not delegate professional work well because he felt he knew it better and would love to be "out in the woodlot again." Watching growing frustration, a wise Agency Manager took Pat aside and said "Pat, you have to stop trying to be the best forester around here! Your role is to help others be as great a professional as you are. Remember your new skills when you left forestry school? Well, there's a new skill set for this new job. I can coach you on these skills, if you'd like." Pat has now happily made the switch from Level 2 to Level 3—a rewarding role of coaching less experienced professionals become excellent foresters.

The career model in this chapter will outline changes you need to make, and the rewards you will accrue, if you wish to make the transition from Level 2 to Level 3.

Level 2 to Level 3—"Don't Compete. Inspire!"

When professionals are asked to think of their best-ever project leader or supervisor and their worst, the characteristics that they state indicate that the best have their heads and hearts at Level 3: their success was your success. The worst, of course, had their heads and hearts at Level 2: seeing you as a professional competitor!

One sure way you know a person is in Level 3 is when that person stops competing for technical excellence and contributes by helping others be technically excellent.

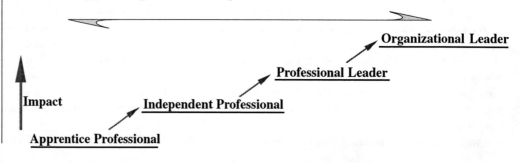

208

THE FOUR LEVELS OF CAREER DEVELOPMENT FOR PROFESSIONALS

Level 1 **The Apprentice**	*Level 2* **The Professional Expert**	*Level 3* **The Professional Leader**	*Level 4* **The Organizational Leader**
'Learning the Rules'	'Establishing One's Reputation'	'Helping Others be Successful'	'Helping the Organization be Successful'
• Willingly accepts supervision and direction.	• Works independently and produces results; amasses expertise.	• Sees own success as the success of others; gives expertise away.	• Shapes strategic direction of the organization in professional area.
• Demonstrates competence in a portion of a project or activity overseen by more senior professionals.	• Assumes responsibility for a definable portion of the project, area, or clients.	• Develops and influences others: as a project leader, a consultant, a coach to more junior professionals.	• Effectively exercises professional power for the benefit of the organization by initiating and influencing decisions in area of expertise.
• Effectively performs detailed and routine work.	• Demonstrates technical competence, credibility, and a reputation for good professional work.	• Demonstrates a breadth of professional and business understanding and insight.	• Uses the tools of the organization to set strategies and to obtain organizational commitment and results.
• Shows directed creativity and initiative.	• Relies less on the supervisor or mentor, develops his or her own expertise to solve technical problems.	• Represents the professional work group to internal clients, other work groups, industry associations, middle management.	• Acquires sponsors for projects; sets new professional directions; mentors and coaches others for key roles in the organization.
• Is a good learner within a professional group.	• Builds collegial relations with coworkers and peers.	• Builds a strong network of organizational and industry relationships.	• Represents the organization both internally and externally.
• Is a junior member of a consulting team.	• Negotiates and contracts fixed projects with clients.	• Builds relationships with a range of clients.	• Has senior management/ executive clients.
• Expects others to contract with clients and define work.	• Expects *others* to market professional work to clients.	• Leads consulting teams; markets to clients.	• Consults and leads the organization in professional area; markets to organization.
• Assists others with their results.	• Produces individual results.	• Leads group results.	• Produces organizational results.
• Expects others to think strategically in area of expertise.	• Contributes to the strategies formulated by others.	• Formulates strategies for groups.	• Formulates organizational strategies in area of expertise.

12

209

Level 2 Lament—'But I Love What I Do Professionally ...'

It is OK to remain a professional specialist at Level 2, but you will often get pressure to contribute through others at Level 3. In addition, you will have to forego some rewards that others receive when they move to Level 3. Many professionals are satisfied with Level 2 careers and do not want the increased responsibilities of Level 3, saying "Just let me do my job," or "I love what I do." Most organizations require the largest group of professionals to be in Level 2. The difficulty often comes with longtime Level 2 professionals feeling unrecognized and unrewarded, saying "This isn't the organization I started with. Those political types (Level 3) are a pain in the butt and don't do anything." Performance appraisals, which in recent years placed great value on professional work, are now slipping.

What can a professional do who wants to stay at Level 2?
- Make a conscious choice to stay in Level 2 and forfeit recognition and rewards afforded those in Level 3.
- Discuss this career choice with management so they understand you and what you want.
- Continue to keep your professional knowledge and skills sharp.
- We have heard of many professionals who find Level 3 satisfaction outside their organization by, for example, organizing and leading volunteer organizations.

Implications and Applications

Implications of the discontinuous Four Levels career model for professionals are:
- If professionals want to *remain highly valued* by their organizations and clients over time, they have two options: be technically brilliant (a 'super Level 2') or leverage the contributions of others (Level 3). Expectations of others change as professionals progress in their careers. Professionals have to learn to leverage the contributions of others to satisfy increasing expectations over time.

- Trying to *skip a Level can undermine credibility*. Professional reputations and credibility are built in earlier career levels. Performing well in your current job is the foundation to future opportunities. Starting to perform the activities of the next higher level is the best way to be considered for a promotion.

- Sometimes *recycling is necessary* between jobs and levels. In order to move to the next level, professionals may need to broaden their areas of expertise by moving laterally. A new role in a new location for a Level 3 contributor can lead to revisiting Levels 1 and 2 to once more reach the contribution of Level 3. Experience shows that once you have made a particular level transition, it is much easier to do the second time.

- *Coaching and mentoring assist development* at all levels. Coaching helps a professional learn to work effectively through the informal systems of the organization. It also provides feedback essential to ongoing growth and progression. Developing within a level or making a Level change, a professional can really benefit from coaching—especially when moving from Level 2 to 3, or from 3 to 4.

- Movement through the levels requires *giving up completely some work and responsibilities while taking on others*. It can be scary letting go of proven skills and approaches and venturing into unproven areas, but necessary for a productive and satisfying professional career. Discuss these intentions with your management to ensure they are aware of, and value, your higher level activities.

- *Promotion is NOT the only way to gro*w, nor to maximize personal satisfaction. Level changes can take place independent of promotions. Usually level change precedes promotion. While management positions may be limited in an organization, there is virtually no limit to the number of informal Level 3 and 4 individuals an organization can utilize.

- *Job assignment is critical*. Think back in your career. Where did you learn your most valuable lessons? Probably while you were engaged in a challenging job that forced you to stretch. Career Levels Model research indicates that job assignment, or what you make of a job, is the sole factor that best correlates with continued high performance.

- What makes professionals *successful at one level can become the millstone preventing progress to the next*. Valued and rewarded dependency of a good learner at Level 1 needs to be discarded in favor of taking responsibility for the independent sources of learning at Level 2. This independence must in turn be discarded in favor of interdependence and helping others to learn at Level 3. Finally, at Level 4 you must help your organization to learn what it needs to be successful in your area of expertise.

12

❝ Quotable Quotes ❞
"Success is getting what you want, happiness is wanting what you get."
– Dale Carnegie

GRAY HAIRS VS. WHIZ KIDS

In a group of self described 'gray hairs' in a major multinational company, a senior engineer bemoaned the fact that he was still a 'slide rule aficionado,' feeling threatened at times by the latest 'whiz kids' who sneered at the slide rule and told him about the latest engineering support software and work stations. His engineering colleagues came up with this list of what the 'gray hair' Level 3 engineers had that the Level 1 and 2 'whiz kids' did not:
- *They know how things work around here.* They know the system, "how to stick handle an idea through the corporate defense."
- *They know Who's Who around here.* They know who to involve to get the job done, ranging from which senior managers are key, to who has what skills for the project.
- *They know how to get funding and budgets around here.* They know how to access money and get projects approved.
- *They know how to marshal groups and teams.* They know where the resources are; internally, in other divisions, in other staff groups and externally.
- *They know the politics of the organization.* They know who can work together and who cannot. They know how to 'smooth ruffled feathers.'
- *They know how to make new knowledge and skills work in the organization.* They understand 'how things really work around here."
- *They are not threatened by complexity.* They don't try to have engineering problems 'fit the textbook mode.' They understand how to take a fuzzy concern through to sustained change.
- *They have a great network.* They can 'cash in favors' when necessary.
- *They know when to take things seriously and when to 'back off.'*
Gray hairs—and Level 3—sound like fun!

There is a huge difference between five years of experience and one year of experience repeated five times.

THE CAREER JOURNEY: APPRENTICE TO MASTER CONSULTANT

Level 1: Apprentice Professional—The Budding Consultant
- Sees success as learning and contributing to the professional work of others.
- Needs work clearly defined by others.
- Needs and wants coaching.
- Needs and wants unambiguous, clear and structured projects.
- Wants others to take leadership and risks.
- Learns under the guidance of others.

Level 2: Independent Professional—The Specialist Consultant
- Sees success as own individual professional or technical contribution.
- Wants to specialize, to become the expert in a knowledge or skill area.
- Is able to do professional work independently.
- Prefers to leave people leadership to others.
- Sets standards by observing peers.
- Wants a rational, unambiguous world; is not comfortable with 'soft' issues.
- Needs to remain at the cutting edge of expertise to remain highly valued.
- Can be threatened when new experts work in the same professional area.
- Expects clients and professional managers to take care of the business side of expertise.
- First order internal consulting: making yourself successful.

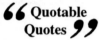

Quotable Quotes

"You become successful by helping others become successful."

*– Bob Ratay
Avery-Dennison*

Level 3: Leadership Professional—The Levered Consultant
- Makes him/herself successful by making others successful.
- Takes on broader professional leadership roles.
- Works through others to get the job done.
- Is not threatened by others' technical/professional expertise.
- Is able to give all his/her hard earned expertise away—others seek his/her opinion.
- Admits he/she doesn't know everything.
- Is OK with unstructured situations.
- Has lots of process tools available; uses those that fit.
- Doesn't expect a rational, unambiguous world; is able to deal with 'gray' issues.
- Is willing to work with issues outside his/her area of expertise.
- Is always willing to learn both technical and process skills.
- Is able to market professional expertise.
- Has mid-level managers as clients.
- Second order consulting: helping other Level 2 consultants be successful.

Level 4: Organizational or Business Consultant—The Guru Consultant
- Sees success as making organization-wide impact in his/her professional expertise.
- Looks long term and strategically at the impact of professional expertise on the organization.
- Is seen as expert outside his/her organization.
- Sponsors, mentors and coaches individuals and groups in expertise.
- Consults with senior managers and executives on the strategic use of professional knowledge and skills.

Career Levels and The Expertise Delivery Model

How does this professional career model tie back to the Expertise Delivery model? Glad you asked!

Step	Level 2 The Professional Specialist	Level 3 The Professional Leader
1. **Exploring the Need**	• Expects others to have thought out the business need and strategy. • Sees problem as having only a technical solution. • Asks self: "Can I do the job or not?" • Tends to want to keep the problem and role narrow.	• Sees the problem needing an organizational as well as a technical solution. • Gets well below the surface concern to root causes. • Asks self: "Who can do the job? What piece, if any, is mine? Who else needs involvement?" • Tries to determine how this concern fits with business and professional strategies. • Looks down the road with the client to the implications of introducing change.
2. **Clarifying Commitments**	• Clarifies role for self only. • Sees role either as expert or pair of hands.	• Clarifies roles for many players. • Determines who else needs involvement or commitment. • Sees role as broker of expertise.
3. **Gathering Information**	• Tries to keep complex problems unambiguous. • Expects client(s) to define priorities and roles.	• Is OK with ambiguity. • Expects to be a partner with client(s) in defining priorities and roles.
4. **Recommending Change**	• Sees self as presenting technical solutions and recommendations—change is client's problem. • Expects that professional logic will sell the recommendation. • Emphasizes technical features. • Sees only immediate client system.	• Sees self as presenting organizational solutions. • Is concerned about commitment. • Expects professional and business logic will sell the recommendation. • Emphasizes features and benefits. • Sees complex client system needed for change. • Shares in change process as appropriate.
5. **Taking Stock/ Closing**	• Tidies up technical parts of the project. • Doesn't use successes to improve the leverage of the role.	• Takes responsibility for wrapping up the project. • Assures that results will be sustained. • Values follow-through to improve strategy. • Asks for feedback. • Thinks how to turn success into a stepping stone to an improved relationship and more consulting work.

WHAT YOU HAVE LEARNED SO FAR ...

- A powerful role is critical to a powerful professional.

- Role flexibility is important. Professional roles can range from Role Taker to Role Maker to Role Shaper—the last being the best long term professional role.

- Professional careers do not proceed in a straight line (as a continuous function) over time but in discrete levels (as a discontinuous function), as described by the Four Levels of professional growth.

- What is helpful and rewarded at one level often becomes a millstone at the next.

- Your leverage, impact, contribution as a professional and personal satisfaction all increase as you progress through the levels.

- The minimum professional level of contribution for a consultant is Level 2. High performing professionals contribute at least at Level 3.

- To contribute at a higher level, you need to change your role. For example, if you want to be recognized as a Level 3 professional, you need to take on group leadership roles and help others be successful.

THE EXPERTISE DELIVERY MODEL

> *"What is the use of running when you are on the wrong road?"*
> *– German Proverb*

CHAPTER 13

YOUR STRATEGY: SAYING YES OR NO

13

Quick Snapshot

Did You Know?
- most professionals don't view their work strategically, yet blame management for the consequences?
- many clients don't know how you, as a professional, can add value to their business?
- professionals unable to say "no" end up doing low value work?

How-to:
- determine which work will create most value.
- know which work is best done by you and which work is best done by others.
- say "no," while continuing to help your clients.
- bring in external resources effectively.

The Bottom Line:
- You will be able to do more powerful and more valued work. In this chapter, you will find models, on-job applications, examples and worksheets to help you do this.

Things Aren't Like They Used To Be

The stark reality is this: either professionals get aligned with the strategies of their organization and the strategy of their clients, or they will be marginalized outside the 'real work' of the organization. Or worse, they'll be outsourced—replaced.

Professionals in organizations are working harder and more diligently than ever. Yet never before has there been more work insecurity, threat of job loss, and work stress. This chapter will address precisely what is wrong with this picture, giving you tools to align your profession and your professional group so that you are valued, recognized and considered key to the lifeblood of your organization. The foundation of such a powerful role is strategic thinking.

Strategic thinking means:
- Thinking long term about the direction of your organization.
- Thinking long term about the direction of your profession.
- Thinking long term about the direction of your career.
- Determining how you add value to your organization.
- Determining what you say "yes" to and what you say "no" to.

How professionals are viewed by others in their organization can vary considerably. For example, Information Technology professionals can go from being referred to as 'nerds' to being seen as key resources in integrated information systems; finance professionals, from being called 'bean counters' to being thought of as financial managers for business units; Human Resource professionals, from 'touchy-feely' to being valued as executive coaches for organizational change. Which view others take of you is mainly up to *you*, the professional, not up to management. Professionals who say "Management doesn't make good use of us" just don't grasp the whole picture.

Invest Wisely!

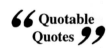

Quotable Quotes

"Helping myself is even harder than helping others."
– Gerald Weinberg

Consider the resources that you have to invest in your consulting efforts: time, effort, energy, and a balance of work with personal/family life. You need to invest these precious resources wisely. Investing wisely means being strategic—that is, being aware of:
- the direction of your organization (if you are unsure about this, read on.)
- the pressures of the environment in which your organization is situated; the resulting pressures on, and direction of, your management.
- the direction of your profession and professional group—how that direction can add value to your clients and to your personal direction.
- your personal direction.

Presently, you may not be aware of all of these directions, yet you need to make good long-term and short-term directional decisions without full information. This chapter will help you do just that.

'Yes' and 'No' Are Key Strategy Words

To be strategic means thoroughly understanding what to say "yes" and "no" to; as well as which of your professional services you must market. To be considered a valued contributor over your whole career, you must regularly re-evaluate how well your work directly supports the strategy of your organization. Strategic thinking requires professionals to be able to say "no" to low-value work. Often professionals *know* they should say "no," but feel pressured or obligated to say "yes." Saying "no" can be difficult, especially if you have had a valued relationship with a client in the past, or if you have a particular desire to do the kind of work that you are turning down. Professionals cannot say "no" successfully, until they know what they should say "yes" to.

Keep the End In Mind

Your goal is to do work which is:
- ✓ valued by your organization
- ✓ valued by your clients
- ✓ satisfying to you personally

This chapter is designed to help you do all of these.

BALANCED, QUALITY WORK

On A Clear Day, You Can See ...

In one organization, professionals challenge each other with questions such as the following, requiring them to draw a 'line of sight' between a work activity and the organizational strategy:

"What is the direction your organization and clients and what contribution are you making to help them be more successful?"

"Can you see a 'line of sight' to your organization's strategy for everything you do?"

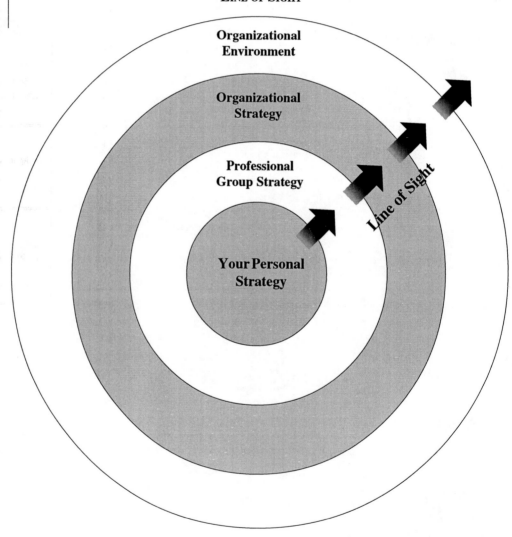

LINE OF SIGHT

Organizational Environment

Organizational Strategy

Professional Group Strategy

Your Personal Strategy

Line of Sight

This model is on the Web Site: www.consultskills.com

THE EXPERTISE DELIVERY MODEL IN A STRATEGIC CONTEXT

13

Organizational Strategy & Environment

Professional Group Strategy & Marketing Plan

Individual Professional Strategy

Taking Stock or Closing

Exploring the Need

Recommending Change

Client Commitment

Clarifying Commitments

Gathering Information

Feedback Systems

Career Development as a Professional & Consultant

Quotable Quotes

"I won't hire a human resource professional who doesn't regularly read a business newspaper."
– A Human Resource manager

This model is inspired by the work of the Novations Group.

Building a Strategic Model for Professionals

We have developed a model specifically designed to help professionals better judge where to concentrate their efforts. Little is currently written on professional strategies, yet in order to remain valued contributors over time, all professionals must think strategically about their contribution.

Our model, however, does not come ready made! We build it piece by piece, using examples. The best insights occur when we put it all together and show how the completed model is actually used.

Part Ⓐ—The Heading at the Top of the Model
> ➧ *Professional Contribution to Organizational Strategy*

We will start building the first piece of the model below. To do this, we need to consider two factors which make up your *Professional Contribution to Organizational Strategy*.

    Ⓑ High Value-Added work   Ⓒ Business Necessity work.

Ⓑ We define Value-Added work as key to the current success of your clients and your organization. Clients see the connection between Value-Added work and their own success. It is visible and clearly hinged to their success.

Ⓒ We define Business Necessity work as must be done, it keeps your client's organization running smoothly but does not add to your clients' future success. It is often called 'base business':

 ✓ every professional role has a fair chunk of it, and it must be done.

 ✓ someone must do it, and there is an automatic expectation that it will be done.

 ✓ it must be done well; it must be done on time. *Yet those who do it well rarely get much*

  recognition.

PROFESSIONAL STRATEGIC MODEL

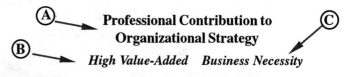

		High Value-Added	Business Necessity
Technology & Expertise	*Unique to/ Best Done by Professional Group*	4. Market!	1. Maintain
	Generic/ Can Be Done By Others	3. Coach or Broker Out	2. Refer or Contract Out

Nobody Notices It Unless It's Not Done!

To illustrate how Business Necessity is distinct from Value-Added, in our workshops we conduct this exchange:

"How many of you received your last four pay remittances on time and completely correct to the last penny?" All put up their hands.

"How many of you telephoned or wrote a note to payroll thanking them for such amazing accuracy?" Sheepishly, no one puts up a hand.

"How long would your organization run if payroll decided not to do this kind of unrecognized work?" *"Not long"* is the response.

(Note that this Business Necessity work is expected, often must be done to a high degree of accuracy, but is usually just expected. We have heard many professionals say they don't even look at their pay notifications—they just assume they are correct!)

"How many of you have ever received a pay notification that was incorrect?" A few hands go up.

"How many minutes did it take before you phoned payroll about the mistake?" (No comment!)

In most organizations, payroll is the epitome of Business Necessity! There is no question that Payroll is business necessity work that must be done. However, carried out consistently by a professional, it won't lead to a powerful professional role. The key question is this: *What business necessity work should done by you and your professional group?* We'll answer this question a little later in the chapter.

The Safe Road may not be the Best Road

Still, many professionals say "We are so busy with Business Necessity that when Value-Added work opportunities come up in our organization, we often outsource that work to external consultants." What a pity! And what a disastrous effect on the credibility of the professional group. Who gets the rewards and recognition? The external group of course!

Chris, a communications professional, takes up her new position in an organization. While becoming oriented, she is happy to smoothly continue the department's routine communication tasks, for example, an internal employee newsletter, corporate donations, event planning and such tasks. Chris does these Business Necessity tasks so well that nobody notices!

The organization announces a merger. Chris is excited about the challenge of her department being a key player in this high-profile event. To her dismay, and that of her professional group, senior management hires an outside communication firm to handle communications around the merger!

Replay:
How could Chris have ensured that her professional group was considered for this important work? As soon as she became oriented, Chris could have drawn a line of sight from each of her department's projects to her organization's strategy. This would probably have led her to challenge and redirect, to outsource or let go, much of the routine business necessity work in order to propose and start work on more strategic projects. Content with her Business Necessity work, senior management did not see her as a 'strategic partner.' By the time of the merger, Chris's department could have become known for its strategic value-added work in this area. Instead, her department was so busy with business necessity tasks...

To make a difference, uncover, market and perform work that has high impact in your organization.

13

Are You Spinning Your Wheels?

Safe is not powerful.

Ironically, professionals can actually collude in their own demise by choosing the safe road. Could it be that professionals and/or managers take the safe road by default? Business Necessity work is by nature generally safe, routine and regular. Value-Added is by nature more exposed and risky.

If *you and your professional group* have not seriously sat down in the last six months to hammer out what is Value-Added work and what is Business Necessity, we can almost guarantee that you are caught up in lower value work—or worse—nonessential work. Note our use of italics in the last sentence. This strategic thinking is always best done in teams, where you get the input of all professionals and commitment to unified action.

But Which is Which Kind of Work?

Professionals often argue about whether work is Value-Added or Business Necessity. If the activity has been done much the same way for a year or more, it is probably now considered Business Necessity by your clients, even though it may not have started out that way.

Viewed strategically, the same work can fall into either category. 'Compensation,' for example, can be either Value-Added or Business Necessity. If Compensation is carried out using the tried and true compensation methods in your organization, then it is Business Necessity, but it can be Value-Added if you are deliberately, strategically using compensation as a way of attracting and retaining the best in your industry.

Part Ⓓ —The Left Side Heading of the Model
➡ *Technology & Expertise*

In the 'Technology & Expertise' axis of the figure on page 223, we distinguish between two kinds of work:

Ⓔ—work which is uniquely best done by you or your professional group. This is work that must be staffed, or is best done by employees in your professional group because of skills required, security, legislation, policy, or because the work is proprietary to your organization. In other words, work that is very difficult to have done by others.

Ⓕ—work which is generic or could be done by others, either inside or outside your organization. This is work which can be done by others, either inside or outside your professional group.

Here is a vital question to pose within your professional group: *Are you doing work best done by you and your professional group, or could it be done by others?*

- More and more professional work is being outsourced. Carrying out most generic work yourself—being considered 'generic' by line management—is a risky way to be seen, a potential death knell for many internal professional groups.
- Many professional groups are finding people *inside* the client's organization, who can do much of the generic work. This raises the modern need to coach and train others in professionals skills—once the territory of managers.

PROFESSIONAL STRATEGIC MODEL

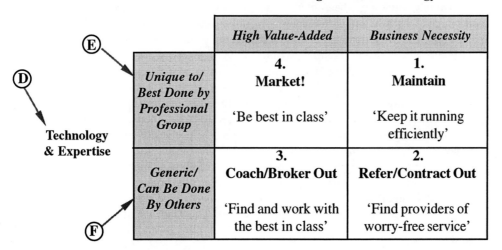

**Professional Contribution to
Organizational Strategy**

		High Value-Added	Business Necessity
	Unique to/ Best Done by Professional Group	**4.** **Market!** 'Be best in class'	**1.** **Maintain** 'Keep it running efficiently'
	Generic/ Can Be Done By Others	**3.** **Coach/Broker Out** 'Find and work with the best in class'	**2.** **Refer/Contract Out** 'Find providers of worry-free service'

Ⓔ
Ⓓ
Technology & Expertise
Ⓕ

The Inner Workings of the Model
➥ *Maintain, Refer, Broker, or Market!*

Now that we have explored the outside of the Professional Strategic Model, let's explore the four inner quadrants of the model.

1. Maintain:
At the intersection of Unique and Business Necessity lies #1, the 'Maintain' quadrant. This is work that is Business Necessity, that is, it needs to be done and done well by the internal professional group.

For better or worse, here's where much professional work is done. For better, because the work is required by the organization. For better, because it can be used as a springboard to higher-value work. Many professionals have pointed out to us that if you don't do this work well, you don't get a chance to do more value-added work. For worse, it takes up most of your time and effort. For worse, you don't get much recognition. For worse, managers will question your contribution!

That leads to our recommendation for Maintain work—keep it running efficiently; use minimum resources. *Efficient* and *minimum* are key words. Here is where professional groups need to fine tune their processes so quality work is done with least resources and at lowest cost.

13

❝ Quotable Quotes ❞
"Just as our industry is being deregulated, so is professional work."
– A manager in a large utility

"Human nature is to spend the most time on what we know best and have done longest. That's why we must constantly challenge ourselves to give up the routine for the strategic."
– Bob Ratay Avery-Dennison

223

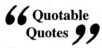

66 Quotable
Quotes 99

'Better to be safe than sorry'? In fast moving organizations 'It's better to be UNsafe than sorry.'

"Internal consultants often get frustrated when the high value-added work goes to external consultants. They complain of not being perceived or treated as valuable consultants like the externals are. Typically the reason is because internals do not look for opportunities and market their services—thus they are never perceived as adding value to projects."

– Bill Sefcik, CPA

2. Refer/Contract Out:

'Refer to Others' means referring this kind of generic, Business Necessity work to others inside the organization. This may require professionals to train and coach others.

Much current outsourcing has been focused on this quadrant. For example, most IS/IT groups have outsourced what was often done internally in the past—basic computer skills. Generic computer training is often done better and more cheaply by external resources. Much of the success of outsourcing has been letting go of this kind of generic work—to service providers outside the organization—to allow internal professionals to take on value-added work.

Professionals in traditional internal staff roles often find this contracting out disconcerting, complaining bitterly "This isn't the organization it used to be." Generic, Business Necessity work appears safe and is comfortable for many. Freeing themselves of generic work can free professionals to get on with the work they really need to do—Value-Added work—another step towards being considered a powerful professional. Our recommendation in this quadrant is to find others who will provide worry free service. If a client calls, you want to be able to say "Talk to so-and-so and they will take care of that." You don't expect to hear from that client again because the need was well met behind the scenes. This leads us into the next quadrant.

3. Broker Out/Coach:

It is crucial to distinguish 'Refer/Contract' from 'Broker/Coach.' The table on the next page summarizes the differences.

When a client calls you with a need in the Refer/Contract quadrant, you quickly *refer* to others. In the Broker/Coach quadrant, when a client calls for a High Value-Added, but Generic need, you will want to *broker* it rather than refer. To Broker Out successfully you need to work with the client and service provider, face-to-face, to ensure that the problem is correctly defined and expectations properly clarified (i.e. carry out at least the first two of six steps of the consulting model). Here you are acting as a 'broker' finding and bringing to the client the resource needed. In order to remain a part of these Value-Added, high recognition activities, you will wish to be at least a minimal part of the project team.

In many ways, the Broker/Coach and Refer/Contract quadrants can be most challenging—and most rewarding. Challenging because:
- You need to give away high Value-Added work to others.
- You may need to coach others—which takes scarce time and energy when it may seem easier and quicker to do the work yourself.

Rewarding because it sets up a 'second level,' much more leveraged consulting practice—one in which when clients call, you are in a position to determine how the work is defined, who will be involved and how quality will be maintained. We fleshed out this powerful role more thoroughly in Chapter 12, *Enhancing Your Role and Career.*

Key issues for professionals around Broker Out/Coach are:
- You have thought through beforehand which work is high Value-Added but won't be done by you.
- When Broker Out situations arise, you know where the 'best in class' resources are externally and you will work with them so you can do this Valued-Added work in the future.
- If the brokered professional resources are internal to your organization, you may need to train and coach them.

	Value Add	Necessity
Unique	4. Market	1. Maintain
Generic	3. Broker	2. Refer

- You need to be able to explain clearly to your clients why your professional group has chosen not to fulfill these needs, yet why you wish to stay involved with the project. (Your own reasons for staying involved are for learning, sharing recognition and quality control.)

DIFFERENCES BETWEEN BROKER OUT/COACH AND REFER/CONTRACT WORK

Activity	*Broker Out/Coach*	*Refer/Contract Out*
The client calls asking for assistance	Explore the need with the client. Offer to find and bring the resource to the client.	Explore the need and refer the client to the resource.
Your involvement	Use your consulting skills to ensure the project captures high value.	Very little or none.
Your personal learning	Keep an appropriate role in the project for quality control and for recognition You will want to learn from the professional resources hired.	Very little or none.
Follow-through	You will be part of the project review to assess your brokering choices and to receive part of the recognition for a job well done.	Periodically, you will want to get feedback and recontract with the resource for improvement.
Your professional capabilities	Know where the best resources are available for high value-added work. Be able to coach other professionals in consulting skills.	Know where the best resources are available for generic, Business Necessity work.
Your professional strategy	Have thoroughly considered beforehand what high value work will be done in the group and what to broker.	Be able to train others if necessary.

13

4. Market!

We consciously chose the title 'Market!' for this quadrant. Who is in the best position to know how you and your profession can contribute Value-Added and Unique work to your clients? You and your professional group, of course!

Before you meet with clients at all, you need to establish and clearly understand your organization's direction, your client's pressure points and direction, and what, for you, is your own professional Value-Added work.

Work in the Market quadrant tends over time to 'drain out' into Business Necessity and other quadrants. This is because what was originally innovative work becomes an automatic expectation. The 'Market' quadrant needs constant replenishment to be kept full. Since clients do not necessarily know how you and your professional group can value-add, **you need to market these activities.**

Professional groups often say "Let's go out and find out what our clients want." Seems like the right thing to do? WRONG! We argue that if you go out and ask the average client "What would like from us?" the average client will mainly ask for Business Necessity work. This is because clients are familiar with these activities and because they need Business Necessity activities to keep their organization humming.

66 **Quotable Quotes** 99

"Sometimes clients don't see/think of ways you can provide value-added activities—they don't know what they can get if you don't let them know! You are in the best position to know your clients' direction and possible needs, as well as knowing what you can do."

– Robin Sober
The Mutual Group

225

Some IT professionals in one organization said "Aha! This model helps us understand why our IT managers act the way they do. They are still treating work which was Market work when they were professionals (before they became managers) as if it still is in that quadrant today." Remember that Value-Added work does not remain static.

The next chapter, Marketing Your Skills Inside Your Organization, contains a wealth of resources on how to market your professional skills.

Should you happen to ask what they want and they request Business Necessity work, you have just raised expectations that you will do the work. Clients can rightfully say "You asked us and we told you. Now you don't want to do the things we asked."

If you offer where you can add value, then it may be appropriate to approach your clients about what they want. "While considering what you may want, here's what we can offer …" Using the session as a negotiation session, you and your clients can agree on a good balance among the four quadrants of the Professional Strategic Model. 'Market!' is where you need to be 'Best in class,' 'Powerful professionals' and 'Professionals of choice.'

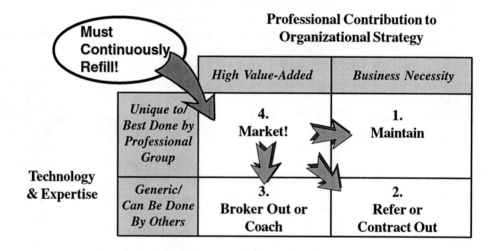

It Takes All Kinds …
'Market' Versus 'Maintain' Personalities
At first blush, the optimum professional group might appear to have *every* professional in the group do a balanced mix of Market and Maintain activities. Some individuals, however, are more suited to and 'turned on' by Market work. Others, by nature, are happier with more routine, behind-the-scenes Maintain work. Even so, professionals who enjoy outgoing, more visible Market work are often disparaged as 'political types.' Professionals doing more behind-the-scenes, routine Maintain work are disparaged as 'bean counters,' or worse. Balancing the portfolio of the whole professional group among Market and Maintain work may be a better use of resources—and meet with less resistance—than going the individual route.

The Professional Strategic Model can help professionals realize that the long-term success of their professional group depends upon *both* contributions. If Maintain work is not done, the group will have little credibility for the Market work. If Market work is not done, the group will get little recognition, or worse, be outsourced. Within the professional group itself, the Market professionals need to give recognition to the contribution of the Maintain professionals, since they will not get much recognition from clients. Visible use of the Strategic Model can improve the spirit of teamwork in the professional group.

Rome Wasn't Built in a Day

"Could you facilitate a half day Strategic Planning meeting for us?" Good intentions, but a half day won't do it (except in special circumstances). Why not? Many professionals implicitly believe that "this kind of thinking should be done by others." In addition, many professionals have been conditioned *not* to ask "Why?" about their jobs—not to think 'big picture.' It takes time for professionals to stand back and ask the bigger questions about their work. Usually a series of meetings, where these ideas are discussed and tentative statements refined, is better than any one-shot deal.

GUIDELINES FOR STRATEGIC PLANNING

❑ Always clarify strategic direction as a group. You need everyone's input and commitment. The best way to get both is by involvement.

❑ Always remind professionals of the 'why'—why this needs to be done.

❑ Do not use the Professional Strategic Model slavishly. Adapt it and its terminology to your own needs.

❑ 80% is OK. You will never 'get it right' 100% of the time. Take strategic statements as proposals which need to be checked out with clients and other 'real world' considerations. At the next meeting, refine them.

❑ Talk to clients, customers and other stakeholders about what you are doing and why.

❑ Take time to step back regularly from the day-to-day work. A half day to a full day every few months is almost certainly better than a three day retreat every 2 years.

❑ Combine this strategic thinking with discussions about the future of your profession and your organization.

❑ Always end the sessions with specific action plans. Many people abhor 'blue sky' thinking if it is not rooted in down-to-earth, practical action.

Resources to Help You Prepare Your Strategy

The next few pages contain a number of resources to help you prepare your own professional strategy.

❶ A one-page summary of the Professional Strategic Model

❷ A Professional Strategic Flowchart

❸ A Strategic Client Analysis Matrix

❹ A real-life example of the model in action

❺ A strategic planning worksheet.

66 Quotable Quotes 99

"You do not merely want to be considered just the best of the best. You want to be considered the only ones who do what you do."
- Jerry Garcia as quoted by Tom Peters

What is the strategy for defining strategy?

❶ AND NOW FOR THE COMPLETED PROFESSIONAL STRATEGIC MODEL …

Definitions:

Value-Added: Is key to the success of your clients and your organization.

Necessity: Must be done, but is not core to your clients' future success; seen as 'base business.'

Unique to Your Professional Group: Must be staffed or is best done by employees in your organization because of security, legislation, or policy, or is proprietary to your organization.

Unique to You: **Must** be done by you because of your unique expertise

Can be Done by Others: Services that are, or could be supplied, by others inside the organization, or by external professionals—that is, generic services.

66 Quotable Quotes 99

"I work very hard; please don't expect me to think as well."
© *Ashleigh Brilliant*

"You will have to invest substantial time and energy in your own learning if you want to remain best in class as work requirements change."
– *George Campbell*

The Model:

Professional Contribution to Organizational Strategy

		High Value-Added	Business Necessity
Technology & Expertise	*Unique to Professional Group*	**Market as a Group** 'Be best in class'	**Maintain** 'Keep it running efficiently'
	Unique to You	**Market Your Skills** 'Be best in class'	**Maintain** 'Use minimum resources'
	Generic/ Can Be Done By Others	**Coach/Broker Out** 'Find & work with the best in class'	**Refer/Contract Out** 'Find providers of worry-free service'

Implications:
- You will be considered a powerful professional to the degree that you do work coming from the Market boxes.
- Be careful about asking your clients "What would you like from me?" because they will often ask for "more of the same"—that is the Maintain, lower value activities.
- You cannot afford to allow low value, generic work to dominate your activities.
- You must continually market activities which are High Value-Added' and Unique to You or Your Professional Group, because clients probably don't know how you and/or your group could add more value.
- Market work is not static, often becoming Business Necessity and/or Generic work over time.

This model is on the Web Site: www.consultskills.com

TO DO OR NOT TO DO?
❷ A PROFESSIONAL STRATEGIC FLOWCHART

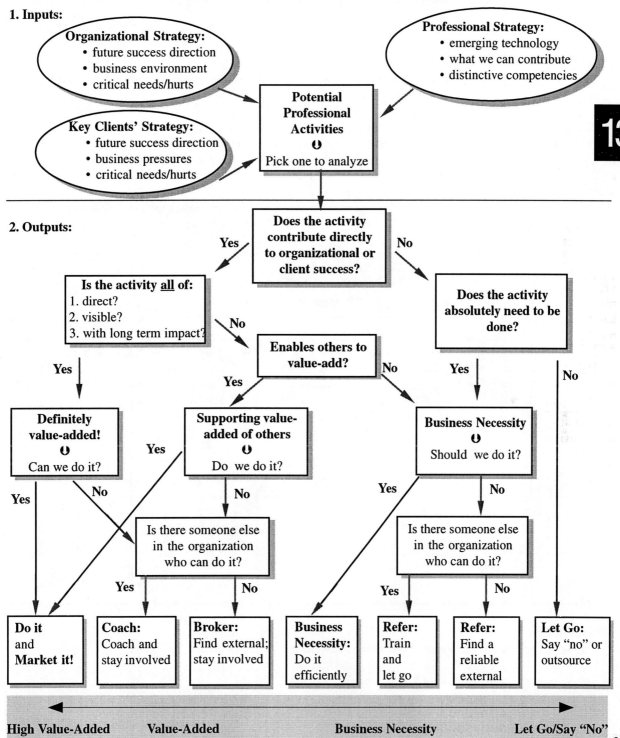

1. Inputs:

Organizational Strategy:
• future success direction
• business environment
• critical needs/hurts

Key Clients' Strategy:
• future success direction
• business pressures
• critical needs/hurts

Professional Strategy:
• emerging technology
• what we can contribute
• distinctive competencies

Potential Professional Activities
↺
Pick one to analyze

13

2. Outputs:

Does the activity contribute directly to organizational or client success?

Yes → Is the activity **all** of:
1. direct?
2. visible?
3. with long term impact?

No → Does the activity absolutely need to be done?

Yes → **Definitely value-added!** ↺ Can we do it?

No → Enables others to value-add?

Yes → **Supporting value-added of others** ↺ Do we do it?

No → **Business Necessity** ↺ Should we do it?

Is there someone else in the organization who can do it?

Do it and **Market it!**

Coach: Coach and stay involved

Broker: Find external; stay involved

Business Necessity: Do it efficiently

Refer: Train and let go

Refer: Find a reliable external

Let Go: Say "no" or outsource

High Value-Added   Value-Added   Business Necessity   Let Go/Say "No"

Who are the Players in Your Strategic Game?

Not all clients are of equal value. Professionals need to regularly examine their client base to ensure offering appropriate services or products to the right people. A good generalization is that 20% of your clients will use 80% of your energy. Are these same 20% also using 80% of your Value-Added work?

In order to establish who the players are in the strategic game, ask these questions:
- ✓ Who are your major clients?
- ✓ Who should be your major clients?
- ✓ Is the type of work you do for your major clients Value-Added work?
- ✓ What should you be doing that you are not?

Answers to these questions are crucial to your success as an internal consultant, as well as to your personal satisfaction.

This model is on the Web Site: www.consultskills.com

Completing the following matrix will help answer the above questions. Write in key names and key activities. Remember the 80-20 rule. Don't get caught up in detail and 'analysis paralysis.'

❸ STRATEGIC CLIENT ANALYSIS MATRIX
Increasing Value-Added ⟶

	Low Value Activities	Necessary But Not Strategic Activities	Brokered or Contracted Activities	Current Value-Added Activities	Strategic & Value-Added Work to Market
Your Current Clients					
Clients You Should Have					

Action Plans:

1. What can you do to add more work on the Strategic and Value-Added side?

2. What can you do to get rid of low leverage work?

④ STRATEGIC MARKETING:
HUMAN RESOURCES EXAMPLE

	Value-Added	**Business Necessity**

Unique Expertise	• Retention strategy:
	  – compensation
	  – benefits
	  – succession planning
	• Organizational effectiveness
	• Recruiting & staffing strategy
	• Affirmative action strategy
	• Change leadership and communication
	• Performance management
		• Compensation and payroll administration
		• Benefits advising
		• Affirmative action plans
		• Labor relations
		• Community relations
		• Performance reviews

	Career development	
Available From Others	• Professional development and training • Employee assistance programs • Special projects we cannot do	• Employee relations services • Employee communications • Benefits administration • Relocation administration • Savings plan administration • Temporary worker administration • Compliance training • Worker's compensation • HRIS input

Work Outsourced or Eliminated

Benefits administration
Salary administration
Data input
Recruiting administration
Personnel files
    administration
Relocation services
Plant tour administration

Activities Assumed by Line Management

Safety
Occupational health
Technical training
Attendance records
Exit interviewing
Filing & retention of
    performance reviews
Educational assistance
    program

Activities Shared with Line Management and/or Other Professional Groups

Regular communications
Newsletter
New hire orientation
Service award program
Educational refund program
On-campus recruitment
School/business partnerships

13

EYE WITNESS REPORT

This is a summary of the Human Resources team strategic marketing plan, for a major unit of a multinational company. It is in no way meant to be a definitive example—every professional group needs to look at its specific circumstances.

Stymied!

A major roadblock to professional strategic analysis is lack of awareness of organizational and/or client strategy. "I could be clearer on my direction if only I got clearer direction from more senior managers" is a recurring remark from professionals. The reality is that senior managers, who should be clear on organizational direction, are often not clear at all! They may implicitly *know* this direction, yet cannot communicate it clearly. They are often unsure how to understand and react to external pressures on their organization. Below are three examples of unclear organizational strategy.

Straightforward
➡ *Strategy unclear because of distance from clients.*
Professionals and professional groups are often separated geographically from their clients. They must work hard at keeping in touch with their clients in order to understand and contribute to their longer term direction. Options here range from more frequent client contact, to physically locating your professional group into your client system. See *101 Marketing Hints and Tips* page 253, in Chapter 14, *Marketing Your Skills Inside Your Organization*.

Impossible!
➡ *Strategy unclear because clients are purposefully withholding directional information.*
Organizations do exist which are so political that crucial information is routinely withheld from professionals. This is a very difficult case for which it is impossible to give easy answers. You might try some of the techniques in Chapter 10, *Dealing with Resistance*. If you work in an organization with this kind of culture move on as soon as you can.

Very Challenging—Very Rewarding!
➡ *Clients and managers are unsure of their strategies.*
Clients and managers buffeted by change feel they cannot set a steady direction. Some have a management style that focuses on the here and now, unwilling to set clear, longer term direction. Strangely enough, experienced professionals often see these situations presenting the most opportunity! Clients unsure of their direction often leave most options open for you to influence the direction. Consider the antithesis of the above: the more certain and fixed your clients and managers are, the fewer options they will be willing to consider.

Realize that:
1. The speed of change makes most long term predictions unreliable.
2. No one will ever 'get it right' 100% of the time. Work with the best information you can.
3. Set a strategy, but be willing to adapt when circumstances change.
4. Help clients make good choices in your area of expertise.
5. Look beyond your specific professional skill to consider the broader issues for your organization. Think of yourself less as, for example, an systems professional than as an organizational systems consultant.

66 Quotable Quotes 99
"If you don't know where you are going, any road will get you there."

"Pick battles big enough to matter, small enough to win."
– Jonathan Kozol

Don't be immobilized waiting for others! No one has it all figured out and is being obnoxious by not telling you.

"Have a destination determined. Knowing exactly how you will get there is less important than being 'directionally correct' along the way."
– Robin Sober
The Mutual Group

❺ A WORKSHEET: LOOKING AT YOUR CONSULTING ROLE STRATEGICALLY

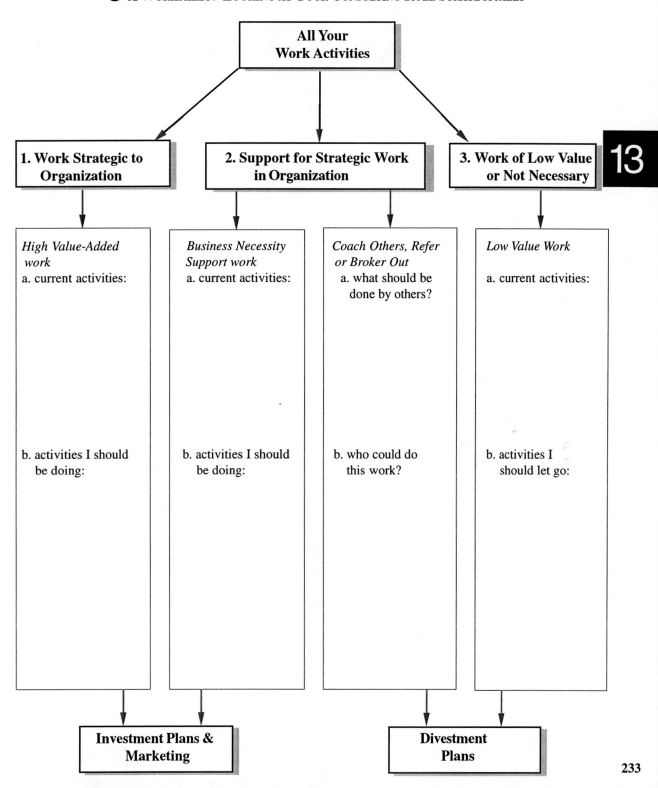

All Your
Work Activities

1. Work Strategic to
Organization

2. Support for Strategic Work
in Organization

3. Work of Low Value
or Not Necessary

13

*High Value-Added
work*
a. current activities:

*Business Necessity
Support work*
a. current activities:

*Coach Others, Refer
or Broker Out*
a. what should be
done by others?

Low Value Work

a. current activities:

b. activities I should
be doing:

b. activities I should
be doing:

b. who could do
this work?

b. activities I
should let go:

Investment Plans &
Marketing

Divestment
Plans

Saying "No"—With Options. Here's Why ...

Having analyzed when to say "yes" helps professionals make (and defend) solid decisions about saying "no." A universal dilemma for internal consultants is to consistently say "yes" to high impact work and to say "no" to clients in a way that maintains the relationship.

In addition to issues of strategic alignment, there are many legitimate reasons why an internal consultant must say "no" to some client requests:

It Just Ain't Right!

- Request is low value
- Wrong solution or wrong problem is being worked
- Insufficient time to do an acceptable, quality job
- Inappropriate skills or expertise to do a quality job
- Request doesn't fit with organizational strategy
- Request is illegal or unethical
- Request doesn't meet professional standards.

It's Scary!

Why an internal professional will not like saying "no":
- Fear the client won't come back
- Fear of loss of stature and perceived value
- Fear of being labeled a 'poor teamplayer'
- Fear of job loss
- Apprehension about client response—anger, threats, etc.
- Fear the client will circumvent
- Fear the client will spread negative remarks.

So, Can We Still Be Friends?

Benefits of saying "no" in a skilful manner:
- The client will at least understand why you need to say "no."
- The client will, in the future, request more strategic work from you.
- The client has some options for getting the need met.

But I *CAN* Still Help You …

Once you are satisfied that you should say "no", the difficult skill is how to say it effectively. The goal is to say "no" in a way that the client will still feel served.

Saying "no" need not be a black or white proposition. There is a range of potential responses calling for varying levels of involvement:

Some important principles underlying saying "no" successfully are:
- Establish, in your own mind and with your supervisor, your right to say "no" on the basis of:
    - quality of work
    - your department's priorities and strategy
    - ethics
    - professional standards.
- Be clear on your group's strategy, that is, to what you say "yes" and "no," and why.
- Always give a reason why you are saying "no."
- Try to give your client alternatives (see below).
- Always discuss a "no" with your supervisor.

66 **Quotable Quotes** 99

"A 'no' uttered from the deepest conviction is better than a 'yes' merely uttered to please, or worse, to avoid trouble."
– Mahatma Gandhi

RANGE OF
SAYING "NO" WITH OPTIONS

Direct Refusal	Partial Involvement	Referral/ Contract Out	Broker Out	Deferral	Coaching Others
"No"	"I will do part of it."	"I will give you some names of people you can contact."	"I will find someone who does high quality work, and I will coach him or her on this project."	"I can't do it now, but will later." "I can do part now and part later."	"I can help you or your people to do it."
An outright "no," without options, is the last resort.	Depending on how much you commit to, this can range from almost a "no" to a virtual "yes."	Contracting out refers your client to another provider who may be available or more appropriate as a service provider.	Brokering out is a way to service and interface with your client, but utilize a third party to actually perform the work for you, under your guidance.	Be very careful if you use this option because you are, in fact, saying a future "yes."	With limited resources, helping your clients to help themselves may be a good long-term strategy.

235

WHAT YOU HAVE LEARNED SO FAR ...

- Successful organizations must have a clear strategy—so must professional groups and individual professionals.

- Often professionals cannot see a direct connection between their work and the organization's strategy—they need a 'line of sight.'

- To be recognized as a high performing professional, do work which is clearly High Value-added.

- High Value-added and unique work must be identified, chosen and marketed by professionals and professional groups.

- Asking clients what they want often results in work of the Business Necessity type—the type that must be done, but is not highly recognized.

- High performing professionals must be able to say "no."

- It is very rare to say "no" outright. Your goal is to be able to explain why you're saying "no," as well as to offer options.

THE EXPERTISE DELIVERY MODEL

> *"Professionals will wait for a long time with mouths wide open before a roast chicken flies in."*
> — adapted proverb

CHAPTER 14

MARKETING YOUR SKILLS INSIDE YOUR ORGANIZATION

14

Quick Snapshot

Did You Know?
- effective marketing is carried out in a highly professional manner?
- more and more internal professional groups are taking responsibility for marketing their skills?
- marketing is informing clients how you can meet their needs?

How-to:
- analyze your internal marketplace.
- analyze what you offer as a professional.
- prepare a marketing plan.
- market your professional skills in 101 ways.

The Bottom Line:
- You will be able to market your skills inside your organization, using the models, checklists, assessments and skills of this chapter,

Once Upon A Time ...

Once upon a time professionals were dependent, loyal employees. They were experts, satisfied career professionals. The organization 'took care of you.' No more is this the case. Winds of change are blowing. These winds include downsizing, mergers and flattened structures. These winds are blowing away the old. No more do we find 'parental' organizations, no more traditional employee dependence cycles, no more taken-for-granted expertise, no more lifetime employment. That was once upon a time ...

This is now. Now, being busy is not enough. Now is taking responsibility for your own professional satisfaction and career tracking; now is "Show us how you add value to this organization"; now is "If you want to stay employed, show us that you can deliver what we need!" Now is marketing your professional skills.

What Happened?

- Harsh economic times happened, bringing more competition and bottom line orientation.
- 'Internal deregulation' of professional services happened.
- Internal and external customer service orientation happened.
- Changed expectations happened—expectations that internal professional groups would operate like a business.

So What's A Professional To Do?

Learn to market professional skills, that's what professionals need to do! Yet for most professionals the very words *selling* or *marketing* seem to conjure up images of fast-talking used car salespeople with gaudy ties and loud sports jackets, even though they know that this image of sales and marketing is antiquated. There is no doubt that marketing tends to have a bad name. Even the popular Dilbert cartoonist constantly pokes fun at marketing. In this book, we take the professional aspects of marketing and refocus them for internal use. Much has already been written about marketing for external professionals, but little is written for internal professionals. Our goal is to assist you to effectively market your professional skills within your own organization, while feeling comfortable and confident doing so.

In this chapter, you will learn to:
- Differentiate common terms used in marketing.
- Explore some principles and models of marketing yourself internally.
- Analyze your internal marketplace and outline steps you can take to market your skills internally.
- Formulate, from a checklist, what you have to offer as a professional.
- Analyze your internal client system; assess your ability to market your professional group internally.
- Use worksheets to prepare a marketing plan.
- From our checklist of 101 hints/tips, glean critical and practical marketing ideas to market yourself inside your organization.

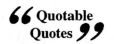 **Quotable Quotes**

Actual comment from a client to a workshop participant: "Doesn't promote his skills. I don't really know what he has to offer."

"I am always amazed when internal professionals are asked what they would do differently if they were running their own external professional group, how many of them will give a long list of things they would do. I ask 'Why don't you just start doing those things now?'"
– Bill Sefcik, CPA

Paddle Your Own Canoe

As a professional, only you know the full extent of what you can offer, or your own expectations and aspirations. No one else knows. To get what you need and want, you have to market skills which can clearly add value. This means taking control of how you work—taking control of your own professional destiny. Effective professionals, internal or external, have always marketed their skills. Marketing skills are learnable skills.

Marketing? Selling? Persuasion? Influence? Strategy?

From our huge database of 35,000 responses, clients have told us what they value from professionals working within their organizations. Two of the top ten items relate to marketing and selling skills:

 i. 'Is able to persuade others.'
 ii. 'Comes up with creative, resourceful solutions to problems …'

From the same database we learn that one of the lowest rated items is for a professional to be 'narrowly focused on the technical part of his/her work.' What do we glean from an analysis of these responses? One finding is that although you may be a great expert in your own field, to be valued you need to demonstrate to others the value and importance of your work; another is that clients *do* value being persuaded (even though they may say they don't, as you will see)!

Marketing is the basis of successfully selling your ideas and proposals. The skills of selling and persuasion, although part of the process, are no substitute for the skills of marketing. You cannot successfully sell your proposals long-term without the bigger picture of marketing in place. Here we differentiate for you a few closely related terms, which often cause confusion to those examining the marketing field.

Marketing:
What you need to think of and do *before* approaching your clients.
- Analyzing what you have to offer professionally, then informing your clients and organization.
- Analyzing client needs, then presenting to clients how you feel you can add value to their business.
- Implementing your strategic thinking.

Sales and Persuasion: (dealt with in Chapter 6, *Recommending Change*)
What you do when face-to-face with clients.
- Persuasively presenting proposals, recommendations and ideas.
- Demonstrating how recommendations fulfill your clients' needs.
- Using tactical here-and-now skills.

Influence and Client Relations:
What you need to do to generate co-operation between you and your prospective internal clients.
- Developing a positive image with internal clients, so they will request your services.
- Ensuring clients 'seek your opinions.' (Another database high-value item.)
- Developing a mutually powerful 50-50 partnership between you and your clients.

"The best way to ensure your future is to create your own."
  – Anon

14

In this chapter, we use the word 'you' to refer to a professional group, a more powerful way to market—though you can use these ideas as an individual professional.

In this chapter ...

- *Why market your skills?*
- *Differentiate some common terms*
- *How to analyze your internal marketplace*
- *How to analyze what your have to offer*
- *Worksheets for your marketing plan*
- *Checklist of 101 ways to market yourself*

Strategic Thinking: (dealt with in Chapter 13, *Your Strategy: Saying Yes or No*)
Thinking long-term about the direction of your profession and organization.
- What you do in preparation for marketing.
- Determining what you market.
- Determining how you gain value-added leverage in your organization.

Marketing is *not* a substitute for strategic thinking—the thinking needed to position your professional skills so that they add value to your organization—that is found in Chapter 13 on *Strategy.* Your most immediate needs may be to come up with ideas on selling a proposal or recommendation to your clients. If this is the case, turn to the chapter *Recommending Change.* In this book, chapters do stand alone. The entire book, however, builds a structure of concepts and models to help you become a more powerful professional.

"Marketing is *not* part of *my* job description!"

The concept of internal marketing is often alien to professional groups and individual professionals. These are some assumptions and 'givens' which may resonate with you. They belie this attitude towards marketing.
- You assume that someone else will do this for you (or you wish they would). Many professionals joined organizations to *escape* marketing and selling!
- It is untraditional; it goes against a number of assumptions:
    - "We are professionals, we shouldn't have to do this."
    - "Engineering shouldn't be pushing their agenda."
    - "This takes us away from our professional work."
- Line management tends to view professionals as 'staff units,' often classified as 'overhead,' with no concept of professionals value-adding to the organization.
- Marketing and sales are associated with negative images: slick, persuasive, 'used-car salesperson' stereotypes.
- An assumption that your clients don't want to be 'sold' on recommendations. (Surprisingly, they do!)
- Lack of vision and passion found in professional groups, who are often more cerebral, conservative and centered on risk avoidance.
- An assumption that professional logic is aligned with business logic; that what professionals think is good for professionals must automatically be good for their clients and for their organization.
- An assumption that marketing is incompatible with teamwork. Although some individuals (or groups) might push their own agenda, teamwork is still a must for modern marketing.

Despite all these marketing myths, survival and career satisfaction are strongly tied to taking responsibility for marketing your professional skills.

"And I don't want you to try and sell to me, either," sayeth the client.

Besides professionals' attitudes, clients *also* tend to be ambivalent about marketing and selling. Asked "Would you like us to market our services to you?" they will almost certainly say "No way!" They, too, have many of the above negative stereotypes of marketing. Yet analysis of our data shows that clients, despite themselves, *do* value being persuaded! This paradox is illustrated in the story below.

There's 'MARKETING' ... and then there's 'marketing.'

14

During a workshop involving a head office group of engineers from a large electrical utility company, much discussion had centered around marketing their engineering services to field facilities. The Plant Manager (a major internal client) of their largest electrical generation plant was invited to be an after-dinner speaker—on the subject of how he saw the client-consultant relationship inside this organization. Spurred on by workshop discussion, one engineer asked "Would you like us to market our services to you?" The Plant Manager quickly shot back "No way!" and subsequently went on to describe how annoying external vendors can be.

During the ensuing discussion, the engineer interspersed a number of questions.
"We are thinking of putting on a 'Brown Bag' luncheon talk series about advances in engineering, geared to your plant personnel. What do you think?"
Plant Manager: "Great idea!"
Later, "When I come around the plant for my projects, would you like me to drop by for a chat?"
Plant Manager: "Sure, that'd be great!"
Still later, "We're thinking of putting together a monthly, one page 'Engineering Hilites' for the company. Would that be helpful for your facility?"
Plant Manager: "Yes, it sure would."

Marketing done well is unobstrusive and satisfying to the client.

Unfortunately, the engineer could not resist asking the consequence question: "Earlier on this evening, you said you didn't want to be marketed to, yet all the marketing initiatives I've suggested, you thought were helpful ..." Why didn't that engineer quit while he was ahead!? The trick is to carry out marketing activities without looking like it's capital-letter Marketing.

"In training a group composed mainly of engineers, when discussing strategic marketing, they suddenly realized that they should have adopted this marketing approach 12 months earlier. They could have had huge impact on the company, they said, but at that time they felt insecure in their internal professional role. Alas, before the 12 months was up, they were informed that they were no longer in the future plans of the company, and most were let go.

What is the moral of this story? Internal professional groups must constantly look strategically at their position within their organizations, and must:
   a. see opportunities to add value to the organization, and
   b. be able to market their roles and ideas.
This will ensure they will be looked upon as a valuable asset to their corporations."

Bill Sefcik, CPA
Consulting Skills for Professionals workshop instructor

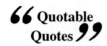

"I could do great things if I weren't so busy doing little things."
© *Ashleigh Brilliant*

Dazzling doesn't work

Marketing techniques are just that—techniques. To work successfully, techniques must be based on solid values, principles and beliefs underlying what you have to offer, otherwise techniques alone will be shallow, stilted and feel phony. If your underlying principles are solid, your tools and techniques will be solid. The best marketing is a 50-50 partnership: your clients win because you are providing an effective service; you win because your service is satisfying to you.

Here are some values, beliefs and principles which we used as our own basis for this chapter:
- It is very difficult to market something that you don't believe in. In order to market well, you must have passion for your professional skill and technology.
- You must have identifiable skills to market. If you are deficient in the knowledge or skills that you wish to market, take steps to upgrade professionally. No amount of marketing can make up for an inferior product or service.
- Marketing is closely tied to strategy. *Strategy* informs you what to emphasize and de-emphasize in your organization. *Marketing* informs you how to implement your *strategy*. The best marketing is about solving significant organizational problems, particularly those with measurable bottom-line results.
- Marketing yourself internally takes time and must be strategically thought out. You cannot 'wing it.'
- You cannot accomplish great things by yourself. In today's complex organizations, you must be part of many teams. Part of your marketing plan must involve the commitment and support of others including:
  - ✓ your professional peers
  - ✓ your support staff
  - ✓ your manager and management
  - ✓ your peers in client units
  - ✓ your clients (of course).

  To ensure professional group commitment, developing marketing plans is always best done by the whole group.
- Higher leverage marketing usually takes place with senior management levels first, but it does not end there. Do not assume that if senior management has bought in, you 'have it made.' In most modern organizations, you need to deal with multiple stakeholder systems. See Chapter 8, *Mapping Client Systems,* for more details.
- Marketing is not 'pulling the wool over management's eyes.' Manipulation just won't work.
- What is valued by you, your clients and your organization keeps changing with time. Think of yourself as a business, keeping up with changing business needs. Think of yourself as 'You, Inc.'

Why a Plan?

"One possible reason why things aren't going according to plan is that there never was a plan."
© *Ashleigh Brilliant*

Having a prepared marketing plan has these benefits:
- You will understand your needs better. Often internal consultants complain about difficulties they have in their professional role.
- A marketing plan results in concrete offers to your clients.
- When you ask for, or you refuse work, you will be able to explain why.
- You will be more focused, more strategic, and you will know where to best invest your energy.

Here's How to Start

There are five steps to preparing a marketing plan:

1. Know your professional group.
2. Know your organization.
3. Know your clients.
4. Formulate your professional group strategy.
5. Integrate the above into a marketing plan.

The next few pages contain a number of tools to help you prepare a plan. You may wish to make some choices depending on your needs:

❶ Before you begin formulating the actual plan, you may wish to complete the *Self Assessment Checklist* overleaf on page 244, which will give you some indication of how well you currently market.

❷ You may wish to surprise yourself by reading about the skill offerings you already possess, but may be ignoring! Use the *Professional Checklist* on page 245.

❸ If you do not have much time, you may wish to take the quick route, using the Express Service Marketing Plan Checklist on page 246 to stimulate ideas for your marketing plan.

❹ We have included a worksheet for each of the five marketing steps on pages 247 - 251. We suggest you write out the answers to the questions on these worksheet pages. (If you have already prepared a strategic plan, many of the questions will already be answered.) We suggest this worksheet method, because thoughts in your head are often vague and can get lost. Written words demand clarity and commitment. Please modify the worksheets to your own needs.

❺ The chapter ends with *Golden Marketing Rules* and *101 Marketing Hints and Tips*.

Although you or your group can prepare a marketing plan on your own, it is better to have someone present who will challenge and coach you.

- It is difficult for you to see yourselves the way others see you. You need feedback.
- You may either underestimate yourself, or overestimate yourself and be foolhardy.
- Others can challenge you to ask yourself difficult questions.
- Someone can record while you and your group think.
- By involving others, you have started the commitment process. The more people who know your plan and its thoughtfulness, the more likely you are to get support for your plan.

Finally, no plan can be written in stone. Circumstance and information will change. We recommend a marketing 'tune-up' at least every six months.

14

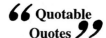

❝ Quotable Quotes ❞

"Chaotic action is better than orderly inaction."
– Karl Weick

These Worksheets are on the Web Site:
www.consultskills.com

*These Checklists are
on the Web Site:
www.consultskills.com*

HOW WELL DO YOU MARKET?
❶ A SELF ASSESSMENT CHECKLIST

This is a 'stocktaking' exercise. Check off those areas that are current strengths of your professional group. Highlight those areas you need to develop.

1. Know your professional group
❏ We know our distinctive skills, competencies and professional passion.
❏ We know which work activities add value to our organization now.
❏ We know which skills will add value to our organization in the future.
❏ We know the long-term direction of our profession.
❏ We know how to leverage our distinctive knowledge, skills and competencies.
❏ We know the constraints of our professional group.

2. Know the business environment of your organization
❏ We know our organization's external pressures, and opportunities.
❏ We know our organization's vision, direction and strategy.
❏ We know our organization's current needs and probable future needs from our profession.
❏ We know what professional work is strategic and value-added for our organization.

3. Know your clients
❏ We know where we currently spend our time and energy.
❏ We know which clients we should have, but do not presently have.
❏ We know the current and probable future needs of our clients.
❏ We know what is strategic and value-added for our clients.
❏ We know what our clients want from us.
❏ We know what we should offer that clients do not currently ask for.
❏ We know how to present the benefits of using our professional skills in our clients' frame of reference.

4. Know your professional group's strategy and goals in terms of business needs
❏ We know which of our current services are essential—business necessity.
❏ We know which of our current services add value to our clients.
❏ We know which services could add value, but are not currently offered, or accepted.
❏ We know which services could be outsourced or contracted out.
❏ We know which activities we need to say "no" to.
❏ We know how to formulate our strategic direction in words our clients can understand and accept.
❏ We all participate in the formation and upgrading of our group's strategic direction.

5. Integrate into a marketing plan
❏ We know our integrated marketing strategy.
❏ We know our long-term marketing goals.
❏ We know our short-term marketing goals.
❏ We know the next steps in our marketing strategy.
❏ We know who we need for support.

❝ Quotable Quotes ❞

*"Market for current
activities, but also
'plant seeds' of ideas
for future work."*
– Robin Sober
The Mutual Group

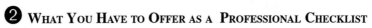

You've Got a Lot to Give!

❷ What You Have to Offer as a Professional Checklist

Often professionals, particularly internal consultants, feel 'one-down' with their clients. Many undervalue what they bring to the table. Use this checklist to reinforce some offerings you may not realize you have!

Professional/Technical Expertise
- ❏ Your knowledge.
- ❏ Your skills.
- ❏ Your experience—how to apply knowledge and skills in your organization.
- ❏ Your professional network—contacts and resources inside and outside your organization.

Leadership
- ❏ Your vision and strategic direction for your professional area.
- ❏ Your values—those values valued by others.
- ❏ Your willingness to lead.
- ❏ Your commitment-building skills—building commitment from project inception to close.
- ❏ Your facilitation skills—skills for leading groups.
- ❏ Your process skills—decision making, problem solving, planning, project management, etc.
- ❏ Your willingness to assume responsibilities for others—seeing your success as the success of others.
- ❏ Your persuasion abilities—ability to sell an idea or project.

Business Expertise
- ❏ Your knowledge of the strategic direction of your organization and how your profession can help strategically—having strategic alignment with your organization.
- ❏ Your knowledge of your client's specific business needs and constraints.
- ❏ Your willingness to adapt your professional expertise to your clients' needs and constraints.
- ❏ Your knowledge of business systems, particularly how they apply to your professional area—budgeting, economics, finance, information systems, problem solving, etc.
- ❏ Your knowledge of, and access to, resources:
  - – others you can delegate to.
  - – access to information and budgets.
  - – expertise, internally or externally, you or your clients need.
  - – knowing how to get things done within the system.

Internal Customer Service
- ❏ Your reliability—you can be depended on.
- ❏ Your integrity—you don't have a hidden agenda.
- ❏ Your responsiveness—you don't give your clients the 'runaround.'
- ❏ Your reputation—you are known as a consultant who delivers.
- ❏ Your quality—you produce excellent work.
- ❏ Your role flexibility—you assume roles that are appropriate to the situation.

Interpersonal Competence
- ❏ You are not threatened by not knowing everything.
- ❏ You are straightforward; you can, with tact, "tell it like it is."
- ❏ You are flexible; at the same time, you can take stands based on well thought-out principles.
- ❏ You raise the self-esteem of others.
- ❏ You keep confidences.
- ❏ You consistently model and live your ethics and values.
- ❏ You are a pleasant person to work with.

14

❝ Quotable Quotes ❞
"Confidence is contagious. So is lack of confidence."
– Michael O'Brien

245

❸ EXPRESS SERVICE MARKETING PLAN CHECKLIST

This is a shortcut if you wish to bypass the worksheets for each step. Use the questions below to stimulate your thinking in the production of a marketing plan. Remember to involve people early and often in your marketing plan. Modify the questions to suit your specific needs.

1. Know your professional group
❏ What are your distinctive skills and competencies?
❏ What are your weaknesses and threats?
❏ For what kind of work does your group have a passion?
❏ Who are your external competitors?
❏ What is your competitive advantage over external competitors?
❏ Where does your group currently spend most of its time?
❏ At present, where are the high payoff, value-added contributions to your organization and clients?
❏ For the leaders of the professional group:
    – what is your vision for your group?   – are you willing to invest the energy needed to see change through?

2. Know your organization
❏ What are the external pressures on your organization?
❏ What are the direction and strategy of your organization?
❏ What is your organization likely to need from your professional group in the future?
❏ What is the current perception of your professional group by others?

3. Know your clients
❏ Who *are currently* your key clients?
❏ Who *should be* your key clients?
❏ What are the strategies, needs and constraints of each key client?
❏ What do your clients currently ask for? What would you like them to ask for?
❏ What are their future needs? What can you offer that they may not currently know they need?
❏ What do you need to know from clients to complete your understanding of their needs and constraints?

4. Formulate your professional group strategy
Given your analysis of your professional group, your organization and your clients:
❏ Which of your current services are essential, or business necessity?
❏ What services are currently clearly value-added?
❏ What services could value-add, but are not currently offered to, or accepted by, your clients?
❏ What services could be outsourced or contracted out?
❏ What activities do you need to say "no" to?
❏ How will you formulate the strategic change in words so that your clients can understand?
❏ What benefits will you offer your clients for participating in the change?
❏ What are the major changes that need to be made in order to implement this strategy?
❏ For leaders, what behaviors will you use to coach and support the new change?

5. Integrate the above into a marketing plan
❏ What are the long-term marketing goals for your group?
❏ What are the short-term marketing goals for your group?
❏ What is your 'next steps' plan for marketing the new professional strategy?
❏ How will you communicate the new strategy to your clients in a way that supports acceptance?
❏ How will you get feedback in order to take corrective action on the inevitable problems that will crop up?

❹ WORKSHEET 1

KNOW YOUR PROFESSIONAL GROUP

The first step of marketing is to know yourself. Obviously, you can know your skills in many ways. Modify the questions as needed. You will benefit most by writing down the answers to the following questions. WARNING—there is no prize for elegant statements. Don't get caught up in analysis paralysis!

1. What are your distinctive skills and competencies? What sets you apart from your professional competitors?

2. People put more energy into what they really like. What are your distinctive interests? What 'turns your crank?' What is your passion (professionally, of course)?

3. Realistically, what are your weaknesses and constraints?

4. Where do you spend most of your time and energy?

5. How does your organization currently benefit from employing your professional services?

6. In our internal marketing workshops, a real eye-opener is to ask participants to think how they would act differently if they were external consultants to their organization. If you were external professionals providing similar professional services to your organization what would you:

   • Stop doing?

   • Start doing?

   • Continue to do?

(While using this worksheet, an engineering manager stopped at step #6 and said to his group "Why don't we start doing these things right now?")

14

WORKSHEET 2:
KNOW THE BUSINESS ENVIRONMENT OF YOUR ORGANIZATION

Your ultimate client is your organization. We often hear professionals complain of unclear and confusing signals sent out by senior management. Successful internal consulting groups have to deal with the differing, often conflicting, needs of professional group members, individual clients, the organization, and the organization's customers. To expect all these needs to be 'in sync' and in agreement at all times is unrealistic. The best you can do is to optimize complex and shifting needs and expectations.

A good marketing plan understands the current and future business environment of your organization. Here are some questions to help your environmental scan:

1. What are the external pressures and opportunities for your organization?

2. What is the current vision, direction and strategy of your organization?

3. Given the external pressures on your organization, what direction will it likely take in the future?

4. How will your professional skills contribute to the strategy of your organization?

5. What does this analysis say about your marketing plan and your skill development?

WORKSHEET 3
KNOW YOUR CLIENTS

The third step to successful marketing is to understand your clients and their needs, including those they are, as yet, unaware of. The most common complaint of clients is the lack of understanding of their business. Understanding the needs of your clients takes an investment of time and energy. The payoff is leveraged work which is valued by the client. Most internal consultants deal with multiple and complex client systems. Another chapter in this book, *Mapping Client Systems,* page 117, will be helpful for those situations.

1. Who are your current key clients?

2. Who are not yet your clients, but should be?

3. For each group of clients:
   • What is their vision, direction and strategy?

   • What are their external pressures and opportunities?

   • What do they currently ask for?

   • What are their probable future needs?

• What can you offer that they are unlikely to ask for, because they don't know they need it, or they think it is too risky?

3. What do you need to know from your clients to complete your understanding of their needs and constraints?

14

WORKSHEET 4
KNOW YOUR PROFESSIONAL GROUP STRATEGY

As much as internal consulting groups wish their clients and their organization would be clearer about direction, to become more powerful, internal consulting groups need to get their own act in order first. Information will never be perfect and static anyway.

Note: Another version of this worksheet which you may find more useful, called *Strategic Client Analysis Matrix,* is contained in the previous chapter, *Your Strategy: Saying Yes or No,* on page 230. Given your analysis of your group, your organization and your clients:

1. Which of your current services are essential and must be continued?

2. Which services are currently clearly value-added?

3. Which services could value-add, but are not currently offered to your clients?

4. Which services could be discontinued, outsourced or contracted out?

5. Which activities do you need to say "no" to?

6. How will you formulate the strategic change in words your clients can understand? What benefits will you offer to your clients for participating in the change?

7. What are the major changes that need to be made in order to implement this strategy?

8. For professional group leaders, how will you coach and support the new directions?

WORKSHEET 5
INTEGRATE INTO A MARKETING PLAN

Now you need to pull all this information together into an integrated and realistic marketing plan.

1. Given your analysis from the previous steps, what are some elements you need to include in an effective marketing strategy? (How are you going to go about marketing your professional skills?)

2. What are your longterm marketing goals inside your organization (a period of three to five years)?

14

3. What are your short term marketing goals inside your organization (in the next six months to one year)?

4. What are your next steps to achieving your goals?

5. How will you communicate your new strategy to your clients in a way that supports acceptance? How will you get feedback in order to take corrective action on the inevitable problems that will crop up?

5. Who and what do you need for support?

❺ Golden Marketing Rules

1. *Know your clients' business*

- Know your clients' business and constraints. The most common complaint of clients is the professional's perceived lack of understanding of their business and its constraints.
- Know your clients' strategic direction. Anticipate critical needs in your area of expertise. Your clients' strategic needs are the source of high leverage work.
- Know your clients' pressure points. Clients greatly value professionals who alleviate pain.
- Think and talk in terms of business benefits as your clients would see them.

2. *Make a marketing plan*

- Have a marketing strategy. The most common reason things do not go according to plan is that there is no plan.
- Separate your longterm marketing strategy (which will change very slowly over time), from tactics (which respond to the situation at hand, within the strategy).
- When you have planned, ask for feedback for a reality check. Lack of good feedback can be fatal to careers.

❝ Quotable Quotes ❞

Inspire and lead, rather than compete and protect.

3. *Build support*

- Share your technical, professional expertise. People give to those who give. People love to work with those who share. Use your energy to inspire and lead, not to compete and protect.
- The best form of marketing is word-of-mouth referrals. The best way to get referrals is to do great, value-added work. The easiest source of more work is through satisfied clients.
- Find a coach in each client group who can help you understand the clients' 'real world.'
- You will meet the odd person on your journey who will use, or even abuse, your openness. Keep moving. Most clients appreciate and reciprocate generosity.

4. *Build partnerships*

- The best client relationships are 50-50 partnerships. Gradually move one-sided clients from 90-10 situations to 80-20, etc.
- Service is not servitude. Most clients want you to, and need you to push back. Push too little and you won't get what you want. Push too much and you won't get what you want, either.
- Don't assume your clients know how to use your expertise. In particular, you need to market to them your value-added services.
- Work from success to success. Build successes starting with your supporters. Don't start with the heaviest resister.

5. *Always be strategic*

- Every job has considerable detail and administration. *Don't get caught up in the details!*
- Have a vision. Know where you are going. Continually test your vision against the reality of your marketplace. It is frustrating to offer services that no one wants.
- Keep strategic. Always look for small gains to your vision. The accumulation of small gains can lead to breakthroughs.
- Get leverage on your work. Coaching and training others are fine ways to free up time for higher value work. (And it can be high value work in its own right!)
- Involve your stakeholders in the formulation of your professional group strategy. There is much more power in group action than in individual action.

6. And a few more:

- Walk your talk. Practice what you preach. Most clients value integrity in the long haul.
- Somewhat understate what you will deliver. Most clients like small, positive surprises.
- Communicate. Lavishly communicate. Do not assume that your clients know how your group can add value.
- Ask for feedback. If it is negative, do not punish those who give it!
- Keep learning. Successful marketers have learned how to learn.

❺ 101 MARKETING HINTS AND TIPS

Professionals often abhor marketing. But there are umpteen things you can do which are excellent marketing tactics, yet you may never have thought of them that way! Many of these are very easy. Here are 101! Check off those you already do. Highlight those you should start doing:

Think about Your Professional Practice
- ❏ Think of yourself as an independent contractor providing professional services to your organization. What would you stop, start and continue doing?
- ❏ Take a half-day per quarter to step back: look at the big picture; plan improvement.
- ❏ Sketch a table of all your current clients and the % of time you spend with each.
- ❏ Sketch a table of who *should* be your clients and the amount of effort you should expend.
- ❏ Continually ask yourself "Is this the best use of my time?"

Build Supportive Networks
- ❏ Don't client bash.
- ❏ Be enthusiastic.
- ❏ Be seen as a solution to, not a contributor to, your clients' problems.
- ❏ Build a powerful informal network of peers, managers, clients, support people, etc.
- ❏ Develop coaches in every client area.
- ❏ Give your expertise away.
- ❏ Inspire and lead, don't control and compete with your clients.

Be 'World-Class'
- ❏ Be committed to being 'world class.'
- ❏ Look down the road with your profession's direction and with your organization's direction. At the intersection of these two roads lies high-value work.
- ❏ Look for 'sweet spots'—value added projects where your distinctive skills are used.
- ❏ Find out what your competitors are doing. Be better in strategic areas.

Expand Your Practice
- ❏ Take every client request as an opportunity to market value-added work.
- ❏ Separate what your clients want from what they need.
- ❏ Never assume that the clients' initial request is all they want or need.
- ❏ Don't assume your clients know what to ask you for.
- ❏ Ask questions which open up new opportunities.
- ❏ Ask questions which get below the 'tip of the iceberg' to more significant concerns and issues.
- ❏ Look for high impact clients and projects.
- ❏ Always talk of the business needs driving your professional services.
- ❏ Talk about the future of your clients and how your profession can help.

14

Feedback keeps your feet in touch with the ground while your eyes are on your vision. Feedback helps you make changes and prevents surprises.

❝ Quotable Quotes ❞

"Business-ing = The process of turning every job into a business, every worker into a businessperson, a business unit of one."

– Tom Peters

253

❝ Quotable Quotes ❞

"Knowing what other professionals outside your organization are doing broadens your awareness and can help when marketing your services. Benchmarking to other organizations can either show what you are doing in addition to them, or may help to demonstrate application of your proposed services."

– Robin Sober
The Mutual Group

Talk Informally With Clients
- ❏ Regularly ask your clients for service improvement feedback.
- ❏ Regularly ask your clients to describe their most pressing concerns.
- ❏ Ask your clients about their business and its concerns.
- ❏ Find out what drives your clients and talk to them in these terms.
- ❏ Continually talk about new ways of looking at your clients' business needs.
- ❏ Continually talk about how you can help with business needs.
- ❏ Listen, then listen some more to your clients.
- ❏ Communicate, then communicate some more with your clients.
- ❏ As an internal professional, remember one of your competitive advantages is 'insider information.'

Set Goals
- ❏ Prepare a marketing plan.
- ❏ Think strategically.
- ❏ Prepare new marketing goals every month.
- ❏ Remember that the 'stairway to heaven' is not an elevator. One step at a time will get you to the top.

Make Yourself Visible
- ❏ Have a 'pizza' professional presentation.
- ❏ Organize 'brown bag lunch' professional presentations.
- ❏ Always tie professional presentations to organizational and business needs.
- ❏ Volunteer to attend the next client meeting.
- ❏ Volunteer to present at the next client meeting.
- ❏ Talk to a client about a new idea every week.
- ❏ Send a short article to your clients. Attach a note connecting the article to a client need.
- ❏ Invite external presenters into your organization.

Make Yourself 'Easy to Work With'
- ❏ Take 100% of the responsibility for marketing yourself and for your career.
- ❏ Coach, mentor or teach someone in your client group.
- ❏ Find out that you can learn from a critic.
- ❏ Work with a colleague who is more competent than you are.

Get Improvement Feedback
- ❏ Ask for feedback from your clients.
- ❏ Ask for project closure meetings—'look back' meetings.
- ❏ Ask for 'taking stock' meetings.
- ❏ Find out about best practices in other organizations.
- ❏ Use client feedback surveys.

Personal Development—Marketing
- ❏ Learn about marketing and selling.
- ❏ Listen to tapes on marketing and selling.
- ❏ Learn about 'call reluctance,' the inhibition of contacting others about what you can do for them.
- ❏ Learn to handle rejection. Nothing works 100% of the time.
- ❏ Learn how to make resistance work for you.
- ❏ Develop your presentation skills.

Personal Development—Leadership
- ❏ Develop yourself technically/professionally.
- ❏ Take a leadership workshop.
- ❏ Develop your project management skills.
- ❏ Develop your business literacy skills.
- ❏ Learn negotiation skills.
- ❏ Develop your interpersonal skills.

- Understand and use the four levels of professional career development:
  1. Apprentice—being a good learner with structured, unambiguous work
  2. Independent Professional—specializing and taking on more complex projects
  3. Professional Leader—getting results through others, leading project teams
  4. Organizational Consultant—helping organizational success in your professional area.

Personal Development—Professional
- Join a professional society.
- Talk to your professional peers in other organizations.
- Learn new business process skills.
- Learn new business skills—finance, budgeting, profit and loss, etc.
- Scan the business pages of a newspaper daily.
- Read a business/leadership book once a month.

Delight Your Clients and Your Manager
- Every month, write up a status report with suggestions for value-added work.
- Continually look for and propose high impact work.
- Tell your clients that you value them. Give your clients some positive feedback.
- Buy the donuts.

Get Commitment to Action
- Present benefits as thoroughly as features.
- Always explain why. History shows people will do anything if you tell them why.
- Make your clients look good.
- Make your peers look good.

Delight Yourself
- Make up a resume outlining your achievements.
- Laugh, loosen up. Marketers are known to have fun!
- Step out—suggest solutions outside your core skill.
- Step out—reframe client concerns.
- Step back—ask 'big picture' questions.
- Say "no," with options, to a low value project.
- Be passionate about your skills.
- Don't be too hard on yourself. Nothing works 100% of the time!

Cultivate a "Small Gains" Approach to Marketing
- Remember you can eat a whole elephant one bite at a time.
- Take a client to lunch every week.
- Have coffee with a client every day.
- Work with supportive clients first. Don't blame yourself—some clients will always be difficult.
- Volunteer to lead the next meeting.
- Think of building a big success by building on small successes.
- Prepare a potential client list. Contact the best bet today.

And A Few More
- Think of yourself running a small consulting business.
- Find a sponsor in every client group.
- Help your group define a professional strategy.
- Develop a professional network inside and outside of your organization.
- Learn about yourself.
- Learn how differences can be made to work for you.
- Learn how to lead change.
- Learn about modern management processes like Total Quality.
- Treat everyone in your organization as you would customers of your own business.

66 Quotable Quotes 99

"Market for current activities but also 'plant seeds' of ideas for future work!"
– Robin Sober

14

Application

1. What marketing activities can you start immediately for short term pay off?

2. What marketing activities do you need to do now for a long term pay off?

255

WHAT YOU'VE LEARNED SO FAR ...

- Professionals must increasingly market their professional expertise if they wish to be valued.

- Marketing is closely tied to professional strategy.

- Marketing your professional services involves a five-step plan:
    1. Know your professional group.
    2. Know your organization.
    3. Know your clients.
    4. Formulate your professional group strategy.
    5. Integrate the above into a marketing plan.

- Marketing your professional skills requires many and varied tactics and techniques.

THE EXPERTISE DELIVERY MODEL

"If things don't improve soon I may have to ask you to stop helping me."

© *Ashleigh Brilliant*

 **CHAPTER 15**

PUTTING IT ALL TOGETHER

15

Quick Snapshot

Did You Know?
- you can choose to have your consultation spiral upwards or downwards?
- powerful professionals 'live at the edge?'
- it's principles that help you adjust techniques to fit novel situations?

How-to:
- give clients feedback.
- raise your chances of receiving model behavior from your clients.
- apply the key principles and skills of the book.

The Bottom Line:
- The last pieces of the powerful professional picture will fall into place for you.

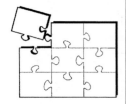

Connections

The purpose of this chapter is to summarize and consolidate the ideas of *Powerful Professionals*. The major topics of this chapter are:

Principles for Powerful Professionals

Techniques are just that—tactical skills, great when the consulting situation is just right. Because each client and situation is unique—and not always straightforward—techniques must be adapted from sound principles. When the going gets rough, or when conditions change, and 'recipes' fail, principles are the sound base for adapting behavior. These are some of the reasons we have been encouraging you to *adapt* the models presented in this book, using your own principles.

What Are Your Foundations?

As an example, one oft repeated principle in this book is that your best longterm role strategy is that of a 50-50 partnership with your clients. To illustrate use of this principle: we have discouraged the pair of hands role because it lacks professional power; and the expert role because it typifies a 'power over' attitude. Yet on occasion, you need to assume the pair of hands role and say "If that's the way you want it done, even though I don't see it as the best way, I'll do it this time." On other occasions, you may have to 'play the heavy' and say "no." It cannot be done that way. It goes against federal legislation."

To help you choose a role, here are some principles:
• You do what is best in the longterm for the organization, clients and yourself.
• You think through what 'You, Inc.' is all about—your strategy, what is important or unimportant, where you draw the line and say "no," and so on.
• You understand the limits of your role flexibility for ethical, professional and business reasons. You can explain your rationale clearly and succinctly.
• You know that you need to model flexibility if you want your clients to be flexible.
• You understand your own need for control.

In the following table, extending to the next page, we have summarized some important principles for powerful consulting. You do not have to agree with every item on the list; rather use it as a springboard for your own list, which in turn becomes a touchstone for your role as a powerful professional in your unique set of circumstances.

The benefits of clarifying and assiduously using your personal set of principles are:

✓ you will be perceived as having integrity.

✓ you will be able to explain your values, your limits and your ethics.

✓ you will be able to explain to others why you are doing what you do.

✓ in explaining to others why you cannot do something, you will be seen as consistent.

✓ you will be perceived as more of a leader because people 'know where you are coming from.'

✓ you will get less stuck in positions where you are arguing over alternatives because you can move the discussion to the underlying principles and needs.

✓ you will find it easier to make choices by getting in touch with your own set of principles.

✓ you will be able to coach others more effectively by coaching not only in techniques but in the whys.

✓ you will be less stuck when novel situations crop up.

66 Quotable Quotes 99

*"Without principles we are leaves in the wind
pushed in every direction
by every new idea."*
– David Bly

15

Some Principles Underlying the *Powerful Professional* Techniques

Principle	If you ignore	Some things to do
Model the behavior you expect from your clients—be recursive. (See the next chapter section.)	If what you say is different from what you do, clients quickly sense this, even if they can't put their finger on it.	The best way to encourage exemplary behavior is to model the behavior you want from others. If you want feedback, accept feedback. If you want openness, be open.
Push too softly and you won't get what you want; push too hard and you won't get what you want.	Too unassertive, you get walked on or over and you feel powerless. Too aggressive and you fight continuously, consequently people will avoid you or work around you.	Here is a place where many professionals need coaching help—it is extremely difficult to assess the impact of one's own behavior. Ask for and accept feedback and coaching.
Become an expert not only in your profession, but also in how to deliver your expertise.	Clients unfortunately are not well skilled (though they ought to be!) in using professional advice. You cannot depend on them to use your own skills effectively.	Learn consulting skills. Watch and model professionals who are strategic and who get the job done in your organization.
Listen with both ears—one for content, the other for process.	Many professionals think mainly in terms of their profession and expertise—content. How that expertise is translated into results is process.	Don't be 'content bound.' When talking about a situation, be as conscious of the process—how the situation is being worked, as you are about the content—what is being worked. Contribute to both content and process.

In this chapter ...

- *Principles of powerful professionals*
- *Recursive behavior*
- *Helping clients be more effective*
- *Living at the edge*
- *Giving and receiving feedback*
- *Power how-tos*
- *The last word*

Principle	If you ignore	Some things to do
Powerful professionals must handle ambiguity, not only for themselves, but often for their clients as well.	Lack of tolerance for ambiguity pushes you and your clients to suboptimal, narrow problem definitions, solutions and roles.	Take the time to explore a narrowly defined issue. Don't panic over an ill-defined issue. Help ambiguity-phobic clients by summarizing content and process frequently.
Be strategic by seeing the big picture and aligning your efforts, while attending to detail and getting things done. Improve both your strategy and your tactics.	Many professionals are detail oriented, leading over the long term to a frustrating pair of hands role. On the other hand 'talking big' and not delivering is not effective either.	If you are detail oriented, frequently ask yourself "Why?" Work with your professional group to prepare longer term strategic plans. Ask Big Picture questions.
Be strategic by thinking of yourself as running a professional services business inside your organization— 'You, Inc.'	Professionals who have not defined their strategy are often frustrated by low value activities and/or blame management for 'not making good use of my skills.'	If you were a small business delivering your expertise inside your organization, what would you stop, start and continue?
Avoid client bashing or blaming your clients.	Stupid clients are assisted by stupid consult-ants—and it will show. When you clash with a client, the only behavior you can control is your own.	Refrain from categorizing people or groups as "They are all ..." See the next principle.
From the clients' perspective, there is always a rationale why they are doing what they are doing.	Without this principle, you may tend to either construct negative motivations or client bash.	If a client is acting 'weird,' talk privately with the client, who will often describe his or her motivation. Client behavior is always rational—as the client sees it.
Inspire and lead; don't protect and compete internally.	Greater leverage as a professional comes from not only being skilled yourself, but from helping others become skilled.	You will be much more valued and much easier to work with if you move to Level 3 of the 4 Level professional career model described in Chapter 12.
Feedback is the breakfast of champion professionals.	Without feedback you will act from false assumptions, leading you to misdirect your limited energy and effort.	Ask for feedback and receive it effectively. See page 267 of this chapter.
The best way to deal with conflict and resistance is to surface them.	Resistance and conflict don't go away if you ignore or suppress them. They just surface in other ways.	'You can pay me now or you can pay me later.' Difficult as it may be to hear, if you are to be effective, you need to know where you and your projects stand.
Understand your personal need for control and the control needs of your clients.	Many professionals' or clients' dysfunctional behaviors can be traced to the need to keep control.	Get feedback on your personal need for control—you may be surprised! Control needs of clients can often be finessed—like the martial arts.
The best consultations have a 50-50 feel, neither one-up nor one-down.	You either withdraw to a low leverage pair of hands role or become a pain in the butt 'know-it-all.'	If you want the project to be 'we' at the end, start with and always talk 'we' throughout the project.
Use every meeting, memo, e-mail and phone call as an opportunity to build commitment.	Many professionals are not really concerned with people commitment until they need it— then they wonder why people are reluctant to give it.	Establish two-way communication and participation; don't talk at, talk with. Always explain why.

More Effective Professional Behavior—Recursion

The toughest principle for powerful professionals is to be recursive. Recursion is a mathematical term, meaning you use a problem as part of its own solution. One type of recursion is 'model the behavior you need from your clients.' This principle will become clearer as you read on. Let's start with some examples, then step back and talk about some benefits and challenges of being a recursive professional.

Some Recursive Elements of Internal Consulting

"Real power is not given; it is taken by earning it."
– Bob Ratay
Avery-Dennison

Clients will find it hard to:
- be open to new ideas with a professional who is not open to new ideas.
- listen to a professional who is not listening to them.
- accept feedback from a professional who does not accept feedback.
- give recognition to a professional who does not give them recognition.
- share confidences with a professional who cannot keep confidences.
- give complex projects to a professional who has a low tolerance for complexity.
- think highly of a professional who does not think highly of them.

15

If you want clients and others to:
- exhibit model behavior, model model behavior.
- lower their resistance, don't resist resistance.
- accept change, be open to change yourself.
- consider you a leader, take leadership roles.
- be strategic with your time, be strategic with theirs.
- understand you, understand yourself and others.
- open up, ask open-ended questions.
- not have hidden agendas with you, don't have hidden agendas with them.
- be reasonable with you, be reasonable with them.
- accept your inadequacies, admit to your own and accept client inadequacies.

And a few more:
- If you want the right to be unreasonable on occasion, accept that others will be unreasonable on occasion.
- Power cannot be given, the powerful assume it. (One common complaint we hear from professionals is "they don't make good use of my skills." The recursive stance is this: "one of my skills is to have my skills used …")

RECURSIVE HUMOR?

If you are interested in recursive sayings, we highly recommend Ashleigh Brilliant's books.

Ordinary life is full of recursive sayings, cartoons, happenings and events. Some examples are:
"All Cretans are liars."– Epimenides the Cretan
"I used to think I was indecisive, but now I'm not so sure." – J. Healy
"I would not dream of belonging to a club that is willing to have me as a member."– Groucho Marx
"I'm just a girl who can't say 'nnn …', nnn …, …" – Joanne Worley
"Worried that your memory is fading? Then write down …" – Time Magazine (Nov. 23, 1998)

Communicate About How You Communicate

Perhaps one of the most powerful and useful skills for professionals is to be able to communicate with clients about how you are communicating or, if you prefer, talk about how you are talking. This skill is known as meta-communication and can help you out of a ton of pickles. When you feel a conversation is bogging down, you can intervene by saying "I think this conversation is going off track. How can we get it back on track?" When you feel you and your clients are getting into conflict, you can say "I don't want to butt heads with you. Can we talk about the impasse we seem to heading into?" Note that these invitations to meta-communication are best put in straightforward language. You want to invite your client to talk about how you are talking. Most clients will respond at this 'meta' level and communicate about the communication problem. You can then use this higher level discussion to help solve the original problem. See the further discussion on the next page for more detail and examples.

This is an illustration of the power of thinking recursively. Clients are quick to sense disconnects between what is said versus what is actually being done. (One of the biggest challenges of this book is to be recursive with our advice to you—to practise what we preach—no mean feat!)

Benefits of Recursive Behavior

- Recursion is at the heart of integrity. Recursive thinking continually challenges a professional: "Is what I say and do congruent with what I say I'm about?" For example, if you want a 50-50 partnership, is everything you say and do congruent with the 50-50?
- Many authors of consulting books talk about 'being authentic' or 'bringing yourself to the job.' For technical professionals, being recursive may be a more accessible concept.
- One of the most powerful ways to elicit model client behavior is to model the behavior you expect in others. Clients will often mirror back your behavior.
- If you act recursively from a well-thought out set of principles, you will be less likely to 'take it personally,' leading to less stress. You will know you have done the best you can.
- Clients will be more likely to accept you 'warts and all' because they know you are willing to accept them 'warts and all.'

Downsides of Recursive Behavior

- Recursive behavior doesn't always work. Some clients, for example, will take your openness as a sign of weakness and try to exploit it. Since we are not writing a book about purposefully difficult clients—see the next section of this chapter on the Range of Clients—we assume that most clients are like you, doing their best to be effective in a complex and often confusing world. This leads us to another principle: nothing works all of the time when it comes to human behavior. Think about it—if behavior 'x' always elicited behavior 'y' on the part of others, you could then manipulate others' behavior.
- Recursive behavior sets a very high, perhaps ideal, standard of professional conduct.

❝ Quotable Quotes ❞

"When an internal professional group has decided on its own sound consulting principles, it is crucial that everyone in the group acts accordingly. Perceiving one of its professionals as being too pushy—asking too many questions, for example—there is a tendency for an individual professional from the group to do what they client is asking for, even if it is not in the best interest of the client. This is usually because the individual professional wants to be accepted. If a professional group is not cohesive in its policies and practice, this can lead to the entire group being 'dumped on,' and ending up in a pair of hands role."

– Bill Sefcik, CPA

Talk About Talking—Meta-Communication

A general and powerful strategy for dealing with difficult situations is to use the technique of meta-communication. A meta-communication is an invitation to your clients to discuss the difficulty at one level deeper than the current level. For example, if you and an indecisive client are in a stall mode over a proposal, you can often unstick the situation by saying "Pat, at our last meeting, you asked for a few days to study this proposal and now you are asking for more time. I am concerned that time is not the real issue. Is there some other concern that you have with the proposal?"

The exact wording is situational but the characteristics of an effective invitation to meta-communicate are:

- A meta-communication calls the client's 'bluff.' The behavior you are seeing is only a symptom of something more fundamental. Be careful here of ascribing negative motives to a client's behavior. Clients often have habitual ways of dealing with situations and they are probably not clear or conscious of their own behavior or motives.
- A meta-communication invites your client 'to come clean.' It invites your client to discuss the issue at a deeper level.
- A meta-communication must be clear enough so your client cannot mistake that you are 'calling' the dysfunctional behavior, yet gentle enough that your client does not feel punished. Push too little and the client may not hear you; push too hard and the client may reject your intervention. Practice with a coach.

If your client does come clean, you must actively listen and support your client. This step is particularly difficult when your client wants to tell you something personal regarding your proposal in which you have invested so much of yourself.

The benefits of a meta-communication are often longterm. If you are known to call clients' dysfunctional behaviors in a supportive manner, you are less likely to get the dysfunctional behavior from clients in the first place! Powerful professionals use this strategy.

15

How Meta-Communication Works

1. There is disagreement or difficulty at the content level:

   e.g. You and your client are disagreeing on the time it takes to complete a phase of the project.

2. Move 'up' a level to discuss the process, that is, how you and your client are dealing with this issue.

   e.g. "Can we step back for a moment? We seem to be going nowhere on this project timeline. How can we solve this difficulty?"

3. After discussing the difficulty at one level up, go back down to the content of the issue to resolve it on the basis of the principles agreed to.

Meta-Communication Schematic

Process Level

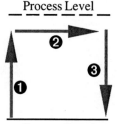

Content Level

Meta-Control?
Control is at the heart of many difficult situations.

Interestingly enough, many (most?) professionals, like clients, have high needs for control. Therefore, difficult situations often have 'control wrestling' underneath the rational words. Meta-control is letting go of control at the content level and, in its place, taking control at the process and context level, for example, asking appropriate questions, thereby establishing a 50/50 role; being open to feedback, surfacing concerns.

Most professionals' first control impulse is to control the professional content of the consultation. In establishing more control over process, the professional content will then take care of itself.

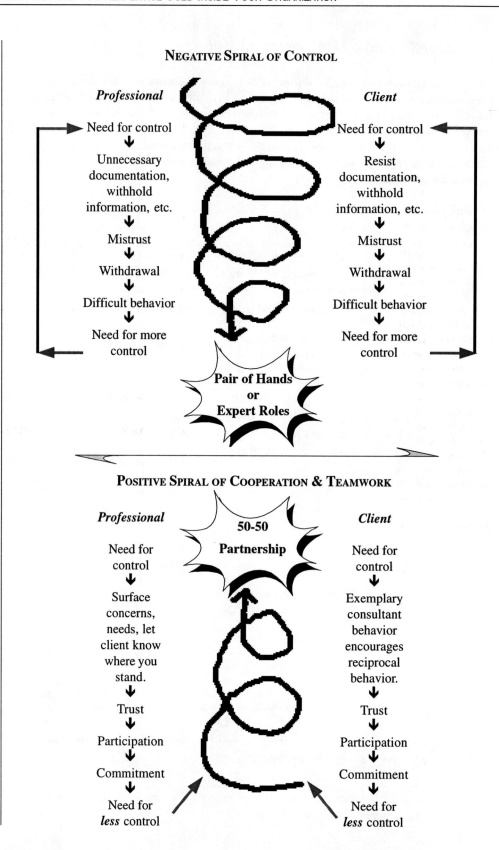

NEGATIVE SPIRAL OF CONTROL

Professional | *Client*

Need for control → Need for control

Unnecessary documentation, withhold information, etc. | Resist documentation, withhold information, etc.

Mistrust | Mistrust

Withdrawal | Withdrawal

Difficult behavior | Difficult behavior

Need for more control | Need for more control

Pair of Hands or Expert Roles

POSITIVE SPIRAL OF COOPERATION & TEAMWORK

Professional | **50-50 Partnership** | *Client*

Need for control | Need for control

Surface concerns, needs, let client know where you stand. | Exemplary consultant behavior encourages reciprocal behavior.

Trust | Trust

Participation | Participation

Commitment | Commitment

Need for *less* control | Need for *less* control

Helping Clients be More Effective—A Range of Clients

It's easy to experience that not all clients are ideal; in fact we have heard that some are downright nasty and dysfunctional. On the other hand, we hope you have a number of clients with whom you 'click' or you 'have great chemistry.'

Clients range from ogres, with whom no legal methods will work, to angels, whose skills make you marvel. The majority of clients are somewhere on a continuum between these two extremes. We have tried to illustrate this distribution by the curves below.

One principle of consulting is that you can't directly change the behavior of clients but you certainly can change your own. This *Powerful Professionals* book is about changing your consulting behaviors to more effective ones, which will have the effect of shifting the curve to the right.

Difficult Client?
One professional told us of a client who had a sign on an office wall: "Spit it out and get out."

15

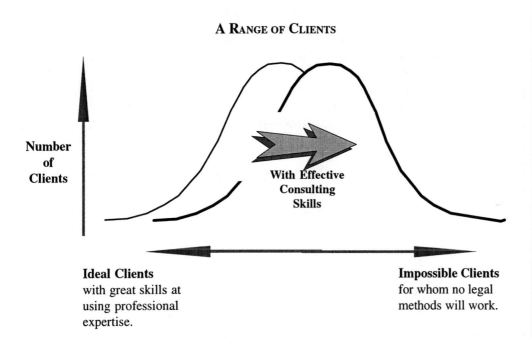

A RANGE OF CLIENTS

Number of Clients

With Effective Consulting Skills

Ideal Clients
with great skills at using professional expertise.

Impossible Clients
for whom no legal methods will work.

For the clients on the right-hand 'impossible' side, you may wish to consult one of the references on dealing with difficult people noted in the *Selected Further Reading* section. The skills and models of this book were designed for the majority of clients—those like yourself, who are trying to be more effective in a fast-moving, complex world.

For clients on the left-hand, 'ideal' side, learn from them. What behaviors do they use that make them ideal clients? Watch their processes; adapt their behaviors to your needs.

One Foot In and One Foot Out—Living at the Edge

Powerful Professionals live at the consulting edge. If all you are is a pair of hands, a role taker, a professional who expects others to define needs, solutions and strategies, and you give predictable advice, you are a 'salt-of-the-earth' professional—but not powerful. If, on the other hand, you give 'far-out' advice, in advance of what the client and the organization are prepared to handle, you will be dismissed as a 'nerd,' a 'geek' or worse.

As you can see from the illustration below, powerful professionals deliver their expertise at the edge. They have one foot firmly planted in the organization or business. They can talk management talk; they are business literate; they understand the environmental pressures on the organization; they understand the direction of the organization and they know when and how to contribute. The other foot pushes clients beyond the 'tried-and-true,' pushes clients and the organization to use your professional expertise for improvement. Two of our top eight survey database items tell how much clients value innovative approaches in the conceptualization and delivery of expertise.

The trick is to live at the edge: one part of you demonstrating to your clients that you can 'start where they are at'; the other part helping clients and the organization with value-added advice in your area of expertise. Note that over time, what was value-added becomes necessity—'the way we do things around here.' Like an amoeba engulfing its food, the circle bulges out to include your recommendations. You continually need to think strategically about how you add value to your clients and organization—how to live at the edge.

Adding value and thinking strategically are dealt with in Chapter 13, Your Strategy: Saying Yes or No.

LIVING AT THE EDGE

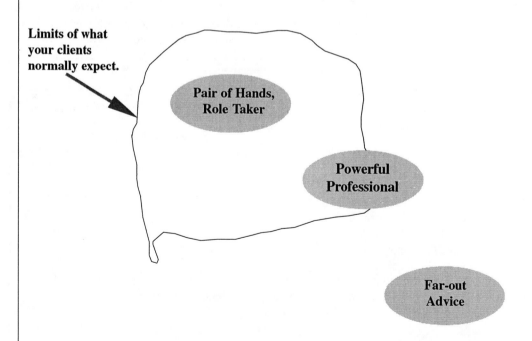

Limits of what your clients normally expect.

Pair of Hands, Role Taker

Powerful Professional

Far-out Advice

Giving and Receiving 'No-fault' Feedback

Performance feedback is the breakfast of powerful professionals. A common complaint of professionals is "I wish I knew better where I stood." As a professional, you also need to be able to give feedback to your clients on what Peter Block calls 'difficult realities.' Giving and receiving feedback can be enhanced by following a few guidelines.

GUIDELINES FOR GIVING FEEDBACK

Usually Well Received	Usually Causes Difficulties
Described concretely in terms of what you saw or heard Described how it impacted you Specific Directed to receiver (eye contact, 'I-You') Balance of things that impacted you—favorably and unfavorably	Described your judgment or evaluation Guessed at another's intent General Described as a third-party event Only negative feedback

For example, after a presentation you have just made, you go up to a colleague and ask "How did my presentation go?" The colleagues turns away and says "It was alright." Immediately you wonder "What does 'alright' mean—good? barely adequate? ..." and "Why did my colleague turn away?" Of course, the feedback would be much more helpful if the colleague looked at you and described your presentation more specifically, e.g. "You started off in a way that got me interested, but you lost me in the middle."

The other side of the coin is receiving feedback. One reason why some professionals do not get feedback is because they cannot receive feedback well. If your response to client feedback appears to be defensive or punishing in any way, clients will avoid giving you feedback. 'Knowing where you stand' can be enhanced by these few simple guidelines.

GUIDELINES FOR RECEIVING FEEDBACK

Usually Well Received	Tends to Put Giver on Defensive
Saying "thank you" Asking for clarification when uncertain Summarizing the feedback Using eye contact	Explaining your behavior Defending your intent

Bad DOG!!

Can you give me an example?

❝ Quotable Quotes ❞

"Thank you for telling me what I didn't want to hear."
© Ashleigh Brilliant

15

Early coaching advice given to the author "If people give you feedback, bite your tongue and count to 10; then bite harder and count again."

Power How-tos for Powerful Professionals

Here is what we perceive as a summary of the most important principles and 'how tos' of the book:

Principles and How-tos	More Info
1. Exploring the Need	
• You have the most leverage and power that you will ever have at the very beginning of a project. Most problems can be traced back to the first few minutes of consulting. Be conscious of both the professional content of the problem and the process by which the problem is being worked.	page 35
• Understand the pressure on your clients to present symptoms or a solution rather than the under-lying problem or need. Take time to surface the underlying issues and causes. Establish sufficient rapport to help your clients speak frankly. Devote as much effort to rapport talk as report talk.	page 30
• Commitment building isn't something you do at the recommendations stage of consulting. Talk of we from the beginning if you want we at the end. Commitments are a matter of the heart, not the head.	page 39
2. Clarifying Commitments	
• Clear expectations means you never have to say you're sorry. Always summarize commitments at the end of every conversation, every meeting and every telephone call—"Just to be sure I understand, what I am going to do is X and what you are going to do is Y." Most clients love clarity as much as you do.	page 57
• Misunderstandings are the bane of your career. For work commitments of more than a few days, confirm with a brief, point-form document or e-mail message. In negotiation, the pen is mightier than the word.	page 58
3. Gathering Information	
• Have a questioning strategy. Know when you are increasing the scope of information by asking big picture questions and when you are decreasing the scope of information by asking closed-ended questions.	page 68
• Every question has a role implied in it. Powerful consultants ask powerful questions. If you need to ask a question to get to the heart of the problem, the issue is not whether to ask the difficult question but how to ask it in a non-punishing way.	page 72
4. Recommending Change	
• Present the benefits of your recommendation as thoroughly as its features. Take time to think of the benefits as your clients would see them. Each type of client can have different expectations and benefits. Executives resonate to quite different benefits than do End Users.	page 88
• Don't resist resistance. It is natural and OK for your clients to think of the advantages of staying with the status quo and the disadvantages of change. Help your clients to surface their reservations such that you can deal with them or at least understand them. You can't do anything about concerns you don't hear.	page 93
5. Taking Stock/Closing	
• Many professionals have ongoing clients. You have most leverage when things are going well. Invest time to sit down with your clients to take stock of your consulting relationship and to propose more leveraged work roles.	page 108
• Most consulting projects fizzle out rather than close. Take responsibility for wrapping up the project so that you get the recognition and feedback you deserve. Remember the best time to negotiate closing is at the beginning. Clear expectations lead to clear closings.	page 109

Principles and How-tos	More Info
Thinking Strategically • Think through your professional practice. Be strategic. Know what you say "yes" to, because it is value-added work for you and your clients. Know what you say "no" to, and why. Try to give your clients options for getting their needs met when you say "no."	page 216
• Your professional power is greatly enhanced by connecting your skills and knowledge to your clients, and organizational needs and direction. Learn about your organization, and about your clients' needs.	page 218
Enhancing Your Role and Career • Leverage in your role and in the commitment of others is best obtained by involving others and getting your results through others. Learn group leadership skills. Leaders lead by taking the lead!	page 205
Sustaining Change • Be a full cycle consultant. Helping your recommendation through sustained change is a key to influence. Changes rarely fail because your recommendations are not technically OK or because people are obtuse. Changes more often fail because the systems surrounding your recommended change are not supportive. Spend as much time considering how to make systems more supportive as you do fine tuning the recommendation.	page 136
• The more important changes take place inside people. Remember the external change is usually quicker than the internal. Give people time to let go of the past. It is natural for them to go through a turmoil period coming to terms with your recommended change before they can embrace it.	page 152

For a list of 101 things to do to enhance your effectiveness and leverage, read *Appendix 1, 101 Ways to Apply the Book.*

The Last Word

We wrote this book from a conviction that professionals are often the overlooked piece of productivity in an organization. This led us to the goal of enabling professionals to become more powerful, to have a resounding impact upon the productivity of their organizations. The wealth of models, checklists, how-tos, and practical suggestions have all been designed with that goal in mind. We thank you for choosing our book, and we wish you every success as a Powerful Professional!

Visit us on the Web Site http://www.consultskills.com for up-to-date news!

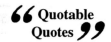

❝ Quotable Quotes ❞

"However much theory you have read, if you don't practice it, you are ignorant."

– Sa'di

WHAT YOU HAVE LEARNED ...

- Techniques and tools must be based in powerful principles for success in the unique situations that you face.

- Recursive behavior is a powerful way of understanding effective consulting behaviors.

- You can make your clients' behavior better by using more effective consulting behaviors.

- Powerful professionals live at the edge, pushing clients to look beyond the usual, but not being dismissed because the advice is too distant from the acceptable.

- Giving and receiving 'no fault' feedback is a valuable skill.

- Powerful professionals have a profound impact on the productivity of their organization.

THE EXPERTISE DELIVERY MODEL

> *"Thunder is good, thunder is impressive, but it is the lightning that does the work."*
> – Mark Twain

APPENDIX 1

101 WAYS TO APPLY THIS BOOK
FOLLOWED BY
101 WAYS TO COACH PROFESSIONALS

The biggest hurdle in professional development is translating good ideas from a book like this into practical, on-job results.

Two factors are critical:
1. You must make plans for improvement. The first checklist will help you do just that.
2. You need support from your manager, supervisor or team leader. The second checklist is designed to help the managers of professionals provide support for professionals.

Appendix 1 concludes with a Meeting Planner to help professionals and their managers have a successful meeting to jointly plan action in a 50-50 way.

Some conditions which assist successful application are:
- **Focus on a few critical issues.** It's better to apply a few ideas and succeed rather than try to apply too many, lose focus and fail.
- **Apply the ideas quickly.** The chances of application go to near zero if you do not or cannot apply the idea soon.
- **Plan changes.** Even writing down a few key words or phrases increases the chances of application. Focus on the application of the idea as much as on the idea itself. Payoffs are in applications. (See the Mark Twain quote above.)
- **Announce the changes.** Many people find that mentioning their applications to a number of people, including clients, greatly increases the chances of actually implementing the changes.

101 APPLICATION IDEAS FOR POWERFUL PROFESSIONALS

The purpose of this Checklist is to help you think of numerous ways in which you can apply the ideas from this *Powerful Professionals* book. Some items will be easy and will produce quick results. Other items will be more difficult but may yield higher results. Others may be impractical. Others may need adaptation for your situation. Use the few most likely to produce the best results for you and your organization. Be aware that working with others, using group action or redesigning your work system is almost always more leveraged than working on your own—although this is important as well.

The Five Stage Expertise Delivery Model

❏ Research shows that people need good 'mental models' to make sense of our complex world. Edit, if you wish, the Five Stage Expertise Delivery model. Print some copies of your working model in a useful size and place them in your office and Planner.

❏ Consciously use the model at the next opportunity.

❏ Resolve not to be a passive professional, expecting others to manage the expertise delivery process. Take responsibility for managing the consulting process.

❏ You cannot depend on managers and clients to 'make good use of my skills,' (although they should!); take responsibility for developing your own professional practice.

❏ Don't blame your clients when things go wrong. Use the skills of this book to make your clients better.

❏ The best way to have ideal clients is for you to use ideal consulting behavior. Model the behavior you expect of others.

❏ Use the Expertise Delivery Model when you are a client using the services of an internal professional or hiring an external consultant.

❏ Although useful at times, neither pair of hands, nor expert roles are functional over the long haul. Use a business partner stance and behavior for every activity, ranging from understanding the organization, to asking questions, to roles.

❏ Leave this book on your desk and use it often.

❏ Place Post-It™ tabs on the pages you will use regularly.

❏ Open the book at random and read a page or two for a for a quick tune-up.

❏ Visit the *Consulting Skills for Professionals* Web Site for a refresher, or when you need help.

❏ The shorter the consultation, the more you need to structure the Expertise Delivery process, because you cannot afford to take the time to wander into dead ends. Use the 'Brief Consultation Checklist' from Chapter 7, *Taking Stock/Closing*, to structure your brief consultations.

Stage 1: Exploring the Need

❏ Clients often present solutions to problems, not the underlying problem. Use questions to get at the underlying needs and open up new options.

❏ Don't ask "Why?" too early and risk putting your clients on the defensive.

❏ If you accept the presented solution instead of the underlying need, one of the side effects is to put yourself into a pair of hands role (and often blame your clients for the narrow role). Ask questions that get at underlying needs, at the same time setting up a 50-50 partner role.

❏ Make a short list of questions which will typically help you and your clients get at the underlying needs and consider more options.

❏ You need to quickly assess whether a client's concern is too narrow, requiring you to ask broadening questions or a client's concern is too broad, requiring you to ask questions which will get at the priorities.

❏ Post a short list of typical *Exploring the Need* questions by your telephone.

❏ Recognize that by asking questions, you can open up options or close off options. Be conscious of the questions you ask.

❑ Framing is a powerful technique for scoping client concerns. Frames are often implied and accepted very early. If the problem is not reframed early, you lose the opportunity for the concern to be seen in a more effective light.

❑ Professionals often struggle with ambiguity and constrict a problem too quickly. Take time to ferret out all the issues, especially those outside your usual area of expertise.

❑ Remember, your clients have fears that result in strange behavior. So do you. Be patient with clients (and yourself).

❑ Professionals often struggle with the 'people side' of work. Spend time on human-to-human rapport and personal relationships.

❑ Establishing trust is crucial to your success. Spend time establishing human-to-human contact, the basis of trust.

Stage 2: Clarifying Commitments

❑ Some of the most embarrassing consulting moments occur over unclear expectations between clients and professionals. Always clarify expectations. Use the checklists and models presented in Chapter 4 to help you do this.

❑ Conflict arises from unclear expectations. Dealing with conflict is one of the weakest skills of professionals. One of the easiest conflict prevention techniques is to clarify commitments.

❑ Too little clarification of expectations leads to misdirected work. Too much can be dysfunctional by taking too much time and making the project inflexible. Use an optimal amount of clarification.

❑ The minimum level of clarification is a verbal agreement. Always end every conversation or meeting by clarifying expectations and establishing the next steps.

❑ The working level of clarification is a simple document. Decide on your guidelines for using documentation. Use simple, non-bureaucratic documentation.

❑ In your word processor, design a *Clarifying Commitments* format for quickly producing a one-page document, to be used when you need it.

❑ Create a folder/directory on your computer hard drive to store samples of confirming documents, so that you don't have to generate them from scratch very often.

Stage 3: Gathering Information

❑ Our high performance database tells us that 'sorting out complex situations' is a skill highly valued by clients. Use the skills of verbally clarifying complex requests.

❑ Be careful using Triage questions. They can be very useful for creating credibility, relieving client stress and demonstrating an action orientation. However, be aware they can also lead to narrow roles and frustratingly recurring problems, because the underlying causes are not dealt with.

❑ Professionals often struggle with ambiguity and constrict a complex problem too quickly. Take the time to ask Big Picture questions.

❑ By asking a Big Picture question, you increase ambiguity and complexity, often difficult for clients and professionals to handle. The best way to keep ambiguity stress at a minimum is to always summarize what you have heard or make visible the information *before* asking a Big Picture question.

❑ Every question has a role implied in it. Avoid inadvertently asking "Tell me what to do, boss" questions (and getting angry with your clients when they tell you what to do).

❑ Be careful about using close-ended questions as an subtle means of keeping control.

❑ Use the hourglass questioning model for sorting out complex situations with your clients.

❑ Edit the hourglass model; print some copies of your model in a useful size; place them in your office and Planner.

Stage 4: Recommending Change

❑ From our survey database, the item 'Is able to persuade others' is unique. It is on the clients' most discriminating list of professional attributes, yet professionals are rated very low on this item. In other words, clients want to be persuaded by your recommendations, but professionals are generally lousy at persuading! Use the skills of effectively selling your recommendations and proposals.

❑ If you have some improvements for the Selling Wheel in Chapter 6, design your own.

❏ Post a copy of the Selling Wheel on your office wall.

❏ Professionals, by nature, tend to emphasize the features of their recommendations, not the benefits. Yet it is the benefits which sell your clients. Distinguish between features and benefits by writing them out in categories.

❏ Push yourself to think beyond the benefits which appeal to you, to the benefits which appeal to your clients' point-of-view. Use the Benefits Checklist.

❏ Get feedback and coaching from people *outside* your department on your balance of features and benefits. People in your department think like you, not like your clients.

❏ Dealing with the inevitable reservations and resistance to recommended change is again one of the lowest scored items from our survey database. Resistance can be helpful. Don't resist resistance.

❏ Professionals, like many people, tend to avoid conflict. There are multiple benefits to surfacing client conflict early in the form of concerns, reservations and resistance. Always give your clients an opportunity to surface their concerns.

❏ Use the Change Window with your clients to get a balanced view of the change—all the upsides plus all the downsides.

Stage 5: Taking Stock/Closing

❏ Closing projects is often poorly done. Closing is set up during the *Clarifying Commitments* stage of consulting. Consciously plan for the wrapping up of projects.

❏ Many professionals have continuing clients. You have the best leverage to improve a relationship when things are going well. Have a Taking Stock meeting with your clients when things are going well. This is your chance to suggest improvements to the consulting relationship.

❏ Use the *Taking Stock/Closing* Checklist for the critical items to discuss with clients at this stage.

Mapping Client Systems

❏ Because different client groups see different benefits and have different reservations, diagram your complex client system, listing the chief benefits and potential reservations for each group.

❏ Benefits that appeal to one client group may turn off another group.

❏ Think how different stakeholders would see the benefits of a recommendation.

❏ Think how different stakeholders would assess the risks, downsides and reservations to your recommended changes.

Sustaining Change

❏ Don't drop the ball at implementation. Think of yourself as a 'full cycle consultant'—one who starts by taking shared responsibility, from helping clients define their needs, right through to the shared responsibility for setting up and facilitating change.

❏ Too little involvement in change can be as dysfunctional as too much. Maintain a business partner approach to change: neither take from your clients too much responsibility for the change, nor wash your hands of the need to help your clients with the change.

❏ Use the Change Equation to assist you and your clients plan successful change.

❏ Post a copy of the Change Equation on your office wall.

❏ Most change fails, not because the recommendation was technically poor, but because the change was not supported by other systems which were barriers to the change. Diagram the interacting systems needed to support the recommended change.

❏ The question from the survey database, 'Understands and helps others deal with the stress of changes resulting from his/her recommendations' is among the lowest scored item on our survey database. Changes inside people—transitions—typically lag behind the external physical change. If you want the change to be smooth, lead people through personal transitions.

Listening Skills for Professionals
- ❏ Listening for understanding is a crucial skill for powerful professionals. Get feedback on your listening skills.
- ❏ There is no point in asking a great question and not listening to the answer. Use listening techniques in Chapter 11.
- ❏ Ask a colleague to give you feedback if he/she perceives you are not listening in a meeting.
- ❏ Use all of the levels of listening at appropriate times.

Enhancing Your Role and Your Career
- ❏ Be a Role Shaper—a professional who works hard to establish 50-50 partnerships with clients, neither one-up nor one-down.
- ❏ Research shows that professional development does not occur in a linear, continuous manner but rather in a nonlinear, discontinuous manner described by the four levels of career growth.
- ❏ Plan your move from Level 2—a good individual contributor—to a much more leveraged Level 3—getting results through others.
- ❏ Operate out of at least Level 3, where your success is the success of others.
- ❏ Be aware that what is considered helpful and high performance at one career level can become a problem at the next. Make a list of the new behaviors you want to use and the old behaviors you wish to let go of at each level transition.
- ❏ One of the lowest scored items from the survey database is the question 'Has a wider perspective than his/her expertise.' Most professionals need to see themselves less as experts and more as internal consultants with a professional expertise. Think of ways to be a business or organizational consultant, rather than an expert consultant.
- ❏ Consider using Novations' Four Stages Model™ as your professional group's career development model. This career model is specifically geared to professional productivity.

High Performance Consulting Competencies
- ❏ Review the *Professional Credibility Sequence* in Chapter 1 which tells you the process that clients use to evaluate professionals.
    - – What does it tell you about client expectations?
    - – What does it tell you and your professional group about what you are already good at and where you need development?

Strategic, Long Term Results
- ❏ Leveraged results can only be obtained by examining and updating your professional strategic direction and that of your professional group.
- ❏ Think and talk strategically about the direction of yourself, your profession and your organization.
- ❏ Use the strategic models in Chapter 13 to plan your professional strategy. They will help you distinguish between value-added work, business necessity work and work better done by others.
- ❏ Use the strategic models in Chapter 13 to work with your professional group.
- ❏ Use the strategic models in Chapter 13 to work with your clients.
- ❏ Besides asking your clients what they want and need, make offers of value-added work—clients may be unaware that your professional group can offer these.
- ❏ Look at your clients strategically. Which clients add more value to you, your professional group and your organization? How can less important clients get their needs met in other ways?
- ❏ Remember customer service does not mean saying "yes" to all requests.
- ❏ Saying "no" is often difficult for professionals (and their managers). Review the suggestions in Chapter 13 for saying "no" successfully.
- ❏ Help your work group design itself around core business processes. Ensure that your professional group's structure supports your work.

Marketing Your Skills

❑ More and more professionals and professional groups are marketing their professional skills. Start marketing yours.

❑ Think of yourself and your professional group as if you were an independent consulting group contracted to your organization. What would you stop doing? What would you start doing? What would you continue? Why not carry out these behaviors now?

❑ Use the Checklist of *101 Ways of Marketing Yourself* in Chapter 14 to inspire ideas for marketing value-added work.

Working with Your Manager, Supervisor or Team Leader

❑ Educational research shows that the learner's work environment is crucial to on-job application. In your work environment, the support and coaching of your supervisor or team leader is critical. Meet with your supervisor or team leader to discuss this *Powerful Professionals* book—your reactions, learnings, concerns, on-job applications and action plans.

❑ Ask your manager, team leader, or supervisor to use the *101 Ways to Coach Professionals* later in this Appendix.

❑ Ask for support with your applications.

❑ Enroll in a *Consulting Skills for Professionals* workshop. Contacts and public workshops are listed on the web site—http://www.consultskills.com.

❑ Don't forget the positives—those skills you already use, which were reiterated in the book.

❑ Plan follow-through. A major reason why things don't happen is that there is no plan.

❑ Discuss the Credibility Sequence—established from over 7,500 professionals who received feedback from over 50,000 others. What do these items tell you about future development needs?

❑ End the meeting by clarifying and documenting expectations—model the Expertise Delivery Model.

❑ You will have started thinking about a strategic approach to your professional performance. Discuss these more strategic approaches to your professional work with your manager and clients.

Working with Your Professional Group/Team

❑ Although one-on-one coaching is useful and necessary, you can obtain more leveraged results through group participation and group action.

❑ Meet with your professional group to discuss your reactions, learnings, concerns and applications from this *Powerful Professionals* book.

❑ As a group, complete the worksheet Looking at Your Consulting Role Strategically, Chapter 13, page 233.

❑ As a group, set goals and specific performance standards. Plan follow-through; include your own responsibilities.

❑ Clarify and document plans and follow-through items.

❑ With your team, design Expertise Delivery job aids that will expedite work without adding bureaucratic overhead. Some examples are:
  – simple project clarification forms
  – simple job tracking forms
  – simple communication/update forms
  – sample questions for getting at the underlying needs
  – sample benefits for your expertise.

❑ You will have started thinking about a strategic approach to professional performance. Discuss more strategic approaches to your group's work.

Systemic Work Results

❑ Although many performance problems are blamed on the employee, performance research shows that barriers in the system are more often the underlying cause. Aligning work systems to produce results is usually the most difficult area to change—but also the most rewarding.

❑ Ensure, where possible, that all performance systems are aligned to support the professional performance you expect—systems such as:
  – training and development
  – career development
  – work assignments
  – work unit goals and strategy
  – work unit values and culture
  – compensation
  – promotion
  – performance appraisal/performance management.

❑ One of the most common reasons for poor performance is mixed messages—'Expecting A while rewarding B.' Align rewards with value-added work.

❑ Remove or reduce barriers to professional performance, such as:
  – lack of mutually agreed-to work goals and priorities
  – understanding the strategic direction for your group and your organization
  – not having direct access to your clients
  – not having the opportunity to contract with your clients for your services.

❑ Client systems are becoming more and more complex. Use the models from Chapter 8, *Mapping Client Systems,* to understand and work with complex stakeholders.

❑ Organize support and follow-through systems, such as:
  – 'no fault' project debriefing sessions
  – self-coaching groups to share wisdom and skills
  – simulated consulting sessions with peer coaching.

❑ Many professional groups have formed support groups in the working environment to discuss consulting difficulties, to celebrate successes, to simulate or role play difficult situations and talk about the professional strategy for your group. Form a support group, or use part of your group's scheduled meetings to talk about consulting issues.

Your Own Personal Consulting Behavior

❑ The most powerful form of leading is by way of modeling. What you do speaks much louder than what you say. Lead by modeling the behavior you expect in others.

❑ Learn more about professional performance:
  – consulting skills
  – professional career development.

❑ Help others to listen by being a good listener yourself. 'Listening is your ticket to talk.'

❑ Help others receive feedback by asking for feedback yourself.

❑ Avoid client bashing, using names like 'bean counters.' Calling your clients names does nothing for client relationships and certainly sends the wrong message.

❑ See your success as the success of others.

❑ Learn the skills of group leadership. One of the most discriminating skills from the survey database is group leadership.

❑ Learn the skills of persuasion. Another of the most discriminating skills from the survey database is the skill of persuasion.

❑ Learn more about the skills of coaching.

Giving/Getting Feedback
- ❏ Feedback is the breakfast of consulting champions. The best way to continue to get feedback is to say "Thank you" for the feedback you get, rather than defending what you did.
- ❏ Ask for feedback.
- ❏ Ask one or two people to sit down with you to discuss some Self Assessments of this book in more detail. Ask for examples where you are unclear what the data means. Ask for feedback on your action plans. Ask for support.
- ❏ Role play difficult client situations with a colleague or colleagues.

HIGH GRADING YOUR APPLICATIONS

Look back at the checkmarked ideas. If you checked more than 10, the 80-20 rule probably applies—80% of your payoff from the book will come from 20% of the ideas. To ensure the few high payoff actions occur, jot down the critical few below along with some specific application times and places.

Application idea	Where to apply	When I will apply

101 COACHING TIPS CHECKLIST
FOR MANAGERS, SUPERVISORS & TEAM LEADERS OF PROFESSIONALS

The purpose of this Checklist is to help you, as a coach, think of the numerous ways in which you can help professional development. Some items will be easy and produce quick results. Other items will be more difficult but yield higher results. Others may be impractical or need adaptation for your situation. Use the few most likely to produce the best results for you and your organization. Be aware that using group action or redesigning the work system is almost always more leveraged than working with individuals one-on-one—although this is important as well. This checklist assumes that the professional you are coaching has read much of this book.

One-on-One Coaching
The quickest and easiest results can usually be obtained through one-on-one coaching. The biggest concern with one-on-one coaching is that it does not deal with systemic and group barriers to personal performance. Yet individual coaching is very helpful and the information you receive can help you plan more leveraged team and systemic interventions.

- ❏ Ask each reader to read part of this book then meet with each reader individually to discuss his/her reactions, learnings, concerns, on-job applications and action plans.
- ❏ Be sure you listen first. Readers of this book will have learned that people often jump to solutions without understanding the underlying problems. Do not jump to solutions yourself.
- ❏ Readers may have thought of applications as they read. Listen to their diagnosis of their concerns and what they have considered for action plans. Coach them with support, new ideas, reality checks, potential problems and follow-through.
- ❏ Readers will have started thinking about a more strategic approach to professional performance. Discuss these more strategic approaches to professional work.
- ❏ Don't forget the positive. Every professional will already be using some of the best practices presented in this book. Celebrate and build on the positive.
- ❏ Ask readers about the best practices of professionals from our survey database of over 7,500 professionals who received feedback from over 50,000 others. What does the *Credibility Sequence* in Chapter 1 tell you and the professional about future development needs?
- ❏ Give ongoing feedback on performance. Give both positive feedback, when goals and commitments are met, and improvement feedback when behaviors are not appropriate. See the *Guidelines for Feedback* in Chapter 15.
- ❏ Use 'no fault' feedback techniques. Clearly separate performance evaluation from coaching support.
- ❏ Set goals and specific performance standards. Plan follow-through, including your own responsibilities.
- ❏ End the meeting by clarifying and documenting expectations. Readers have learned the need to clarify commitments as part of effective consulting.

Group/Team Coaching
Although one-on-one coaching is useful and necessary, you can often obtain more leveraged results through group participation and group action. Most of the tips for one-on-one coaching above will also apply to the professional group.

- ❏ Give every member of your professional group a copy of *Powerful Professionals* to read. Assign reading of a section or two and discuss applications during your regular meetings.
- ❏ Work with the readers as a group to discuss their reactions, learnings, concerns and applications.
- ❏ Give professionals the floor to present their ideas. Remember that listening is *your* ticket to talk!
- ❏ Give both positive and improvement feedback on team performance—positive, when goals and standards are met; improvement feedback when behaviors are not appropriate.
- ❏ With your team, design job aids that will expedite work without adding bureaucratic overhead. Some examples are:
  - – simple project clarification forms
  - – simple job tracking forms
  - – simple communication/update forms

❏ Readers will have started thinking about a strategic approach to professional performance. Discuss more strategic approaches to your group's work. (See the following sections.)

❏ With the group, set goals and specific performance standards. Plan follow-through; include your own responsibilities.

❏ Clarify and document plans and follow-through items.

Systemic Work Results

Although many performance problems are blamed on the employee, performance research shows that barriers in the system are more often the underlying cause. Aligning work systems to produce results is usually the most difficult area to coach—but also the most rewarding.

❏ Ensure, to the degree possible, that all performance systems such as:

– training and development	– compensation
– career development	– promotion
– work assignments	– performance appraisal/performance management
– work unit goals and strategy	– work unit values and culture

are aligned to support the professional performance you expect. One of the most common reasons for poor performance is mixed messages—'Expecting A while rewarding B.'

❏ Remove barriers to performance like:
  – lack of mutually agreed-to work goals and priorities
  – misunderstanding the strategic direction for your group and your organization
  – not giving the professionals direct access to their clients
  – not giving professionals the opportunity to do some contracting with their clients for their services.

❏ Client systems are becoming more and more complex. Use the complex/multiple client models from Chapter 8, *Mapping Client Systems,* to understand and work with complex stakeholders.

❏ Organize support and follow-through systems like:
  – 'no fault' project debriefing sessions
  – coaching groups to share wisdom and skills
  – simulated consulting sessions with peer coaching.

Strategic, Longterm Results

❏ Think and talk strategically about the direction of your profession and organization.

❏ Use the strategic models in Chapter 13 in working with your group. They will help you and your team distinguish between value-added work, business necessity work and work better done by others.

❏ Besides asking your clients what they want and need, make offers of value-added work that your clients may be unaware that your professional group can offer.

❏ Look at your clients strategically. Which clients add more value to your organization? How can less value-added clients get their needs met in other ways?

❏ Remember 'customer service' does not mean saying "yes" to all requests.

❏ Often, saying "no" is difficult for professionals and their managers. Review the suggestions in Chapter 13 for saying "no" successfully. Model saying "no" appropriately.

❏ Design the structure of your work group around core business processes. Be sure that your organizational structure supports your work.

❏ More and more professional groups are marketing their professional skills. Read Chapter 14 on how to market professional skills.

❏ Think of your professional group as if you were an independent consulting group contracted to your organization. What would you stop doing? What would you start doing? What would you continue? Why not carry out these behaviors now?

High Performance Consulting Competencies

Through the use of the *Consulting Skills Profile* for over ten years internationally, we have amassed the best database in the world (over 35,000 surveys) on what clients value most from professionals.

❑ Review the *Professional Credibility Sequence,* which tells you the implied process clients use to evaluate professionals. This sequence is in Chapter 1. What does it tell you about client expectations? What does it tell you and your professional group about what you are already good at and where you need development?

Career Development Coaching for Professionals

Research shows that professional development does not occur in a linear, continuous manner but rather in a nonlinear, discontinuous manner as described in Chapter 12.

❑ Provide coaching assistance to help professionals move from Level 2—good individual contributors—to a more leveraged Level 3— getting results through others.

❑ Be sure you are operating out of at least Level 3 yourself, where your success is the success of others.

❑ Consider using the Novations' Four Stages Model™ as your professional group's career development model. This career model is specifically geared to professional productivity.

❑ One of the lowest scored items in the survey database is the question 'Has a wider perspective than his/her expertise.' Most professionals need to see themselves less as experts and more as business consultants with a professional expertise.

Your Own Personal Leadership Behavior

The most powerful form of coaching is by way of modeling. What you do speaks much louder than what you say.

❑ Model the behaviors you expect from others, by scrupulously behaving as you want others to behave.

❑ Learn more about professional performance:
    – consulting skills
    – professional career development (see Chapter 12).

❑ Help others to listen by being a good listener yourself. Read Chapter 11, *Listening Skills for Professionals,* if you need assistance in this area.

❑ Help others to receive feedback by asking for feedback yourself.

❑ Do not 'client bash,' using names like 'bean counters.' Calling clients names does nothing for client relationships and certainly sends the wrong message.

❑ See your success as the success of others. Do not compete with your professionals. Your rewards are helping professionals to be successful.

❑ Learn the skills of group leadership. One of the most discriminating skills from the survey database is group leadership.

❑ Learn the skills of persuasion. Another of the most discriminating skills from the survey database is the skill of persuasion.

❑ Learn more about the skills of coaching.

Now some specific coaching tips for each step of the Expertise Delivery Model.

Stage 1: Exploring the Need

❑ Clients often present solutions to problems, not the underlying problem. Coach professionals on the use of skilful questions to get at the underlying needs.

❑ One of the side effects of taking the presented solution as the underlying need is to put oneself into a pair of hands role (and often blame clients for the narrow role). Help professionals ask questions which get at underlying needs, at the same time setting up a business partner role.

❑ Professionals often struggle with the 'people side' of their work. Coach the need for human-to-human rapport and personal relationships.

❑ Professionals often struggle with ambiguity and constrict a problem too quickly. Coach professionals to ferret out all the issues, especially those outside their area of expertise.

❏ In this book, we present the powerful concept of framing client concerns. Frames are often implied and accepted very early. If the problem is not reframed early, you lose the opportunity to see the problem in a more effective light. Help your professionals understand the concept of problem frames.

❏ Listening for understanding is a crucial skill at this first step. Give feedback to, and coach professionals on, their listening skills.

Stage 2: Clarifying Commitments

❏ Some of the most embarrassing and bitter consulting incidents occur over unclear expectations between clients and professionals. Ensure that professionals always clarify commitments. Use the checklists and models presented in Chapter 4.

❏ Much conflict arises from unclear expectations. Dealing with conflict is one of professionals' weakest skills. Coach professionals on this easy-to-use conflict prevention technique.

❏ Too little clarification of expectations leads to problems. Too much can be just as dysfunctional by making the project inflexible. Coach for the optimal amount of clarification.

❏ The minimum level of clarification is a verbal agreement. Always end your conversations and meetings by clarifying commitments and establishing the next steps.

❏ The working level of clarification is a simple written document. Clarify guidelines for the amount of clarification expected.

Stage 3: Gathering Information

❏ Our high performance database tells us that sorting out complex situations is a skill highly valued by clients. Coach your professionals on the skills of verbally clarifying complex requests.

❏ Learn more about this skill yourself. Read Chapter 5.

❏ Readers will have learned that every question has a role implied in it. Coach professionals on the skills of questioning. Give feedback to professionals who want a more powerful role but inadvertently ask "Tell me what to do boss" questions (then often get angry with their clients).

Stage 4: Recommending Change

❏ From our survey database, the item 'Is able to persuade others' is unique. It is on the clients' most discriminating list of professional attributes, yet professionals are scored lowest on this item. In other words, clients want to be sold on recommendations but professionals are lousy at it! Coach on the skills of effectively selling recommendations and proposals.

❏ Professionals, by nature, tend to present the features of their recommendations, not the benefits. Yet it is the benefits which sell your clients. Help your professionals distinguish between features and benefits.

❏ Push your professionals to think of the benefits from the clients' point-of-view.

❏ Think of multiple/complex client systems. Benefits which appeal to one client group may turn off another group. Coach professionals to think of all the stakeholders involved in a recommendation.

❏ Dealing with the inevitable reservations and objections to recommending change is again one of the lowest scored items from the survey database. In this book, readers learn that resistance can be helpful. Work with your professionals on how to handle resistance.

Stage 5: Taking Stock/Closing

❏ Closing projects is often poorly done. Closing is set up during the *Clarifying Commitment* phase of the Expertise Delivery Model. Coach professionals on the need for wrapping up projects.

❏ Many professionals have continuing clients. Professionals have the best leverage to improve a relationship when things are going well. Coach professionals to have a Taking Stock meeting with their clients when things are going well. This is their chance to suggest improvements to the consulting relationship.

Sustaining Change
- ❏ Most change fails, not because the recommendation was technically inadequate, but because the change was not supported by other systems that were barriers to the change. Help professionals look at the systems which are needed to support the recommended change.
- ❏ The question from the survey database 'Understands and helps others deal with the stress of changes resulting from his/her recommendations' is one of the lowest scored items on the survey database. Book readers have learned a process for minimizing the stress of change. Coach professionals on the need to lead people through personal transitions if change is to stick.

HIGH GRADING YOUR COACHING

Look back at your checkmarked ideas. If you checked more than 10, the 80-20 rule probably applies—80% of your payoff from your coaching will come from 20% of the ideas. To ensure the few high payoff actions occur, jot down the critical few below along with some specific application times and places.

Coaching idea	Where to apply	When I will apply

MEETING PLANNER

NOTE: Here is a suggested plan for a successful follow-on meeting with an individual reader. Modify the words for your particular situation.

Purpose
- The purpose of this meeting is to get a manyfold return on the investment in the *Powerful Professionals* book.

Expected results from the meeting
By the end of the meeting, we expect to have:
- described the major insights from this *Powerful Professionals* book
- discussed any concerns the book may have raised
- refined application ideas from the book
- refined and documented follow-through plans for both reader and coach.

Important reminder
Strike a balance between skill improvement and building on what is already positive.

Agenda
1. Reader's reactions:
    - the major insights and learnings from the book
    - concerns raised by the book.
2. Coach's reactions:
    - what the coach hears from the reader's reactions
    - how this confirms or raises concerns from the coach's point-of-view.
3. Resolving the differences:
    - discussion of how to resolve any differences of perception.
4. Agreeing to and documenting follow-through actions:
    - clarifying and documenting improvement commitments of the professional
    - clarifying and documenting support from coach
    - setting a follow-up meeting.

Improvement actions (be as specific as possible):

Coaching Support Commitments:

Follow-through meeting date:

*"The more I learn about myself
the more I become a different
self."*

© Ashleigh Brilliant

APPENDIX 2

SELECTED FURTHER READING

General References on Internal Consulting

Flawless Consulting: A Guide to Getting Your Expertise Used (Second Edition) by Peter Block
Jossey-Bass; San Francisco, 1999. ISBN #0787948039
Block wrote the very first book specifically geared to internal consultants. With good humor, Block discusses consulting from A to Z. He is particularly strong on the topics of contracting and resistance. This second edition is *the* classic for internal consultants.

Getting Things Done When You Are Not in Charge, by Geoffrey Bellman
Berrett-Koehler Publishers, San Francisco, 1992. ISBN #1-881052-02-8
A personal and practical look at the issues of an internal consultant. Bellman writes in an easy-to-read, how-to and personal style. Highly recommended.

The Internal Consultant: Drawing on Inside Expertise by Marcia Meislin
Crisp Publications, Inc., Menlo Park, CA, 1997. ISBN #1-56052-417-0
This Fifty-Minute™ series book is a very brief introduction to internal consulting with lots of worksheets.

Shared Services/Professional Services

Shared Services: Mining for Corporate Gold by Barbara Quinn, Andrew Kris, & Robert S. Cooke
Financial Times Prentice Hall Publishing; Edinburgh, 2000. ISBN 0-273-64455-6
A practical introduction to the shared services concept by outlining how to assess its viability for an organization and how to proceed with planning and implementing it.

True Professionalism: The Courage to Care About Your People, Your Clients, and Your Career by David H. Maister
Touchstone Books, 2000. ISBN #0684840049
 One of his many books and although focussed on external consultants, Maister has become an authority about the role of the professional and the professional services firm.

Specific References

Internal/External Consulting

Consultant's Calling: Bringing Who You Are to What You Do by Geoffrey Bellman
Jossey-Bass Publishers, San Francisco, 1990. ISBN #1-55542-411-2
In his very personal look at consulting as a vocation, Bellman discusses how to make consulting meaningful, fulfilling and rewarding. Highly recommended, especially if you are seeking balance in your career and life.

High-Impact Consulting: How Clients and Consultants Can Leverage Rapid Results into Long-Term Gains by Robert Schaffer
Jossey-Bass Publishers, San Francisco, 1997. ISBN #0-7879-0341-8
Chock-full of examples, Schaffer makes a strong case for changing the consulting role from a consultant/expert focus to a results-based focus. His strong emphasis on creating sustainable and lasting change makes this book a must for senior internal and external consultants. Recommended.

Consultative Budgeting: How to Get the Funds You Need From Tight-Fisted Management by Mack Hanan
AMACON, New York, 1994. ISBN #0-8144-0257-7
The title says it like it is. This book focuses on how to get the budgets you need for professional projects.

Framing Problems

Decision Traps: The Ten Barriers to Brilliant Decision-Making & How to Overcome Them by J. E. Russo & P. J. Schoemaker
Doubleday/Currency, New York, 1989. ISBN #0-385-24835-0
This book, besides having good ideas on decision making, has two very good chapters on framing and reframing.

Getting Past No: Negotiating Your Way From Confrontation to Cooperation by W. Ury
Bantam Books, New York, 1993. ISBN #0-553-37131-2
Ury has an excellent chapter on reframing. The chapter is full of examples—well worth the price of the paperback on its own.

Negotiating

Getting to Yes: Negotiating Agreement without Giving In by R. Fisher & W. Ury
Penguin Books, New York, 1981. ISBN #0-14-015735-2
A best seller and widely used as the basis for negotiation skills workshops. This book is recommended for internal consultants because of its 50-50 orientation. It teaches the skills of principled negotiation, neither 'hard' nor 'soft.' If you only have time to look at one reference book on negotiating, this very readable paperback is the one.

Getting Past No: Negotiating Your Way From Confrontation to Cooperation by W. Ury
Bantam Books, 1993. ISBN #0-553-37131-2
This book builds on and goes beyond *Getting to Yes*. This paperback is particularly strong on breaking through barriers and reframing.

Negotiate to Close: How to Make More Successful Deals by Gary Karrass
Simon and Schuster, 1985.
This book takes a more competitive and aggressive approach to negotiating and is more oriented to sales people. You probably have seen the Karrass seminars advertised in in-flight magazines. The tape by the same title would be a particularly good way to psych you up for a difficult negotiation.

Selling and Marketing

These books are recommended even though they are all written from an *external* sales point-of-view. There are no books on internal sales as yet—that we are aware of.

Spin Selling by Neil Rackham
McGraw-Hill Book Company, New York, 1988. ISBN #0-07-051113-6
A must for senior consultants for at least two reasons. First, it describes the difference between a traditional small sale and a large sale. The skills of one are often a problem in the other! Second, the book is particularly strong on questioning skills.

The SPIN® Selling Fieldbook by Neil Rackham
McGraw-Hill Book Company, New York, 1996. ISBN #0-07-052235-9
A very accessible how-to version of the original. Highly recommended if you are selling large projects.

Strategic Selling by R. B. Miller and S. E. Heiman
Warner Books, New York, 1985. ISBN #0-446-38627-8
An excellent introduction to the whole field of selling. You could replace the word 'selling' with 'consulting' and have another good book. Particularly strong on the subject of understanding and working with multiple and complex client systems.

Ziglar on Selling by Zig Ziglar
Oliver Nelson, Nashville, 1991. ISBN #0-8407-9131-3
A very readable, modern book on selling. It contains an overview of selling from finding prospective clients to closing a sale. Ziglar emphasizes the professionalism of selling.

Selling the Dream by Guy Kawasaki
Harper Collins, New York, 1991. ISBN #0-06-016632-0
Written by a former member of the original Macintosh™ marketing team, this book is fun to read. Its strength is in describing the passion it takes to market and sell an idea or product. The examples are worth the price of the book.

Change

Leading Change by John P. Kotter
Harvard Business School Press, Boston, MA, 1996. ISBN #0-87584-747-1
Although written for managers, this book contains easy-to-read practical advice on leading change, especially the need for vision and building commitment to change.

Creating Paths of Change: Managing Issues and Resolving Problems in Organizations by W. McWhinney, James Webber, Douglas Smith and Bernie Novokowsky
SAGE Publications, Thousand Oaks, CA, 1997. ISBN #0-7619-1007-7
A book that looks at change from fresh perspectives, it will provide you with a number of strategies and a wealth of tools through which change can be achieved and conflicts resolved.

Organizational Change

Managing Transitions: Making the Most of Change by William Bridges
Addison-Wesley, Reading, MA 1991. ISBN #0-201-55073-3
The follow-up to Bridges' first, more personal *Transitions,* this book provides practical suggestions on how to help people you are working with make changes with minimum stress. This book addresses personal change in an organizational setting.

Personal Change

Transitions: Making Sense of Life's Changes by William Bridges
Addison-Wesley, Reading, MA 1980. ISBN #0-201-00082-2
A book about personal transitions that can be read to help you lead business transitions. *The* classic resource on the 'people' side of change.

Simple Living in a Complex World: Balancing Life's Achievements by David Irvine
Red Stone Ventures, Inc., Calgary, Canada 1997. ISBN #0-9680504-1-7
A thoughtful, personal book on bringing about a balance between achievement and personal life. (David is also an excellent speaker for your conferences.)

Turning Feedback into Change by Joe Folkman
NOVATIONS, Provo, Utah, 1995. ISBN #0-9634917-2-5
In an easy-to-read format, Folkman offers 31 principles for bringing feedback forward into sustainable change.

Influence

Influence without Authority by Allan Cohen and David Bradford
John Wiley & Sons, Inc., New York, 1991. ISBN #0-471-54894-4
An extensive and readable reference on influence, with lots of examples. Recommended as a personal journey of what you can accomplish without direct control.

Principle-Centered Leadership by Stephen Covey
Summit Books, New York, 1991. ISBN #0-671-74910-2
A wide ranging book dealing with the principles of leading a good life as well as leading in business. On the topic of influence, Chapter 11, *Thirty Methods of Influence,* is good set of suggestions for getting results without direct control.

Group Leadership

The TEAM Handbook by P. S. Scholtes
Joiner Associates, Madison, WI, 1988. ISBN #0-9622264-8-0
This book simply describes and illustrates basic statistical quality tools and other group processes.

The Leader's Handbook by P. S. Scholtes
McGraw-Hill Book Company, New York, 1998. ISBN #0-07-058028-6
A wide-ranging book in down-to-earth terms, filled with models of leadership.

Cross-Functional Teams: Working with Allies, Enemies & Other Strangers by Glenn Parker
Jossey-Bass Publishers, San Francisco, 1994. ISBN #1-55542-609-3
Parker provides practical advice for the formation and operation of cross-functional teams.

The Wisdom of Teams by J.R. Katzenbach and D.K. Smith
HarperBusiness, New York, 1993. ISBN #0-88730-676-4
A best seller on what it takes to nourish high performance teams. Recommended.

How to Lead Work Teams: Facilitation Skills by Fran Rees
Pfeiffer & Company, San Diego, 1991. ISBN #0-88390-056-4
Although written from the perspective of a person in a supervisory role, this book contains the basics of group leadership.

Career Development
Novations: Strategies for Career Management by G. W. Dalton and P. H. Thompson
Originally published by Scott Foresman and Company, Glenview, Illinois, 1986.
Now only available from NOVATIONS, Provo, Utah (801) 375-7525. ISBN #0-673-18181-2
This ground breaking book describes the research and application of ideas crucial to professional career development. Successful and productive technical careers do not proceed in straight lines. They develop in distinct stages. Each stage requires different activities, skills, relationships and strategies. A must for understanding the careers of professionals.

Strategy and Future of the White Collar Professional
If you want to put your role as a consultant in a larger context, these are good references:
Shifting Gears: Thriving in the New Economy by Nuala Beck
HarperCollins Publishers Ltd., Toronto, 1992. ISBN #0-00-215785-3
An easily readable book that has a particularly good chapter on the 'knowledge worker.' Well worth a read to position your job in the modern economy.

Human Resource Champions by Dave Ulrich
Harvard Business School Press, Boston, MA 1997. ISBN #0-87584-719-6
In this 'must-read' for human resource professionals, leading researcher Ulrich outlines the current issues and strategies in human resources.

Real-Time Strategy: Improvising Team-Based Planning for a Fast-Changing World by L. Perry, R. Stott & W. N. Smallwood
John Wiley, New York, 1993. ISBN #0-471-58564-5
An easy-to-read book with lots of examples of the role of the individual in strategic thinking. The book uses a colorful jazz metaphor for formulating strategy.

The Work of Nations by Robert B. Reich
Vintage Books, New York, 1992. ISBN #0-679-73615-8
An interesting perspective on the workforce North America needs in order to be competitive in the future. The role of white collar professionals—consultants—is seen to be paramount.

Time/Priority Management
First Things First by S. Covey et al
Fireside, New York, 1994. ISBN #0-684-80203-1
THE book on managing your time and priorities.

Accountability: Getting a Grip on Results by Bruce Klatt, Shaun Murphy and David Irvine
RedStone Publishing/Stoddart Publishing, Toronto, 1998. ISBN #0-7737-6012-1
A very practical book, full of examples of why and how to write 'no excuses' accountability agreements—particularly helpful when negotiating project, roles or services agreements.

Coaching
Coaching for Teams by Nigel Bristow
Cascade Press, 1996 ISBN# 1-886662-07-X
One of the new skills of internal consultants is not only to deliver your expertise yourself, but also to help others deliver their expertise. This book is full of good how-to advice for coaching others, especially in a team setting.

Communication
The 7 Habits of Highly Effective People by S. Covey
Fireside, New York, 1985. ISBN #0-671-70863-5
Read the whole book! The chapter 'Seek first to understand then to be understood' is excellent reading on empathic communication.

That's Not What I Meant: How Conversational Style Makes or Breaks Relationships by D. Tannen
Ballantine Books, New York, 1986. ISBN #0-345-37972-1
This very understandable book on linguistics is filled with excellent examples of communication difficulties and solutions. This is one of the many practical and very readable Tannen books. Recommended.

Dealing with Differences
The next two books are very readable paperbacks with many examples for dealing with differences and applications to everyday life.
Type Talk by Otto Kroeger and Janet Thuesen
Delta Books, New York, 1988. ISBN #0-385-29828-5
Please Understand Me by Marilyn Bates and David Keirsey
Prometheus Nemesis Book Co., Del Mar, CA 1978. ISBN #0-9606954-0-0

Type Talk at Work by Otto Kroeger with J. Thuesen
Delacorte Press, New York, 1992. ISBN# 0-385-30174-X
A practical guide to understanding your own preferences at work and also understanding and working with others more effectively. A highly recommended book.

The Myers-Briggs Type Indicator (MBTI)
The 'real thing' upon which the above books are based. The *Indicator* is published by Consulting Psychologists Press of Palo Alto, CA. Often you will find local educational institutions sponsoring workshop sessions with certified instructors. An MBTI workshop is strongly recommended for those of you who wish to become thoroughly familiar with the model. For those of you who would just like an introduction or more information, the above books are very readable and helpful.

Cross-Cultural Communication
Kiss, Bow or Shake Hands: How to do Business in Sixty Countries by Terri Morrison, et al
Adams Media Corporation, Holbrook, MA 1994. ISBN #1-55850-444-3
If you do out-of-country or cross cultural consulting and business, this book is an invaluable resource.

Assertive Behavior
Your Perfect Right: A Guide to Assertive Living by Robert Alberti & Michael Emmons
Impact Publishers, 1982. ISBN #0-915166-05-4
One of many references on the topic of assertion, Alberti and Emmons present a practical and readable overview. If you have difficulty asserting yourself as a consultant, this is a good introduction. (We also highly recommend you take a good workshop where you can practice assertiveness skills.)

Difficult People

Coping with Difficult People by Robert Bramson
Dell Publishing, New York, 1981. ISBN #0-440-20201-9
A very practical paperback full of examples from everyday and business life. Bramson describes a variety of difficult people with humor and practical suggestions. Your best read here. Also available in a cassette tape version.

Dinosaur Brains: Dealing With All Those Impossible People At Work by Albert J. Bernstein & Sydney Craft Rozen
Ballantine Books, New York, 1989. ISBN #0-345-36713-8
A very readable book, focusing on your dysfunctional, reptilian reactions to dysfunctional people and situations.

Difficult People: How to Deal With Impossible Clients, Bosses and Employees by Roberta Cava
Key Porter Books, Toronto, 1990. ISBN #1-55013-186-9
Another very readable book about difficult situations which also discusses the interrelated issues of stress, listening, communication skills, public speaking, and so forth.

Working with Difficult People by Muriel Solomon
Prentice Hall, Englewood Cliffs, New Jersey, 1990. ISBN #0-13-957390-9
Solomon categorizes dozens of types of difficult people. You may find a category which describes your particular situation very closely.

Leadership

The Encyclopedia of Leadership: A Practical Guide to Popular Leadership Theories and Techniques by Murray Hiebert & Bruce Klatt
McGraw-Hill, New York, 2001. ISBN #1-881052-02-8
Designed to provide modern, busy leaders with practical help in 15 minutes or less, this easy-to-use desktop reference includes 130 classical and modern leadership tools, each summarized in a few pages, including application worksheets. An accompanying *Coaching Guide* will provide content and application focus for many successful coaching meetings. Leadership development materials are also available.

Results-Based Leadership by Dave Ulrich, Jack Zenger & Norm Smallwood
Harvard Business School Press, Boston, MA, 1999. ISBN #0-87584-871-0
A book which challenges the conventional wisdom of leadership and places emphasis on producing results.

Internet Web Site

Consulting Skills for Professionals Web Site
http://www.consultskills.com
The web site contains all the current information about the *Powerful Professionals* book and the *Consulting Skills for Professionals* workshop. The *Desktop Workshop* section contain dozens of on-job resources hypertext linked for ease of access. The web site also contains links to other professional and internal consulting resources.

NOTES

> *"Proper words in proper places."*
> *– Jonathan Swift*

FINDING WHAT YOU WANT:

Symbols

 Actual consulting incidents and examples

 Pay attention to this

 Checklist

 (Additional) Information

 Warning

 Web Site Resources

Numerical Items

A

B

C

COMPETENCY/SKILL AND
POWERFUL PROFESSIONALS RESOURCES MATRIX

The Resources start on the pages indicated.

Competency/Skill Area by Chapter	How tos/ Information	Model/ Principles	Checklist	Assessment/ Application/ Worksheet
High Performing Professionals				
Understands what clients value from a professional	12	11		
Is able to make role change from expert to internal consultant	4	8	272	278
Understands what is driving professional role change	3			
Expertise Delivery Model				
Understands the need for an Expertise Delivery model	16	16		
Uses an Expertise Delivery Model	17	16	272	278
Is able to adapt model to suit the situation	21, 114		114. 272	
Exploring the Need				
Understands the need for Exploring the Need	24	27, 29		45
Understands fears and their impact	30	33	30	
Is able to clarify underlying concerns and client needs	33, 86	38		
Is able to ask effective opening questions	33		34	
Is able to frame/reframe problems	35	36	37	
Is able to establish rapport	39		40, 41	45
Clarifying Commitments				
Understands the need to Clarify Commitments	48	51		
Knows what to clarify			52, 53	
Knows how much to clarify	54	57		
Uses most appropriate form of clarification	58	57		61
Can ask for what is needed for a successful project	62	62		
Is able to establish 50-50 client partnerships	63	6, 63, 73		
Gathering Information				
Is able to ask powerful questions	68	78		70, 78
Is able to quickly sort out complex situations face-to-face with clients	68	77		78
Understands the connection between roles and questions	75	77		75

303

Competency/Skill Area by Chapter	How tos/ Information	Model/ Principles	Checklist	Assessment/ Application/ Worksheet
Recommending Change				
Understands the need to sell recommended changes	82			
Is able to sell proposals and ideas to clients	83	84	85, 91	103
Can present persuasively	87	88	91	
Is able to deal with reservations or resistance	93	94	95, 96	
Is able to introduce change	98	98		103
Taking Stock/Closing				
Understands the need for following through & wrapping up projects	108	109		
Knows when and how to take stock in an ongoing relationship	110		111	
Knows when and how to close a project	110			
Can lead a closing/taking stock meeting with a client			113	
Mapping Client Systems				
Understands the complexity of modern stakeholder interests	118			
Can categorize the types of clients to a project	121	121		
Can diagram complex client systems to assist change	128	129-132		129,130
Can deal with conflict between stakeholders	133		133	
Sustaining Change				
Is able to negotiate an appropriate role in change	138	138		
Can state and use change principles	140		140	
Can assess the ease of change	143		141, 143	143
Can use a number of change models	144	145	147	
Can lead the 'people' side of change	152	153	158	
Is able to establish appropriate level of participation in change	159	160	161	161
Is able to lead systemic change	148	149		149
Dealing with Resistance				
Can distinguish between direct and indirect resistance	165	166		
Understands the sources and types of indirect resistance	167		168	
Is able to surface indirect resistance	169, 172	168, 173	174	

Competency/Skill Area by Chapter	How tos/ Information	Model/ Principles	Checklist	Assessment/ Application/ Worksheet
Listening Skills for Professionals				
Understands why listening is important to a powerful professional	178			
Is able to use appropriate listening skills	181	181, 190	187	182
Enhancing Your Role and Career				
Is able to connect roles and professional behavior	201	202		
Can propose most appropriate role for the situation	202	202, 204		204
Understands the changes required in developing a professional career	205	206		
Is adapting and growing in impact as a powerful professional	213	212		
Your Strategy: Saying Yes or No				
Has a wider perspective than professional expertise	218	219		
Is strategic as an individual	220	220, 229	227	
Contributes to professional group strategy	228	229		233
Understands and contributes to client and organizational strategies	218	220		230, 233
Is able to say "no" appropriately	234	235		
Marketing Your Skills				
Understands the modern need to market skills	238, 240	243		
Can analyze the organizational needs	248		245	244, 248
Is able to prepare a marketing plan	243		246	247
Can market professional skills effectively	252		253	255
Putting It All Together				
Has a set of effective principles to use to deliver expertise	258	259		
Can meta-communicate when needed	263	263		
Avoids control problems with clients	264	264		
Is able to give and receive feedback	267	267		
Is able to receive coaching or coach others in Powerful Professional skills	279		279	283

NOTES

ABOUT THE AUTHORS

Murray and Eilis Hiebert manage a consulting organization specializing in professional development and organizational effectiveness from their Calgary, Canada office. Murray has published a world-class internal *Consulting Skills for Professionals Workshop,* part of which are client feedback surveys, which have provided Murray with the world's largest database on high performance skills of professionals—as seen by their own internal customers. The constantly upgraded *Consulting Skills for Professionals Workshop* is presented by associates in the U.S.A., Canada, Europe and Asia in English, German, French and Spanish.

Murray's second book, *The Encyclopedia of Leadership,* coauthored with Bruce Klatt was released in 2001 by McGraw-Hill Business Books. Designed to provide modern, busy leaders with practical help in 15 minutes or less, it includes 130 classical and modern leadership tools, each summarized in a few pages, including application worksheets. An accompanying *Coaching Guide* will provide content and application focus for many successful coaching meetings. Leadership development materials are also available.

Murray's skills and experience cover a wide range, with proven specialty in professional productivity—developing internal professionals and world-class internal consulting groups. With clients ranging from multinational petrochemical companies through very large utilities to small entrepreneurial organizations, Murray consults in the strategy of professional groups, marketing internal professional groups, internal customer service, career management, change management, organizational and work redesign and strategy development.

During his several years in a multinational company, Murray's positions included technical training advisor, senior management development advisor, organizational effectiveness consultant and human resources manager. Also widely experienced as an external consultant, Murray has worked with a wide range of organizations in Canada, U.S.A. and worldwide. He has consulted and presented workshops from the Arctic Circle to Brazil and across the Atlantic and Pacific oceans.

Murray, who has a Masters Degree in Science, has published numerous articles in scientific journals, professional newsmagazines, international human resource development journals, *Executive Excellence, The Wall Street Journal* and the *AIMC Forum.* His work has been selected for the American Society for Training and Development's *The Best of...* series. He has written a comprehensive computer-based resources for professionals called the *Desktop Workshop*— a unique continuous learning and application resource accessible through the workshop Web Site, http://www.consultskills.com.

1991 Winner of the prestigious *Practitioner of the Year Award* from Human Resource Development Canada, Murray has presented on the topic of internal consulting and professional productivity at professional gatherings all over North America. He has presented at conferences for ASTD, the Association for Internal Management Consultants, and Linkage Inc.'s Consulting Skills Institute.

Eilis Hiebert has worked in international development for many years, living and working in North America, Europe, Africa, India and Singapore. She designs and delivers programs in the area of cross-cultural relations to diverse groups. Her extensive writing and editing experience includes publishing a series of brochures on world religions and production of an award winning TV series. She has been Murray's writing (and life) partner for many years.

ABOUT THE
CONSULTING SKILLS FOR PROFESSIONALS WORKSHOP

If you have read this book from cover-to-cover, you will have seen many references to a 'workshop' and a 'database.' The over 700 *Consulting Skills for Professionals* workshops with nearly 10,000 participants worldwide provided the field testing and honing of these book materials. The over 7,500 participants who received performance and development feedback from over 50,000 clients, managers, peers and others provided the database from which we quoted.

If you are looking for a skill-building workshop to support the concepts of this book, you need go no further than the *Consulting Skills for Professionals* workshop:

- **The How-to Approach and the Field-Tested models.** The genius of the workshop lies in its hands-on approach. We continue to emphasize user-friendly consulting processes by emphasizing tips, hints and down-to-earth applications. Like the book, the workshop is peppered with checklists, mini-applications, simulations, etc. that professionals find so practical and useful.

- **The Appeal to Professionals Working Inside Organizations.** We know there are dozens of workshops available for the managers of professionals or external consultants. We find our 'niche' is the internal professional with a professional skill who needs improved skills to deliver that expertise within his/her sphere of work. Our workshop speaks a language that professionals understand, developing skills to deliver expertise in a logical, learnable framework for engineers, systems analysts, geologists, human resource professionals, financial professionals, public affairs advisors—almost any internal professional you can think of. We have found that these professionals arrive at our workshop eager to change their ways of working, but unsure of how to do so.

- **The Support of the *Consulting Skills Profile*.** Without a doubt, when we ask participants what stood out for them on the workshop, the 20+ pages of personal, confidential, no-fault feedback report is cited most often. This thoroughly tested customer/client feedback survey contains 64 numeric items and 2 open-ended questions.

- **Continuous Upgrade of the Workshop.** The workshop is now in version 7. We continuously upgrade the materials, using what we learn from our clients and reflecting current concerns of professionals working inside organizations. The *Consulting Skills Profile* is in version 5. It meets or exceeds the standard statistical requirements. More importantly, it passes the client feedback test "How could we improve this survey?"

- **The 'Blue-Ribbon' List of Clients.** We are proud of our Client List. It includes many Fortune 500 companies, not-for-profit organizations, government and professional service organizations. We are proud of the variety of professionals—the who's who of professional occupations—who have participated. Our workshops continue to be presented all over the world.

- **The Support of Local Associates.** Rather than form a large organization with lock-step, foolproof instruction, we have chosen to develop associations with successful, practicing consultants worldwide. Your local Associates practice what we preach and provide a consultative approach to deal with your specific needs and with the instruction of the workshop. See the Web Site at http://www.consultskills.com for the current List of Associates and how to contact them.

- **The Support for Organizational Change Initiatives.** Many professional groups are undergoing improvement pressure from within and without—re-engineering, internal customer service, business process design, business unit, shared services. Many organizations have used the workshop to assist change.

- **The Support for On-Job Application.** We realize the success of the workshop is measured by how well the skills are used real-time, on-the-job. *Consulting Skills for Professionals* has many application and follow-through tools.

- **The Support from this Book.** If you learned from this book, you will certainly enjoy the in-depth skill building, practice and application discussions of the workshop.

Visit the Web Site for the latest information:
http://www.consultskills.com